THE GLOBAL BRAND

THE GLOBAL BRAND

How to Create and Develop
Lasting Brand Value in the
World Market

Nigel Hollis
Chief Global Analyst
Millward Brown

THE GLOBAL BRAND
Copyright © Millward Brown, 2008.

All rights reserved.

First published in 2008 by
PALGRAVE MACMILLAN®
in the US—a division of St. Martin's Press LLC,
175 Fifth Avenue, New York, NY 10010.

Where this book is distributed in the UK, Europe and the rest of the world,
this is by Palgrave Macmillan, a division of Macmillan Publishers Limited,
registered in England, company number 785998, of Houndmills,
Basingstoke, Hampshire RG21 6XS.

Palgrave Macmillan is the global academic imprint of the above companies
and has companies and representatives throughout the world.

Palgrave® and Macmillan® are registered trademarks in the United States,
the United Kingdom, Europe and other countries.

ISBN-13: 978–0–230–60622–7
ISBN-10: 0–230–60622–9

Library of Congress Cataloging-in-Publication Data

Hollis, Nigel.
   The global brand : how to create and develop lasting brand value in the
world market / Nigel Hollis.
     p. cm.
   ISBN 0–230–60622–9
    1. Brand name products. 2. Branding (Marketing) I. Title.

HD69.B7H646 2008
658.8′27—dc22   2008009927

A catalogue record of the book is available from the British Library.

Design by Newgen Imaging Systems (P) Ltd., Chennai, India.

First edition: October 2008

10 9 8 7 6 5 4 3 2 1

Printed in the United States of America.

Dedicated to Sue Gardiner

Contents

List of Tables

List of Figures

Foreword

In the same way that I can never remember whether I should feed a cold and starve a fever, I also tend to forget whether I'm meant to think globally and act locally. (Or is it the other way around?) But I'm in good company. I share this quandary with many of the world's greatest marketers. Brand owners everywhere are struggling to strike the right balance between global and local when it comes to managing their precious brand assets.

On the surface, global brand management sounds so easy, doesn't it? Simply insist on global brand consistency, develop a common channel strategy, and generate demand with a universally compelling message. But therein lies the rub. People around the world are, indeed, different in many ways. We eat different foods, we shop in different ways and different places, we form households differently, and we certainly laugh at different jokes. These infinite variations make the world a truly magical place. Its endless diversity drives our wanderlust and provides us with a lifetime of fascinating friendships and enriching experiences. But it sure doesn't make a marketer's life easy!

My good friend and colleague Nigel Hollis has spent the last year studying and writing in an attempt to remedy this problem—in short, to make life a little easier for global marketers. He has mined the many and massive international databases we maintain at Millward Brown, conducted important new primary research, and talked to literally hundreds of people involved in marketing, either as brand owners or in the many agencies that support them.

Not surprisingly, he found that global brand management is a bit like geopolitics. It is characterized by an endless litany of seemingly unanswerable questions and a dazzling array of opinions, often divergent. But amid all of this cacophony, Nigel has come up with a pretty startling thesis: There's no such thing as a "global brand"!

"What?" you say. "Isn't the book called *The Global Brand*?" Indeed. What Nigel will help marketers understand is that while brands can succeed globally, they can't do it without being incredibly adaptive. In the same way that a sports team can deliver an undefeated season, marketers can win on many fronts by understanding the specific playing field, studying the local competition, and tailoring their game plan accordingly. But be forewarned: Trotting out the same old game plan on every field will rarely be the route to sustained success.

So what are marketers to do? Start from scratch in every market they enter? Of course not! There are often huge operational benefits to scale. Simply being able to amortize things like research and development, innovation investment, and manufacturing capacity over a larger global buying population can have immense payback. And going back to my sporting analogy, there will almost always be some plays in your arsenal that are fail-safe and will work every time. By all means, use them! But listen to Nigel when he advises you to mix them up with a few new moves designed to endear you to the local crowd.

"Endear" is not a word I choose lightly. Increasingly, we are seeing that brands must connect on an emotional level in order to succeed. And very few things are tougher to do with a one-size-fits-all strategy than win hearts. Nigel's message, quite clearly articulated in this book, is one of balancing that which can be truly global with that which *must* be genuinely local. For this reason alone, *The Global Brand* deserves a place on every marketer's (and perhaps every diplomat's) bookshelf.

So with Nigel's sage counsel, we are reminded of the essential need to think locally before acting globally. It's perhaps not as pithy on a bumper sticker, but it's damned good marketing advice!

EILEEN CAMPBELL
Chief Executive Officer
Millward Brown

Acknowledgments

First, my grateful thanks to my colleagues who provided contributions for this book:

Matthew Angus, Account Manager, Millward Brown South Africa

Judith Kapanga, Senior Research Executive, Millward Brown South Africa

Joanna Seddon, Executive Vice President, Millward Brown Optimor

Dominic Twose, Global Head of Knowledge Management, Millward Brown

I should like to thank the following people who kindly agreed to an interview for this book and provided valuable ideas and observations on the subject of global brands:

Dilek Dölek Başarir, Marketing Director, Efes Turkey Beer Group

Jeben Berg, Product Marketing Manager, YouTube

Ralph Blessing, Senior Partner, Arbor Strategy Group

Peter Brabeck-Letmathe, Chairman and Chief Executive Officer, Nestlé SA

Brian Fetherstonhaugh, Chairman and Chief Executive Officer, OgilvyOne Worldwide

Karen Hamilton, Regional Category Vice President, Deodorants Europe, Unilever

Ben Haxworth, Marketing Consultant

Mike Keyes, Global Jack Daniel's Brand Director, Brown Forman

Del Levin, Marketing Director, Colgate-Palmolive South Africa

Ross MacDonald, Executive Planning Director, Rivet Global

Christene McCauley, Global Consumer Planning Director, Brand Building, Diageo

Jim Murphy, Director of Global Marketing, Jack Daniel's, Brown Forman

Tony Palmer, Chief Marketing Officer, Kimberly-Clark

Simon Rothon, Senior Vice President, Unilever Marketing Services, Unilever

Eric Salama, Chief Executive Officer, Kantar Group

Dan Schapker, Group Manager, Consumer Insights Group, Jack Daniel's Brown Forman

John Seifert, Chairman, Global Brand Community, Ogilvy & Mather Worldwide

Bill Sidwell, Director of Global Brand Strategy and Management, Hewlett Packard

Sir Martin Sorrell, Chief Executive Officer, WPP

Richard Thorogood, Director Consumer and Shopper Insights; Europe and South Pacific Division, Colgate-Palmolive

David Wheldon, Global Director of Brand, Vodafone Group Services Limited

I would also like to thank the participants in Millward Brown's seminar on global advertising, "Where Great Minds Meet: Global vs Local," held on November 20, 2007 in London. Their commentary provided some valuable examples on the practice of developing global advertising.

Jaroslav Cír, Global Consumer and Market Insight Director for the Rexona brand, Unilever

Dr. Valerie Curtis, London School of Hygiene & Tropical Medicine (an expert in evolutionary psychology)

James Eadie, Integrated Marketing Communications Director, Coca-Cola Great Britain

Richard Swaab, Executive Vice Chairman, AMV BBDO

I have talked with and listened to many other practitioners and academics in meetings and conferences around the world. They are far too many to acknowledge by name here, but I thank them nonetheless.

To Anne Hedde, CEO of Lightspeed Research, North America, my sincere thanks for her assistance on the Global Brand Survey.

Numerous colleagues have provided me with ideas and feedback on the book. In particular, I would like to single out Gordon Pincott and Warwick Nash, who offered both ideas and feedback on several chapters. I would also like to thank: Jorge Alagón, Lisa Bartlett, Dale Beaton, Andrea Bielli, Sandeep Budhiraja, Deepender Rana, Sue Elms, Manuel Gonzalez, Ann Green, Jean McDougall, Erika Nemethi, Graham Page, Lisa Parente, Kyril Petrin (A/R/M/I-Marketing), Petra Prusova, Erik du Plessis, Felipe Ramirez, Anita Valdes, Peter Walshe, Dan White, Geoff Wicken (Development Director,

KMR Group), Gordon Wyner, and all the others who responded to my e-mails with ideas and examples for the book.

Thank you to Jill Davies for her patience while I was writing the book and for providing valuable feedback on the final draft.

And last, but certainly not least, I would like to thank Dede Fitch, without whose help this book would be unstructured and unreadable.

Introduction

Going Global: A Business Imperative, a Big Challenge

The brand-globalization movement continues apace, as increasing numbers of companies expand their brand footprints to foreign markets. The logic behind this trend seems compelling. New markets hold the promise of new opportunities, new customers, and new revenue. New markets, particularly those in developing countries, offer growth prospects that seem attractive, if not unparalleled. Expanding a brand's presence to multiple countries mitigates the risks associated with launching a completely new brand and also brings with it the possibility of benefiting from advantages of scale.

The success of companies that have marketed their brands effectively in different cultures is seductive and appealing. Brands like Coca-Cola, McDonald's, and Toyota, which have created strong connections with consumers across cultures, add incredible value to the companies that own them. But very few of today's global brands were developed with the objective of "going global" in mind. Most were well-established brands in their countries of origin when their owners sought to take advantage of developing markets abroad. They ventured into foreign markets with a history of success at home, but not necessarily with the tools they needed to replicate that success in a new place. As a result, their ultimate success was dearly won, the result of considerable trial and error.

In today's competitive global marketplace, however, companies can't afford to stumble as they enter new markets. They need to hit the ground running. Therefore, companies with global aspirations for their brands need to plan carefully to turn those visions into reality, because success is far from guaranteed. Few brands succeed in creating a strong connection with consumers across multiple countries. The formula that makes a brand strong in one country may not travel well. Consumer needs and values still differ dramatically from place to place. Few brand positionings readily stretch across different cultures. The process of going global not only magnifies the complexity of building a strong brand but adds new barriers to success.

Finding the Right Balance

The fundamental challenge for brand marketers is to distinguish between the aspects of a brand that can be exported successfully and those that must be adapted. In the words of Geoffrey Probert, a senior vice president at Unilever, "The challenge is to find the right balance between mindlessly global and hopelessly local."[1] Companies competing on the world stage need to find that optimal balance in order to stimulate and maintain profitable growth for their brands. They must weigh the efficiency of developing one global marketing campaign against the need to be sensitive to local countries and cultures. Go too far in the direction of local adaptation and all efficiencies are lost; a company might just as well launch a completely new brand in each country. Fail to adapt the offer sufficiently and the opportunity cost of lost sales and wasted marketing investment could be significant.

Identifying the ideal point of balance between global and local is not an easy task. A thorough understanding of local needs, values, and desires is necessary to successfully manage a brand on the global stage.

Brands Need to Act Local

The vast majority of people in the world live very local lives. Though they may be exposed to international news, media, and brands, their frame of reference still tends to be insular. Just watch the TV news in New York, Buenos Aires, or Bangkok. Most content is local: local events, local sports results, sales in local stores. People relate best to local brands. After all, they grew up with them. Their friends use them. Local brands understand their needs.

To be successful, brands need to engage people at the local level, whether that is in the brand's "home" country or elsewhere. Doing this requires an understanding of the local culture, which is best obtained through people on the ground in the region. Yet while seeking to reduce costs, many companies have consolidated and centralized resources, particularly those supporting innovation and marketing. If local brand teams have been eliminated, and the savings already have been passed to the bottom line, companies will face a major challenge in undoing what has been done. Investors will not applaud an about-turn that apparently adds cost back into the business.

Marketing Is Not Getting Any Easier

Globalization of markets makes the world of brands more cluttered and competitive. It requires marketers to come to grips with new issues and different cultures while they are already grappling with a raft of challenging issues at home: growing retailer power, the accelerating pace of innovation, the increasing fragmentation of media, and the advent of new technologies. All these issues have converged to make the world of marketing more complex and chaotic than ever before. Brand marketers have contributed to this complexity by presenting consumers with a bewildering number of alternatives, not just in the domain of the supermarket but also in service offerings, such as calling plans and credit cards. As brands are forced to stretch across so many variants, it becomes increasingly difficult for them to clearly communicate what they stand for.

Globalization presents threats as well as opportunities as successful companies based in Asia and elsewhere grow and copy the tactics of the western multinational corporations. For example, western marketers, who have tended to view China and India as "new" markets for their goods and services, often have used acquisition as an entry strategy. This is no longer a one-way street. Asian companies Lenovo, Haier, and Tata are now viewing western companies as fair game. In the last few years we have seen Tata buy the venerable British tea brand Tetley and set its sights on Jaguar and Land Rover. Lenovo bought the IBM Thinkpad division and Haier made a bid for Maytag. This is a trend that is only likely to accelerate.

The difficulties presented by these challenges are intensified by the greater uncertainty facing the world as a whole. The new century has brought a growing acceptance that the threat of global warming is real. As governments look for ways to mitigate the effects of greenhouse gas emissions, companies will need to reconsider production and outsourcing strategies for economic reasons. Consumer attitudes are also likely to demand changes from brand manufacturers. As consumers become more sensitive to the issue of global warming, we can expect to see a stronger desire to buy local and to buy green.

Human Nature: A Reassuring Constant

Faced with this increasingly challenging environment, we must ask: Is the glass half empty or half full? If consumers are dissatisfied and confused by too many choices, then a brand that offers a clear, compelling proposition will have a significant advantage over competitors.

In the furor over what is changing in the domains of retailing, media, and technology, many people forget the one thing that is not changing: human nature. Human beings around the world have a core set of motivations, and the brands that best address their needs and desires will emerge as the global leaders. The means by which brands do this may change, but the nature of the connection they forge with consumers will not.

One of the most basic facets of human nature is the desire to minimize effort. In modern times, this desire expresses itself in a preference for convenience. Marketers have long known that convenience sells when it comes to food preparation, retail locations, and travel, but behind such examples lies an even more basic truth: People want shopping to be simple. Most people want to invest the minimum amount of effort in thinking about, shopping for, and selecting brands for purchase. Purchase decisions are mental work that take up an increasingly precious resource: time. Brands are valuable because they provide convenient shortcuts to decision making.

The Role of Brands

The critical role of marketing, therefore, is to make a brand's proposition as clear and compelling as possible. In many cases, doing this means highlighting the positive aspects of using, consuming, or interacting with the brand. In others, it requires differentiating the brand through the personality it projects. The specific tasks will vary according to brand and market, but all actions must work toward the ultimate goal: to create strong emotional bonds with consumers.

No longer can these emotional bonds be created simply by running TV ads and making sure the brand is available at the right price. Marketers need to draw on all of the available touch points to engage their customers at every step of the purchase process, starting before a need is even recognized and concluding only after the purchase is made. Mobile phones, in-store media, sponsored search links, social networks, word of mouth, viral videos, radio and outdoor ads—all of these have roles to play. We just need to understand what those roles are and how they can best be used to turn a potential buyer into a loyal repeat purchaser.

Will Global Brands Continue to Be a Worthwhile Investment?

In *The Global Brand*, I will explore the ways brands compete on a global stage. Globalization will remain an imperative, but *how* brands approach globalization may need to change.

The Global Brand considers the tension between effective branding and business efficiency and identifies the practices that will help aspiring global brands become successful on the world stage. For over 20 years, Millward Brown[2] has conducted market research for some of the biggest global brands, accumulating a vast wealth of information on effective practices for growing and maintaining brands. I have drawn on that experience and augmented the knowledge gained with new research, case studies, and interviews with the architects of some of today's most successful global brands.

I have organized the book into three parts. In Part One, I describe the ways in which strong global brands create lasting value. In Part Two, I focus on the challenges faced by marketers in building strong global brands. And finally, in Part Three, I describe some practices that can help marketers overcome the difficulties they will face in the process of building strong global brands.

The dynamics of building a strong brand on a global basis are complex and challenging, as well as confounding to many marketers, especially in light of social trends that seem to suggest that, rather than becoming more homogenous, the world is fragmenting. For some product and service categories, a strong, local brand may be far more profitable than a global one. Whatever the future holds, however, one thing remains true: Without a good understanding of people's needs, wants, and desires at a local level, marketers of global brands stand little chance of success.

Part One

Part One

Strong Global Brands
Create Lasting Value

A strong brand is not the same as a business or a trademark. A brand—global or local—derives its value from creating a strong relationship with consumers. The strength of that relationship is determined by ideas and associations in people's minds. For that reason, marketers must use every available "touch point"—that is, every available point of contact between a brand and a consumer—to reinforce relevant, differentiating, and motivating perceptions about their brands.

Successful global brands are strong brands that transcend their origins and create enduring relationships with consumers across countries and cultures. On this basis, many brands are global, but very few are globally successful. In this first section of the book, I examine a model for measuring brand success and apply that model to identify the world's strongest global brands.

In Chapter 1, I amend the accepted definition of a brand ("a brand exists in the minds of consumers") by suggesting that the ideas and memories that constitute a brand must drive behavior and create value for a business. Although perceptions held by individual consumers matter, shared impressions are necessary for brands to have social meaning. I discuss what this means for marketers and include the implications of new learning from cognitive science.

A global brand is one that transcends its cultural origins to develop strong relationships with consumers in multiple countries, even though it may not show a consistent face in every market. In Chapter 2, I review several examples of brands that have been successful on the global stage.

In Chapter 3, I outline the five steps to a strong brand that are represented in the BrandDynamics™ Pyramid. The stronger the relationship consumers have with a brand, the more value the brand can create. In the short term, this value is reflected in incremental volume and price premiums; in the longer term, through increased market share.

In Chapter 4, I use "bonding"—the top level of the BrandDynamics Pyramid—to create a Global Brand Power Score representing a brand's ability to create a strong bond with consumers across countries and cultures. I use case studies based on the highest-ranked brands to highlight the drivers of global success: a strong, scalable business model; innovation; a great brand experience; clarity of positioning; a sense of dynamism; authenticity; and a strong corporate culture.

To close the first part of the book, Joanna Seddon, executive vice president of Millward Brown Optimor, explains how a strong brand leads to a consistent and growing revenue stream, improved shareholder value, and other, less tangible benefits, such as resilience in adverse conditions and the ability to extend to new categories. This chapter includes a review of the 2008 BrandZ™ Top 100 Most Valuable Brands and highlights the different means by which brands deliver long-term value.

Chapter 1

What Is a Brand?

Judging by their actions, few people in business really understand what a brand is. Yes, people have all read the definitions in a myriad of business books, but have they really absorbed the true implications of those definitions? A brand is not the same as a business. A brand is not the same as a trademark or corporate identity. A brand is not a veneer to be applied to a business or something to be ignored when it does not suit or budgets are tight. In this chapter I review the latest understanding of what a brand is and outline some of the implications resulting from that understanding.

So What Is a Brand?

The U.K. brand planning guru Paul Feldwick defined a brand this way: "A brand is simply a collection of perceptions in the mind of the consumer."[1]

That definition is fine, as far as it goes. The core idea contained in the definition, that a brand exists in the mind of a consumer, is used repeatedly in discussions of branding. But why would you invest millions on brand identity and marketing to build nothing more than a collection of perceptions?

What's missing from Feldwick's definition is the idea that this collection of perceptions must somehow make the associated product or service more salient, more interesting, or more compelling than it would be otherwise. These mental associations must make the branded product valuable to potential buyers, valuable enough to inspire them to choose it over alternatives. The associations people have with a brand must make them want to buy it.

Associations Can Be Many and Varied

In research and development work conducted by Millward Brown in Mexico and the United Kingdom, we asked two open-ended questions of people who had expressed a preference for a brand. The questions were:

1. When you think of (brand), what memories and associations come to mind? You might want to consider images, pictures, feelings, sensations, words, people, places or occasions.
2. What do you know about (brand)? You might want to consider things like the product itself, its packaging and how much it costs.

On average, for each brand, people offered eight associations. These associations differed markedly across brands, even among those in the same product category. They included such things as product attributes, rational and emotional benefits, places and events where the brand was used, the brand's price, its perceived value, and the type of people who use it. Marketing activities were also mentioned, giving us a useful indication of their relative importance to different types of brands and confirming that impulse brands are more likely to be defined by their communications than products or services involving more complex selection processes. In Mexico, 19 percent of our sample mentioned marketing—primarily TV advertising—in relation to a soft drink brand, while only 1 percent mentioned any form of marketing in relation to a hotel chain.

The origins of brand associations are legion. They may be rooted in nostalgic memories from childhood or shaped by messages from the brand's advertising. They may be based on direct experience with a brand or on observations of a brand in use. Positive associations make people more inclined to buy the brand and, importantly, to do so repeatedly in the future. Positive brand associations create loyal customers.

The latest findings from neuroscience (see the box) confirm that the stronger and more positive these associations are, the more likely it is that the brand will stand out and be purchased. The same research also suggests that the strength of a brand is related to the degree to which a brand's associations are balanced across three important areas: the brand's physical cues, its functional benefits, and its emotional connotations. However these associations were formed, the marketer's job is to understand which ones strengthen the brand and then to reinforce those beneficial associations through marketing.

What Marketing Can Learn from Neuroscience

At the 2006 ESOMAR Congress, the annual gathering of the world association of research professionals, Graham Page, Millward Brown's executive vice president, Global Solutions, and Professor Jane Raymond

➡

received the Best Paper Award for "Cognitive Neuroscience, Marketing and Research: Separating Fact from Fiction."[2] In their paper, they review what neuroscience tells us about the workings of the brain and apply that learning to the practice of marketing and market research. In so doing, Page and Raymond provide a science-based rationale for some long-established marketing practices. Their paper begins to shed some light on why these techniques have been effective, and, in particular, it highlights the critical roles of both brand experience and clarity in determining loyalty.

Critical to the world of marketing is the finding that people use "representations" to understand, make decisions, and interact with the world around them. Representations are made up of little bits of information that may be externally perceived or remembered. Different types of information are processed by different parts of the brain, in clusters of neurons known as modules. One module might handle visual stimuli while another sorts out auditory inputs. These modules progressively share information with each other in a hierarchical structure, culminating at the top in three "mega-modules": one that handles knowledge about the physical properties of objects; one that deals with actions, such as how an object is used; and one that works with emotional responses or evaluations.

According to Page and Raymond, a representation of something, whether it's an object, a concept, or a brand, is put together using information from each of the three mega-modules: knowledge, actions, and feelings. The greater the strength and clarity of the representation, the more likely it is to take priority in what is called the "workspace," the brain system that integrates ideas into long-term memory and allows them to be used in decision making. A representation of something exceptionally powerful to an individual, such as the face of a loved one, may become "superfamiliar," meaning that it is constructed more readily than other representations.

Page and Raymond's paper helps us understand how differentiation relates to the way the human brain makes choices. Brands that readily form strong, differentiated representations have the best chance of being chosen in a cluttered environment. Critically, however, the strength of those representations depends on people having a balanced understanding of the brand: one that includes its physical cues, its functional benefits, and the emotions it evokes. While we tend to think of marketing in terms of visual and verbal communication, this new understanding makes it

➡

clear that it is the total sensory experience that matters. Memories of a positive brand experience can be reinforced directly, through exposure to the relevant sensory experience, or indirectly, through communication designed to remind people of the experience.

The paper builds on this point with some new analysis. Drawing on over 8500 interviews, Page and Raymond examined people's responses to open-ended questions about the thoughts and feelings that came to mind for 42 specific brands. Answers were coded into the three key groups, Knowledge, Action, and Emotion. Brands were then scored on two dimensions: the degree to which associations came to mind and the degree to which the distribution of associations was balanced across the three mega-modules.

Brands were assigned to one of four groups based on their scores.

1. Many associations, well balanced across the three groups
2. Many associations, not balanced across groups
3. Fewer associations, but well balanced across the three groups
4. Fewer associations, not balanced across groups

The group of brands that was best, on average, at increasing the consumer predisposition to purchase was the first group, in which associations were many and balanced. Intriguingly, the group that was next-strongest in this regard was the third group, composed of brands with fewer associations but a good balance across the three mega-modules.

The two groups with unbalanced associations were both dramatically weaker. This fact strongly supports the implication of the neuroscience findings: Brands need to be strong in all three mega-modules to maximize their potential for success.

Brand Associations Must Be Shared

Jeremy Bullmore, a well-known author on brands and branding, and a board member at WPP and the Guardian Media Group plc, says this about brand perceptions: "The image of a brand is a subjective thing. No two people, however similar, hold precisely the same view of the same brand."[3]

That's true enough—a brand is experienced in a unique and personal way. But without some collective understanding among individuals, can brands have any value at all?

Imagine we are having a conversation, and I mention the name "Bombril." Does that name mean anything to you? If it doesn't, your brain will either "bleep over" the name or deliver vague impressions related to what the name sounds like . . . a drum beat, a reference to Tom Bombadil from Tolkien's *The Lord of the Rings*, or the name of a patent medicine. Without a common understanding of what it means, the name can add no value to the conversation. Rather than being a shortcut to a relevant idea, the name Bombril becomes something I need to explain.[4]

With this idea in mind, Faris Yakob, a strategist at Naked Communications, reformulated Paul Feldwick's brand definition in this way: "A brand is a *collective* perception in the minds of consumers."[5] Yakob compares brands to money, which has value only because we agree it does. The cash in your pocket is just paper, with little intrinsic value, but others will happily exchange goods and services for it. Yakob concludes that "a brand is a form of socially constructed reality that has attained an objective reality, which is why it can have a cash value that is dependent on the totality of perceptions held about it."

While I think it is slightly oversimplified, this definition adds a lot to our understanding of why marketers need to imbue brands with clarity. Any symbolic power wielded by brands is rooted in a collective understanding of what they represent. Perceptions of powerful brands, such as Coca-Cola, Apple's iPod, and Harley-Davidson, consist of well-known and widely shared associations, which form a base on which people add their own individual, subjective reactions. The significance of the shared understanding is most apparent when considering "identity" brands, ones that openly indicate something about a person's lifestyle and attitudes. The person who chooses a Rolex signals something different about himself from someone who chooses a Swatch. Buying Patagonia clothing makes a different statement from buying Billabong. And in both developed and developing countries, hosts signal both their own status and their respect for their guests through their choice of food and drink brands.

Because this shared understanding is critical to a brand's meaning, culture is a key factor in determining the success of global brands. Throughout the remainder of the book, I examine the role of local culture, both as a driver to the development of a strong local brand and as a barrier to global brand success.

Amending the Accepted Definition

Based on all the available evidence, I propose the following definition of a brand:

> A brand consists of a set of enduring and shared perceptions in the minds of consumers. The stronger, more coherent and motivating those perceptions are, the more likely they will be to influence purchase decisions and add value to a business.

As a market researcher I see the brand from a consumer viewpoint. But a brand does not spring into being in consumers' minds without a marketer who creates a product, identity and positioning to which people then respond. Peter Brabeck, chairman and chief executive officer of Nestlé SA, puts it this way: "A brand is both what it gives to the consumer but also what it gets from the brand owner. You cannot easily separate the two."[6]

In the remainder of this chapter I consider the other side of the equation. What are the implications for marketers trying to build strong brands?

The Implications of This Definition for Marketers

While it is widely accepted that a brand consists of a set of perceptions, the implications of this idea are often misunderstood. Understanding that brands exist only in the minds of consumers, many people now wrongly conclude that brands can no longer be controlled by marketers and suggest that in this age of consumer-generated content, marketers should just "let go" of their brands. In my opinion, that advice is not only dangerous but reflects a fundamental lack of understanding of what marketing is all about. Let me briefly explain why.

In his collection of essays *Apples, Insights and Mad Inventors*, Jeremy Bullmore refers to an analogy he once made, which became widely quoted: "People build brands as birds build nests, from scraps and straws we chance upon."[7]

As Bullmore admits, this statement is demonstrably untrue: Birds build a wide variety of nests, and they are often very selective in their use of building materials. But you do get the main idea, which is that a mental concept of a brand is a montage of images, impressions, and experiences.

Those unordered impressions are neither consciously chosen nor limited to ideas expressed in the brand's marketing communications. Rather, they are acquired from experience, from scores of seemingly trivial encounters with the brand. Impressions are formed at the point of purchase, during the use or consumption of the product, when encountering the brand's marketing communications, or when other people are heard talking about the brand.

A Unifying Theme

Random and disorganized impressions won't enhance a brand's value. The marketer's job is to provide the unifying theme around which brand associations form, to frame people's experience of the brand so that they focus on the positive aspects of it, not the negative. To return to Bullmore's analogy, marketers need to ensure that when people are building their brand "nests," they have a structure around which to build. The last thing marketers can afford to do is to let brand associations pile up in an untidy heap.

Therefore, marketers must work to shape people's day-to-day encounters with a brand to ensure that the cumulative impression is a desirable one. Of course, some encounters are more powerful than others, and some are easier to control.

Personal experience of the brand itself is the dominant source of impressions—but what constitutes that experience? For a car, it might be the first impressions gained on a test drive or the lasting memories formed by the daily commute. It might simply be the sight of the car on the street. Even a 30-second video ad can create an imagined experience with the power to shape impressions. The marketer must consider how all of these experiences mold perceptions of a brand.

The Brand Promise: A Magnet for Associations

Agencies often refer to a concept called the "brand promise." Sometimes this idea is also referred to as the "brand essence," or "brand idea." Whatever name is used, this outward expression of the brand exists to help provide structure to all brand impressions, controlled or uncontrolled. If it is to do this effectively, the brand promise must be strong enough to pull all impressions together and focus them toward an emotional connection with the brand. An effective brand promise provides a foundation on which marketers can build a deep and compelling impression of a brand. Once a compelling promise is identified, it should not be changed lightly. If it is, all the prior efforts to build and frame people's perceptions will be undermined.

Maurice Saatchi, a co-founder of the advertising agency Saatchi and Saatchi and currently a partner in M&C Saatchi, would have us boil the promise down to one word. Referring to the new world of branding in an infamous 2006 *Financial Times* article, he states: "In this new business model, companies seek to build one-word equity—to define the one characteristic they most want instantly associated with their brand around the world, and then own it. That is one-word equity."[8]

It is the modern equivalent of the best location on the main street, except the location is in the mind. Speaking at a Millward Brown seminar on global advertising held in London in 2007, Richard Swaab, executive vice chairman at AMV BBDO, expressed a similar point of view but acknowledged the need for that promise to motivate potential buyers. He said: "We try and distill any campaign these days down to a verb because verbs are behaviorally driven."[9]

A brand promise needs to speak to the target audience; it does not need to appeal to everyone. In fact, many branding experts suggest that a more segmenting brand promise will produce a stronger appeal to the brand's real target.

Table 1.1 Brand Promises and Taglines

Brand	Brand Promise	Tagline
Guinness	Anticipation of enjoyment	"Good things come to those who wait"
Nike	Win	"Just do it"
Coca-Cola	Optimism	"The Coke side of life"
Apple	Computing made human	"Think different"
Nicorette	Start (giving up)	"Beat cigarettes one at a time"

Some well-known brand promises and their related taglines are shown in Table 1.1.

Brand Associations Need Repeating

An enduring brand impression is not formed overnight. Over time, through experience and engaging communication, beneficial associations must be established in people's memories. Shaping impressions must be a continuing process, because memories are malleable and impermanent things.

Consider the fact that when I'm staying in a hotel, I rarely forget my room number. That is a pretty amazing feat, considering that I often stay in as many hotels (and cities) as there are days in the week. What I may not be able to remember is the number of the hotel room I stayed in the night before. And last week? Forget it. Why do I remember the current room number and forget the rest? Because the current one is relevant and important to me, and the others no longer are.

This example points to the fact that humans have good reasons to forget things. If we remembered the number of every single hotel room we had ever stayed in, we would get confused. We need to remember the most relevant one. But that is a problem when it comes to building brands. Few brands are relevant to us all the time. Our need for them comes and goes, and in between those occasions, our memories of what brands stand for starts to shift and fade. Even when we use a brand on a regular basis, we probably do not pay conscious attention to the experience, as we come to accept it and take it for granted. I love driving my Audi TT, but I don't often think about the components of the experience that make it different from driving a BMW Z5. An important function of advertising, then, is to refocus attention on the positive, differentiating aspects of a brand experience.

Building Coherence through 360 Marketing

The brand promise reflects the essence of what the brand stands for and provides the unifying theme for brand associations. However, the brand promise alone is not enough. It must be fleshed out if consumers are to understand all of a brand's physical associations, functional benefits, and emotional connotations. The understanding that this task is too big for any one communication channel has led to the emergence over the past several years of the disciplines known as 360 marketing and touch-point planning.

No one touch point can hope to convey every aspect of a brand. Therefore, each potential brand contact needs to be crafted to work in synergy across the whole brand experience. Personal experience is best for conveying a brand's physical properties while the Internet, print advertising, product demonstrations, and public relations may be better suited to communicate a brand's functional benefits. Video advertising may be ideal for evoking an emotional response. All these channels need to work in concert in order to create a balanced representation of the brand.

The best mix of channels will vary from brand to brand and country to country. To ensure that the most positive and motivating memories come readily to mind when consumers think about buying the brand, marketers need to:

- Establish the most motivating brand associations possible prior to purchase and keep them fresh until the purchase is made.
- Cue recognition of the brand and its associated memories at the point of purchase.
- Over time, constantly refresh the positive impressions held by brand loyalists.

Next I explain how a strong brand impression helps consumers make purchase decisions. Human nature, it seems, is biased in favor of a strong brand.

Shortcuts to Decision Making

According to Procter & Gamble, shoppers make up their minds about a product in three to seven seconds, which is just about the time it takes for a shopper to notice a product on a store shelf. P&G calls this time lapse the "first moment of truth" and considers it to be the brand's most important marketing opportunity.

In such a short period of time, people can't undertake a reasoned analysis of their options. Rather, under these conditions, people rely on shortcuts, called heuristics, to help them make brand choices.

Too Much Information, Too Little Time

Making conscious, thought-out decisions takes knowledge, time, and effort. It requires us to search for relevant information, assess it, and weigh up the pros and cons. For critical decisions, such as choosing the hospital where your child will undergo major surgery, the effort seems worthwhile. But everyday decisions, such as which brand of coffee to buy, don't warrant so much time and effort.

Furthermore, it's a fallacy to believe that we can find and evaluate all the relevant information for even the most important decisions. That goal is laudable but unachievable. We cannot possibly process all of the things that may bear on our decision. Instead we focus on a few, readily appreciable facts. In the case of brands that we buy on a regular basis, we may hardly give the decision any thought, buying solely on the basis of habit.

Brands Help Make Decisions Simple

Gerd Gigerenzer and Peter M. Todd at the Max Planck Institute for Human Development in Berlin propose that all human decisions use what they call "fast and frugal heuristics" to reach conclusions that are satisfactory if not always optimal.[10] These heuristics are fast in the sense that they facilitate quick decision-making. They are frugal in the sense that they allow decisions to be taken based on limited information. Fast and frugal heuristics help us make choices in spite of the fact that we lack perfect knowledge and unlimited time. Early in their book, *Simple Heuristics That Make Us Smart*, Gigerenzer and Todd describe a very simple decision tree, comprising three yes/no questions, used by doctors to classify incoming heart attack patients. Importantly, the decision tree has clear stopping points that determine what action is to be taken. If the patient's blood pressure is greater than 91 and the patient's age is less than 62.5, that patient is at low risk. If the patient is older, a further question needs to be asked to assess the risk level. The decision tree's simple, step-by-step approach allows doctors to make critical decisions quickly, when time is of the essence. It is far easier to apply under stress than alternative systems that rely on inter-locking predictors to reach the same conclusions. Gigerenzer and Todd propose that this is how humans make all decisions.

The concept of heuristics is interesting because it is so helpful in explaining why strong brands are important. Brands, like heuristics, provide convenient shortcuts for decision making. To illustrate this idea, let's consider the example of buying coffee.

A basic heuristic that governs choice among alternatives is recognition. Let's say your preferred coffee brand is out of stock at the local store. How will you choose an alternative? If you recognize only one brand of coffee on the shelf, then recognition may become your decision heuristic. You are much more likely to choose the brand you recognize. If you recognize more than one brand, then recognition will not suffice to make the decision, but it will have winnowed down the set of alternatives. You will then need another criterion in order to reach the stopping point and make your choice.

Another common heuristic is "take the one chosen last," better known to us as habit. But what if you did not like the coffee you chose last time? Then you might resort to a heuristic called "take the best." Drawing on your knowledge of the alternatives, you would assess the options according to the criteria that are important to you until you find one that is discriminating. Say you prefer a rich-tasting coffee. Then you would search for the cues that best differentiate the coffee brands on that criterion. If that route yields a dead end, you might turn to other heuristics, such as "take the cheapest," "take the most attractive," and so on.

The heuristics we've mentioned thus far have been very rational ones, but Gigerenzer and Todd also propose that heuristics based on emotions, social norms, and imitation belong in our decision-making toolbox.

Let us now consider the selection of an analgesic painkiller. Faced with a branded analgesic and a private-label product, most people will choose the branded alternative, even though both products contain identical ingredients. Rationally there seems to be only one criterion on which to make a choice—price—but most people do not use that heuristic. Few people admit to buying analgesics on price. Instead, most people make an emotionally driven choice and select the brand that is most recognizable, has the strongest product credentials, or seems most trustworthy.

Although social norms may seem to apply better to the realm of interpersonal relations than branding, Gigerenzer and Todd suggest that they also underlie heuristics that can help us make decisions. Let's go back to our coffee example. Lacking any other decision criteria, you might choose the brand that you think is the most popular (a safe choice), or you might even watch what other people are choosing, or ask for advice. If you happen to be a fan of George Clooney, you might choose the brand he advertises, Nespresso. If it's good enough for the man twice voted Sexiest Man Alive by *People Magazine* (1997 and 2006), it should be good enough for you, right?

So how do we choose a heuristic to apply in a certain situation? Gigerenzer and Todd point out that there are actually relatively few alternatives for any one situation, saying: "Each heuristic is specialized for certain classes of problems, which means that most of them are not applicable in a given situation." When more than one heuristic does apply, it may be a combination that determines the ultimate choice. In the case of frequently purchased goods and services, repeated exposure and response to a set of heuristics should lead to the decision becoming habitual, requiring consumers to waste hardly any thought on the purchase decision. Marketers need to ensure that for their brands, motivating associations are triggered by whatever heuristics might be used. Brand cues have an important role to play in that process.

Cues that Aid Recognition

The role of recognition in the purchase process goes beyond that of a simple decision heuristic to be used when little else is known. Recognition is the cue that triggers other brand associations to come to mind.

In his book *The Advertised Mind*, my good colleague Erik du Plessis reviews how our senses help direct our attention by stimulating instinctive, emotional reactions to the world around us.[11] This process determines how we react to our surroundings and helps explain why recognition is such an important component of branding. Whether it is the distinctive styling of a Cadillac, the Nike swoosh, or the stylized silhouette of someone listening to their Apple iPod depicted on billboards, recognition is a precursor to triggering motivating memories of the brand.

Brands with distinctive properties from their packaging, advertising, or product can leverage them to good effect to ensure instant recognition. For example, in the United Kingdom, Guinness recognized that its loyal drinkers needed little prompting to buy the brand. Others, however, who considered Guinness an acceptable choice but didn't drink it regularly needed a reminder. To encourage those customers to buy Guinness, large replicas of glasses of ice-cold Guinness were added to either side of the shelf display. Spanning multiple shelves, the models were visible from every point in the beer aisle. Instantly recognizable, they helped disrupt people's established shopping habits, cued positive associations, and helped to increase sales by 27 percent.

Research conducted by the U.K. research company RMS found that a similar display helped Unilever's Pot Noodle brand generate a 19 percent increase in sales. Extending perpendicular from the shelves into the aisle, banners adorned with giant Pot Noodle cups faced shoppers as they moved down the aisle and served to lure them to the section. In these cases, simple recognition was enough to make the sale. In more considered purchases, other heuristics will come into play.

Cues that Aid Differentiation

The heuristic that is ultimately relied on in decision making will depend on the context for the decision (e.g., which brands are known and available), the cues presented by the different brands, and the first relevant point that differentiates one brand from the rest.

The last factor is critical to the process of how brands help make a sale. The concept of fast and frugal heuristics suggests that a brand should try to gain exclusive association with key decision criteria in its product or service category. But in this day and age, it is unlikely that any brand will maintain a unique "product" benefit for long. Failing that, we need to ensure that our brand has parity on the most important criteria while aiming for ownership of less easily judged criteria, such as a sense of dynamism, a unique design, or emotional appeal. To help it stand out from the clutter, a brand needs a differentiating promise, either rational or emotional.

The Second Moment of Truth

The first moment of truth is only a small part of the brand story. While the marketing world has turned its attention to those first precious seconds, it may have lost sight of the "second moment of truth": the repeated experience of the product. As the 2002 P&G chairman's address stated, "The second moment of truth occurs two billion times a day when consumers use P&G brands. Every usage experience is our chance to delight consumers."[12] So while the first moment of truth is an opportunity to encourage trial, the second moment of truth will determine continued brand loyalty, priming consumers to use the "same as last time" heuristic next time they buy the category. Just as important as triggering the right associations at the point of purchase is ensuring a positive response to the continued brand experience.

Effective marketing communication is often based on product truths—that is, rational benefits that are translated into emotional benefits. Equally, advertising can effectively shape customers' experience of a brand by focusing their attention on specific aspects of that experience.

The importance of this route was demonstrated by my former Millward Brown colleagues Andy Farr and Gordon Brown in their award-winning paper "Persuasion or Enhancement" describing an experiment that demonstrated that a product which performed exactly the same as competing products could gain a perceived edge through advertising.[13] By enhancing people's perceptions at the time of use, advertising helped to lift their perceptions of the brand from "as good as other brands" to "better than other brands." Work by John Deighton[14] at the University of Chicago showed the same effect for car advertising. He showed that a group of people exposed to Ford's print advertising campaign "Quality is Job 1" were more likely to conclude from *Consumer Reports'* reliability data that Ford's vehicles were reliable. The interaction of the claim and the independent data created the effect, not just hearing the claim.

All in the Mind

A brand, then, is a complex entity. A brand exists as clusters of associations in individual minds, but only when fundamental brand perceptions are widely shared can that brand realize its full potential. Marketers must shape these perceptions as best they can to maximize a brand's value to their business.

Key Points to Take Away

- Consumers and customers do not put a lot of thought into most brand decisions.
- You need to create strong, coherent, and motivating perceptions of your brand at all points of contact in order to influence consumers' purchase decisions and create brand value.

Questions to Consider

1. What heuristics apply in your brand's product or service category today?
2. What heuristics might apply? Can you change the playing field on which decisions are made?
3. Which heuristics might benefit your brand more than others?
4. Which cues will identify that heuristic most obviously to potential buyers?

For more information related to these questions, visit theglobalbrandonline.com.

Chapter 2

So What *Is* a Global Brand?

Surely a global brand is simply a brand that is sold and marketed consistently around the world? Unfortunately, things are not that simple. As Simon Rothon, senior vice president of Unilever Marketing Services, says, "A wide geographic footprint does not qualify you as a global brand. You also need all the other aspects of what makes a brand a brand."[1] And those aspects may well vary depending on the nature of the brand, its category, and local culture.

One Size Does Not Fit All

A decade ago, a global brand would have been one that used the same product, packaging, and positioning in countries around the world. Encouraged by Theodore "Ted" Levitt's 1983 prediction that the future of brands was global,[2] and expecting to reap tremendous economies of scale, multinationals sought to standardize their brands. But to their chagrin, they found that the future Levitt predicted had not yet arrived. The world was still a very complex and diverse place.

Professor Pankaj Ghemawat of Harvard Business School, an expert on global strategy, refers to the belief that the world is flat as "globaloney." He points to the history of Coca-Cola to highlight the risks associated with that assumption.[3] In the 1980s, Coke chief executive Roberto Goizueta instituted an aggressive policy of centralization and standardization in the hope of leveraging economies of scale. Ghemawat writes, "It took Coke the better part of a decade to figure out that globaloney and its strategic implications were hazards to its health—in the course of which its market value declined by about $100 billion, or more than 40 percent from its peak."

Today, Coke pursues a much more balanced strategy, one that seeks to recognize differences between markets while still leveraging the advantages of scale.

From Consistent to Highly Adapted

As companies like Coke have learned, the globalization of a brand is no simple task. Companies must identify and maintain the delicate balance between the business advantages of scale and the branding advantages of a localized offer. Because the challenges posed by globalization vary according to brand and category, today we observe a continuum of brands, with those that are consistent around the world at one end and those that have been highly adapted to different regions at the other.

The beer brand Heineken is firmly positioned at the consistent end of the scale. In his article "Forging a Global Strategy for a Global Brand," Daniel Tearno states:

> Heineken has become the world's most international beer brand because of its quality. Beer drinkers know that when they get a Heineken, they get a great beer, no matter where they are in the world. That consistency is an important factor in the brand's global success. The unstinting devotion to achieving that quality is summed up in a comment by the late Freddy Heineken: "A bad bottle of beer is a personal insult." The images of Heineken—the distinctive green bottle, the five-pointed red star, the tilted "smiling" e in the Heineken logo—all welcome the consumer to the brand.[4]

Bill Ramsay, who had an extensive career both at General Foods and in academia, suggested that food brands might achieve global success without consistency in product formulation, positioning or even brand name.[5] For that to be true, however, a company must be able to derive great value from the business advantages offered by scale, such as cheaper sourcing costs or production efficiencies, since savings in production must counterbalance the expense of marketing brands separately in different countries. Most food brands try to maintain a degree of consistency but often have to adapt their product to meet local tastes. The Kit Kat candy bar, now owned by Nestlé, was invented in York, England, in the early 1930s and is reported to be available in versions that match Japanese, German, Australian, Canadian, and American tastes.[6]

No Single Recipe for Success

The aim of successful global brands is to strike a balance between business scale and brand strength that allows them to connect with consumers around the world. With this in mind, branding expert Martin Lindstrom proposes that a global brand needs to maintain a consistent name, logo, and color scheme in order to combine marketing efficiencies with the flexibility to localize positioning and communications.[7] At face value, this seems to be an appealing proposition, but there are many examples of brands sold globally that flout these guidelines.

History has left Unilever with several brands that share the same positioning but have different names in different parts of the world. Here are some examples:

- Unilever's male grooming brand is known everywhere in the world as Axe—except in the United Kingdom, Ireland, and Australia, where it is called Lynx. The name Axe worked well in France, where the product was first launched, but in the United Kingdom, that name didn't cut it. Apart from the name, the only other significant aspect of the brand altered to meet local needs is the fragrance level. Otherwise, the color scheme, logo, and packaging are consistent worldwide.
- Rexona, the world's largest deodorant brand in terms of sales, is known in the United States as Degree, in the United Kingdom as Sure, and in South Africa as Shield, because Unilever acquired established brands with those names in each market. In some Asian countries, the brand is known as Rexena because of local difficulties in pronouncing "RexOna." But in all locations, the deodorant's positioning, product formulation, packaging, and advertising are the same.

On the surface, this proliferation of brand names may seem odd, but it has enabled Unilever to marry up a promise that has global "legs" with a brand name that's familiar to a local population. It is the result of a consistent strategy that seeks to combine local appeal with global efficiency.

If something as fundamental as a brand name can vary across countries, what happened to the need for people to have a common understanding of what a brand stands for? That still applies, but only among people who are likely to interact around the brand. Where the brand appeals to an international and cosmopolitan group, a common brand understanding is a must. For example, Apple, Starbucks, and Red Bull all appeal to a relatively homogeneous audience and therefore have more of a need to maintain a common image.

The understanding of food brands, however, often differs. Bournvita is a brand of malted chocolate drink traditionally sold in the United Kingdom as a relaxing bedtime drink. In Nigeria, however, the brand's appeal used to be that it "made the blood strong." Bedtime associations, while present, had little to do with sleeping or relaxing. (In other words, the brand was seen as a predecessor of Viagra.) The differing perceptions of the benefits in the two countries did no harm to the brand's sales; there was no need for Nigerians and Brits to agree on the meaning of Bournvita.

My Definition of a Global Brand

Given the wide variation in how global brands are marketed today, consistency cannot form the basis of a definition. I define a global brand as one that has transcended its cultural origins to develop strong relationships with consumers across different countries and cultures.

■ McDonald's: A Strong Relationship with Consumers across Cultures

In 2003, McDonald's introduced its "Plan to Win" to address lackluster business performance. By 2007, the global giant reported the highest same-store sales growth in a decade in its Asia Pacific, Middle East, and Africa division as well as its third year of consistent global sales growth.

Speaking at the Association of National Advertisers Annual Conference in 2007, Mary Dillon, global chief marketing officer for McDonald's, explained the success in this way: "People's need for what we have to offer, convenience and value, has grown. . . . To truly connect with communities, you have to *be* local."[8]

McDonald's obeys Lindstrom's guidelines by maintaining a consistent name, logo, and color scheme in all its locations, but the brand's offering varies dramatically around the world. In Brazil, the company has an up-market reputation and offers home delivery. McCafés originated in Australia but are now found worldwide, and in Germany, they even outsell Starbucks. All of this will seem alien to those who are familiar only with the typical U.S. fast-food outlet. We might wonder, then, whether McDonald's really qualifies as a global brand, if its image is inconsistent and if many people value it only for the practical benefits of speed and low prices. But such functional benefits can contribute to stronger sales.

Given the choice between a McDonald's and an independent burger joint in a new city, many more people will choose McDonald's. Why do they do so? One senior manager at a major financial services firm explained why, when traveling abroad, he ate only at McDonald's: "You always know what you are going to get, it's safe, and besides, I like the coffee."

People choose McDonald's because it offers them something familiar, consistent, convenient, quick, and cheap. While they might actually prefer the food served next door, people choose McDonald's, the known quantity, because it's a safe bet.

McDonald's seeks to create the maximum return from its investment by balancing the business efficiency of total consistency with the extra demand created by adapting to local tastes. Its business model provides a platform on which the brand can build. In developed economies, where the brand is more familiar and faces strong competition, it must play to its basic strengths of economy and convenience. In developing countries, a similar product lineup can appeal to people aspiring to a western lifestyle. Either way, travelers entering a McDonald's in a foreign country will find something that meets their expectations on both quality and price.

Brands Are More than a Mark of Quality

The days of brands as a mark of quality alone, however, may be limited. Particularly in more developed and marketing-savvy economies, people expect more of a brand, if they are not to buy solely on the basis of price. As Jim Stengel, global marketing officer at P&G, puts it, "If you go back at Procter & Gamble, and in a lot of the industry, we often thought of our brands in terms of functional benefits. But the equity of great brands has to be something that a consumer finds inspirational and an organization finds inspirational."[9]

Inspiration can come from many different sources—as many as there are great brands—but the end result is a strong attitudinal bond with a brand. So while the experience of the past couple of decades suggests that a global brand need not present exactly the same face around the world, it must maintain a strong relationship with its consumers wherever it is found. The challenge to the marketer is to maximize the potential of the brand across countries and cultures on a profitable basis. In many cases, this means adapting the marketing mix just enough to be successful, but not so much that economies of scale are lost or unnecessary costs are incurred.

In the remainder of this chapter, I examine three case studies: Jack Daniel's, Red Bull, and YouTube. Each highlights that adaptation is key to growing a successful global brand. Jack Daniel's has a very strong brand promise in the United States that has transferred well to countries with similar cultures but may now need to be reinterpreted for more collectivist, Asian cultures. By contrast, Red Bull is the result of taking a local product from Asia and completely adapting it to meet the needs of western consumers. The new incarnation and consistent delivery against its brand promise have helped make Red Bull extremely successful. YouTube is already a global platform, but now it is seeking to become local too.

Jack Daniel's: A Brand Rooted in History and Popular Culture

Brown-Forman's Jack Daniel's brand was registered in 1866. Today, this global brand is still produced at one distillery in Lynchburg, Tennessee.

Jack Is Essentially a Brand of Contradictions

On the one hand, there is the town of Lynchburg, where folks make the whiskey. The brand's communications have focused on the charcoal process that mellows the drink and the people who make it and load the trucks. TV ads feature the tagline "Everyday they make it, they make it the best they can."

On the other hand, popular culture makes of the brand what it will. The brand's strong links to popular culture date back to before Frank Sinatra, who not only drank Jack everyday, but was buried with a bottle. Today, you can read *Men's Journal* and find Jake Burton lauding the brand in an interview, or flip through *US Weekly* and learn that Britney Spears swigged Jack Daniel's before going topless in a hotel swimming pool.

Popular culture has helped make Jack a very strong brand in the United States, but the free publicity is not all positive. In his office, Mike Keyes, global Jack Daniel's brand director, keeps what he refers to as "the Jack Daniel's wall of fame and shame," featuring a vast collection of cuttings from popular media around the world. Pointing to the story of John Daly, who blames his lost fortune on his dependence on Jack, Mike explained that it's not possible to control what is said and done to the brand out in the world—you just have to live with it. The iconic nature of the brand makes it a shortcut to signal independence in ads for other brands, such as Andrew Marc, and the label is even featured on the cover of a bootleg Russian copy of Jack Kerouac's *On the Road*.

Jim Murphy, director of global marketing for Jack Daniel's, identifies three levels to the brand's story.

1. You have the brand itself, which tells its own story, embodying the brand's authentic, American, idyllic values.
2. Then there are the consumers who tell stories of their own experiences with the brand. Often these focus on personal and social "rights of passage."
3. Finally, there is the mythos created by popular culture. In many ways this is the most powerful because it keeps the brand top of mind and provides a backdrop for the personal storytelling, a common point of reference.

The combination of the brand's own storytelling and the interpretation by popular culture creates an image of authenticity, independence, and a touch of rebellion. In the United States, the result is that the brand appeals to a wide array of people, from "bikers to bankers," from LDA to DND (Legal Drinking Age to Damn Near Dead). Even people who might otherwise have nothing in common can sit down and enjoy a Jack together.

Taking Jack Global

When Owsley Brown II became chief executive of Brown-Forman in 1993, only 22 percent of the company's net sales revenue was derived from outside the United States. Recognizing that a lot of the company's eggs were in the U.S. basket and that he had brands that had very strong foundations, Brown decided to take the company global, with Jack Daniel's leading the charge. Today, half of Brown-Forman's revenue comes from international markets, even as the company's business in the United States has continued to show healthy gains. During Brown's tenure as head of the company, Jack Daniel's depletions have more than doubled, to close to 10 million cases; the brand is now sold in more than 135 countries.

In the process of going global, the Jack Daniel's brand has encountered another problem that other global marketers will find all too familiar: The appeal of its persona varies by culture.

The global brand team focuses on the core values, such as authenticity, masculinity, and fraternalism that make Jack different and appealing. In the United States, these values resonate with the desire people have to live life on their own terms.

People from other English-speaking cultures typically have an immediate affinity with this positioning, resulting in strong sales in the United Kingdom, Australia, and South Africa. Outside of the Anglo cultures, the appeal of Americana has helped the brand travel to markets like Japan. In China, however, the brand's strong persona is at odds with local values and customs and the culture's concept of individualism. To Chinese consumers, the brand has automatic status as an upscale western brand, but its story does not resonate with them. Recognizing this challenge, the Jack Daniel's global team has invested in research to better understand how the brand's values can be positioned more appropriately.

Jack is definitely not the only brand to find that success at home and abroad may have different origins. Many brands need to reinterpret their promise and values in order to succeed in different cultures. In the next case study, I examine a brand that had its origins in Asia, was re-created in Austria, and now appeals to millions of people around the globe.

Red Bull: Undiluted Brand Building

In the heady days of the late 1990s, when I was running Millward Brown Interactive in San Francisco, I was introduced to a carbonated beverage unlike any other. That beverage was the energy drink Red Bull, the favorite of software engineers, ad execs, and entrepreneurs—in fact, anyone who needed to keep sharp for hours at a time. When it was launched in Austria in 1987, Red Bull didn't just create a new brand, it created a new category, energy drinks. It sold 1.1 million cans in Austria that year. In 2006, 3 billion cans of Red Bull were sold in over 130 countries.

The brand was created by Dietrich Mateschitz, an Austrian entrepreneur. On a trip to Asia, he found that a local Thai drink called Krating Daeng helped to cure his jet lag. Encouraged by the experience, Mateschitz set out to adapt the elixir to western tastes. After three years of intense development, the Red Bull drink that we know today entered the Austrian market. It was less sweet than the original, lightly carbonated, and with a name and packaging designed to appeal to a specific target audience: the youthful and independent-minded.

Red Bull not only tastes different, it makes you feel different. Upon trying Red Bull for the first time, many people comment on its invigorating effects. The company's sampling activity seeks to highlight the drink's impact by ensuring that its ambassadors find people who are exhausted and therefore most likely to benefit from the experience.

Speaking at the 2006 Advertising Research Foundation conference, Thomas Grabner, CEO of Kastner & Partners in America, the agency behind Red Bull, suggested that Red Bull's brand personality was defined very clearly from the start, to the point of being polarizing. Implicit in his comments was the assertion that you cannot create passion by appealing to all people equally. If you stand for something, some people will love you and some will hate you, but the ones who love you will buy your brand and pay a premium for it. This no-compromise attitude extends to the Red Bull business model. Their focus is single-minded: no diversification, no licensing, no brand merchandising, and no umbrella branding. How many brands can you think of that lost their way by trying to spread beyond their core positioning and target group? I suspect Red Bull is one of very few not to try.

From our brand equity research, we know that a differentiated, tightly targeted brand can sustain a premium price that mass-market brands cannot. Red Bull takes this to an extreme by charging three to six times more than Coca-Cola. The premium charged fuels the next growth driver: brand-building activities, which range from simple TV ads designed to create awareness and image, through sponsorship designed to establish credibility, to events created to differentiate and engage the audience. All of these activities support the Red Bull tagline: "Red Bull gives you wings."

Grabner sums up the Red Bull philosophy in this way: "Red Bull seeks to help and support its target group, not sell cans."

He believes that Red Bull has been successful because it has engaged in grassroots marketing—what he called an "intense conversation" with its target group. The brand shuns traditional celebrity endorsements, instead using event sponsorship to engage its audience directly by partnering with leaders in different activities to help them fulfill their dreams. Rather than sponsor other people's events, Red Bull seeks to create its own: from the Red Bull air race to the Last Man Standing 48-hour motocross; from Word Clash street poems to Art of the Can. (The last two are particularly interesting, because they speak to invigorating the mind, not just the body.)

Red Bull has not only identified a promise that appeals across countries and cultures, it has tailored the entire brand around the promise and then communicated it single-mindedly.

YouTube

Everyone in marketing knows YouTube. The number-one name in online video is widely cited as one of the spectacular successes of the new media world. The site now contains hundreds of millions of videos with an average of eight hours of content being uploaded every minute. Every minute! And what's more, that content comes from only 2 percent of the site's user base. These "creators" are at the heart of YouTube's success and sit at the top of the user ecosystem that includes "collectors," who generate playlists for every topic under the sun, "critics," who add their often irreverent and off-color comments to the content, and then finally the "consumers," the silent majority who just watch the videos that have been posted. According to Comscore, in November 2007, in the United States alone, 74 million people watched 39 videos each.

Global in Scope, Now YouTube's Going Local

In spite of YouTube's global reach, Jeben Berg, the company's product marketing manager, says that "localization is absolutely on the agenda. You need to be there with the right language, tone and personalities in order to create a real community."[10] YouTube attracts an extensive global audience via its U.S. site, but it now extends this reach through local sites in 18 countries.

In addition to fully translated sites, local home pages, and local search functions, site features include localized:

- domains
- user interface and help centers
- watch pages
- home pages (including featured videos, directors' videos and promotions)
- user support
- community features (such as video ratings, sharing, and content flagging

With localized search features such as directors' videos, featured videos, and home-page promotions, YouTube sites make it even faster and easier for the local YouTube communities to quickly search and view the most relevant video content. Additionally, content uploaded by local users will show up as "favorites" and "recommended content" on the local sites, giving users the opportunity to become stars by increasing their exposure with the national community.

A complaint often leveled against the global platform, YouTube.com, is that it is too American. While a team of editors works hard to identify creative, engaging, and noncommercial videos to feature on the home page, Berg admits it is a tough challenge to come up with material that works everywhere. "There are some videos that just transcend local culture and appeal to everyone. On the other hand there is content that just does not meet the needs of the local constituencies."

Local Is Part of the Value Proposition

Berg sees local understanding and implementation as a key part of YouTube's value proposition to its clients. Each event is scripted and produced by YouTube, from the rules of each contest to the launch videos. "You can't just translate the content pages into a local language," he says. "They have to be written in such a way that the style and tone sounds local. If we are going to localize something, we want it to be authentic. And the only way I know for that to happen is to have a native of the country do it, someone who is in touch with the local culture. You have to have people on the ground." Just how culturally specific do things get? Berg said that YouTube marketing managers in India had recently asked whether advertising could be targeted by caste in order to better reach upper-income people.

Berg cites the launch of YouTube.de in Germany in November 2007 as an example of good local implementation. For the launch to go well, they needed to find an angle that would light a fire under the local video addicts. Brainstorming resulted in the simple idea of a contest to "share your secret talent." No constraints were applied (other than that people should not do anything that was obscene or involved inflicting pain). The launch video featured the local YouTube product manager asking Germans to show off their talent. To date thousands of submissions have been uploaded.

The three brand examples reviewed here provide some hints on what is required to take a brand global. They also confirm that there is no one way to be successful on the global stage. Jack Daniel's is well on its way to establishing strong relationships with consumers in many countries even though it may need to adapt the way it presents itself to appeal successfully to Chinese consumers. Red Bull has found success in its carefully crafted appeal to a common motivation that transcends countries and culture. YouTube started with the advantage of global reach but is now adapting its service to meet local needs. In the next chapter, I provide a ranking of the strongest global brands, all of which have transcended their cultural origins to develop strong relationships with consumers around the world.

Key Points to Take Away

- It takes more than global distribution and a consistent trademark to make a global brand. A global brand is one that has transcended its cultural origins to develop strong relationships with consumers across different countries and cultures.
- Contrary to the beliefs of 20 years ago, consistency is not always the answer to building a strong brand. Differing cultures can be one of the biggest barriers to global success.

Questions to Consider

1. Has your brand's global growth been limited by centralization and standardization?
2. How well do you understand the different needs, desires, and values of potential consumers around the world?
3. Are you prepared to adapt to local conditions? What about your brand is sacrosanct, and what can be changed?

For more information related to these questions, visit theglobalbrandonline.com.

Chapter 3

Five Steps to a Strong Brand

Finding the right combination of global and local for any one brand is not an easy process. Ultimately it is consumers who vote on the winning combination. Defining whether a brand possesses a strong relationship with consumers, however, is relatively easy. The specific attributes that allow a strong relationship to form may differ from country to country, but the stages of development are very consistent.

This chapter presents a model for understanding brand strength that I use throughout the book. In Chapter 4, the model provides the basis for a ranking of global brand strength (a measure of how well brands develop strong relationships with consumers in multiple countries). In Chapter 5, it forms the foundation for a ranking of brand value, based on how well that brand strength generates current and future earnings. Later in the book, I use the model as a tool to understand how global brands can identify obstacles that might hinder success in local markets.

The Brand Pyramid

The BrandDynamics™ Pyramid, shown in Figure 3.1, describes the progression of a consumer's relationship with a brand. It identifies five key levels of increasing attitudinal loyalty that underpin purchasing behavior. The pyramid and the survey questions that create it are an integral part of Millward Brown's BrandDynamics brand equity framework.[1]

The first level of the pyramid is called *presence*. Consumers who reach the presence level are actively aware of the brand when they think about the product category, either because they've tried it (or know someone who has) or because through some other means they've become aware of what the brand stands for. Consumers reach the second level, *relevance*, when they believe that a brand promises to deliver something of value to them, at a price they consider acceptable. To move to the third level, *performance*, people must believe that the brand delivers satisfactorily on its basic functional promise. Those who reach

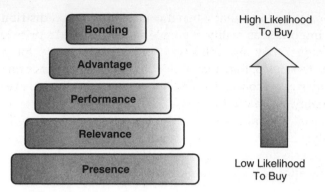

Figure 3.1 Five Steps to a Strong Brand: The Brand Pyramid

the fourth level, *advantage*, believe the brand offers some rational or emotional benefit that distinguishes it from the competition. People who reach the fifth level, *bonding*, believe that the brand offers unique advantages in terms of what is most important in the category; therefore, it is the best brand for them. People are typically at least 10 times more likely to buy a brand they are bonded to than one that they are simply aware of at the presence level.

Each level of the pyramid deals with issues critical to brand success, so it is important to understand the implications of strength and weakness at each one.

Presence

Presence is a fundamental driver of brand performance. People must know what a brand has to offer before they will consider it for purchase. While people do sometimes discover new brands while shopping, they will only try these unfamiliar brands if their promise is readily apparent.

Rather than rely on the vagaries of the shopping experience, brands that want to grow should strive to maximize their familiarity. The U.S. insurance brand Geico achieved a significant increase in business through growing its presence from 57 percent in 2001 to 73 percent in 2006 without otherwise increasing the relative strength of the brand.

Relevance

The step from presence to relevance is an important one. To reach the *relevance* level, people must not reject the brand on account of its price (which may be perceived as too expensive or too cheap), its lack of availability, its ability to meet their needs, or the identity and status (or lack thereof) that it conveys.

It is important to note that when it comes to price and distribution, perceptions are as important as reality. If people believe a brand's price lies outside an acceptable range, they are unlikely to consider the brand for purchase. If a brand seems too cheap, they may think the product is of poor quality, because, even in today's price-conscious world, many people still use price as a benchmark for quality. More often, especially for high-priced infrequent purchases, people will exclude brands from consideration because they think they cost more than they can afford. This is particularly important in higher search categories. Why waste time researching something that you don't think you can pay for? The same applies if you don't believe you can buy the brand locally, unless it is something you can source online.

One of the key tenets of branding success is that you cannot be all things to all people. Many successful brands, including the likes of Guinness, Tommy Hilfiger, Gevalia, and Lexus, lose a significant number of consumers in the step from presence to relevance because they have chosen to keep their price high or to appeal to a particular market segment. Losing customers in this stage, however, should be a conscious decision, not an accident. Inadvertent product or image issues must be addressed if a brand is to maximize its potential for growth.

Performance

Purchase, and critically, repeat purchase relies on a good product or service experience. For people to progress from relevance to *performance*, they must believe that the brand fulfils their basic expectations of product performance. Where cost and perceived risk are low, as with most packaged goods, people will typically try the brand before making a judgment. Where cost and perceived risk are high, people will check out the offering before making a purchase, by taking a test drive, reading consumer ratings online, or asking friends and colleagues for advice.

Advantage

If people are to develop a strong attitudinal relationship with a brand over the long term, they must believe that it offers some advantage over the competition. *Advantage* may take many forms, and is often driven as much by experience as by what brands suggest through marketing communication. Advantage could come from:

- product benefits, when the combination of product or service features makes the brand a better rational choice,
- emotional benefits, when the brand, or the experience of the brand, makes people feel good,

- popularity, which signals that a brand is a safe choice,
- difference, when consumers want something unique or want to signal their allegiance.
- dynamism, for brands that are setting trends or shaking up the status quo,
- price, because when all else fails, a brand will appeal to some people simply because it offers a good deal.

These six basic drivers of advantage do not preclude others, and the nuance of each will differ from brand to brand. The satisfaction that someone feels when relaxing in a Starbucks is a very different emotional experience from that which someone might feel while driving a high-end Mercedes. Each brand must identify and magnify its unique benefits to be successful. Ultimately, if the brand is to grow its market share, those benefits need to make people believe the brand is better than others, more appealing, and different from its competitors.

Bonding

People enter into the strongest attitudinal relationship with a brand, *bonding*, when they believe that it is the brand that delivers best on the most important criteria in the category. People who are bonded to a brand are more likely to buy it, and, as a result, there is a strong relationship between the proportion of people bonded to a brand and its market share.

What Heuristics Matter to Your Brand?

As people progress through the five levels of a brand's pyramid, they develop increased affinity toward the brand. Those who arrive at the bonding level believe the brand is better than the competition in some unique way. The job of the brand team is to identify the barriers that stop people moving up their brand's pyramid and find ways to mitigate them.

Essentially the pyramid is composed of a set of heuristics that consumers might apply to any brand to help them make purchase decisions. This is why the pyramid works so well across brands, categories, and cultures. It applies the same fast and frugal heuristics to brands that people do in their everyday lives. Do I recognize it? Is it going to do the job? Is it better priced? Does it work better? Is it more appealing?

The challenge for the marketer is to get beyond these general heuristics to the ones that specific groups of individuals apply in specific circumstances. They need to identify the most differentiating and motivating idea around which to build their brand, and they need to consider the impact that the shopping context has on decision making. When people are choosing a brand of coffee in the supermarket, do they apply the same heuristics that they would use in a convenience store, where they have far fewer choices? What brand cues will trigger the most differentiating and motivating perceptions?

Maximizing a Brand's Growth Potential

As we noted in the section on relevance, some brands may choose deliberately to exclude potential buyers, but generally a brand should aim to maximize its conversion from one level of the pyramid to the next. A brand that can maximize its presence and subsequently escalate people to bonding (while other brands in the category are trying to do the same) is most likely to grow share and revenues. And growth is critical to both brand and corporate success.

Commenting on an analysis of U.S. company performance from 1984 to 2003 at the sixth CMO Summit in Evanston, Illinois in September 2007, Tom French of McKinsey & Company stated, "This data confirms something we all intuitively know—that growth is essential to corporate survival and value creation. By the way, the data also shows that those companies that can sustain growth and value creation over time reap about 30 percent greater return to shareholders, and increase their survival rate by an astonishing five to six times."[2]

How then can a brand maximize its growth potential?

- By creating stronger presence compared to the competition, thus maximizing the likelihood that people will consider it for purchase.
- By encouraging stronger conversion from presence to bonding compared to competitive brands, which will ensure that an increase in trial will ultimately produce more loyal customers.
- By maximizing the likelihood that people will think the brand is the only one that satisfies important category drivers. The more attitudinal loyalty a brand enjoys versus its competitors, the more likely people will be to stick with it over time.
- By securing the loyalty of the more valuable consumers in the category (those who do not buy on price and who buy more than others).

Brand equity research like BrandDynamics can be an invaluable tool when it comes to diagnosing a brand's current strength and comparing performance across brands. But brand planning also requires us to anticipate future performance. In the next section, I highlight the drivers of future sales success and show how a new measure of brand momentum can help guide brand strategy.

Strong Equity Creates a Higher Probability of Growth

There is no guaranteed way of accurately predicting future sales for a specific brand. Beyond the time frame of a few weeks, unforeseen factors begin to throw any prediction off track. Unanticipated price hikes due to rising commodity prices, changes in interest rates, cuts to the media budget, and, most unpredictable of all, competitive actions can all serve to undermine predictions based on current data relationships. This said, it is possible to use brand equity data to predict a probability of future share gain or loss based on people's existing attitudes to a brand.

Our measure of future brand potential is called Voltage 2.0. A brand with positive Voltage 2.0 is primed for growth. It is in a good position to gain share from its own marketing actions and to resist the actions of competitors. A brand with negative Voltage 2.0 can still grow, but it will have to work harder to do so, and it will be more vulnerable to the actions of other brands. Voltage 2.0 is calculated relative to the performance of other brands in the same category using three metrics:

1. Current brand use and brand salience
2. Emotional attachment
3. Perceived differentiation

For durables and infrequently purchased goods, such as cars, financial services, and computers, we also take into account unexpressed preference (future consideration versus current use or ownership).

That these metrics have a strong relationship with future share gain or loss makes good sense. If you buy a brand today, the chances are that you will stick with it, particularly if it is more salient, more appealing, or in some way different from the competition. These attributes will also attract new people to try the brand. And in the case of infrequently purchased goods, if, when asked what brand they are most likely to purchase in the future, a person mentions some brand other than the one currently owned or used, it seems to indicate that the current brand is not considered satisfactory and is not likely to be selected again. A brand that is not currently owned or used but that is mentioned as a respondent's first choice is more likely to be chosen.

Voltage 2.0 was developed based on an extensive analysis of the relationships between BrandDynamics metrics and shifts in actual market share for 350 brands over the year following the brand equity survey. As part of our validation work, we used chi-square statistical testing to compare Voltage 2.0 estimates of whether a brand's share would grow/remain flat/decline to the actual in-market outcome. The chi-square statistic describes how close the distribution of our prediction is to the actual distribution. The chi-square value was large; therefore our testing found a very strong relationship between the two variables for both frequently and infrequently purchased brands.

Using Presence and Voltage 2.0 to Guide Brand Strategy

In planning, knowing the inherent potential of a brand is vital. For a brand with a high probability of growth, capitalizing on that potential through innovative and unique communication will be important. For a brand with a high probability of decline, understanding and addressing the weaknesses becomes imperative. By combining the predictive power of Voltage 2.0 with another key pyramid metric, presence, we can make additional observations about a brand's prospects and identify an appropriate strategy.

As a starting point for our analysis, we summarized the strength of a brand's relationship with consumers using presence and Voltage 2.0. As I have explained, presence is a measure of how many people know about a brand and understand what it has to offer. A brand with a high level of presence will be considered by more people than one with low presence. Voltage 2.0 describes the probability that a brand is primed for growth or decline.

We plotted brands according to their values on presence and Voltage 2.0 to create a map of brand equity, in which the four quadrants are used to define four groups of brands. Figure 3.2 shows the average scores, by quadrant, on three key metrics: average market value share, net percent of brands that gained or lost share, and share change. The average market value share at the time of the survey confirms the relationship between consumer attitudes and the relative size of brands in their categories. The net gain (or loss) summarizes the extent to which the brands grew or declined in the year following the survey.[3] The average year-on-year percentage share change describes the market performance of each group of brands.

In comparing these metrics across the groups, we see that brands in the upper-right quadrant tend to have high market shares and good growth prospects. Brands that dominate their product categories, such as Coke, Nike, and McDonald's would fall into this quadrant. Clearly these brands should continue to maintain their high profiles and play to their strengths.

By contrast, brands in the lower-right quadrant, which have strong presence but lower Voltage 2.0 scores, tend to lose share year on year, although the size of their market shares helps to reduce their volatility. Many of the brands in this quadrant lack differentiation and appeal compared to other brands in the category; they may be past their prime and in need of restaging (that is, relaunching with changes to various aspects of the marketing mix). The first step to rekindle growth for these brands is an honest evaluation of their

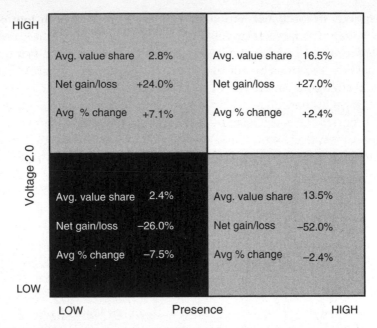

Figure 3.2 Brand Strength and Market Share Growth Prospects

Source: Millward Brown.

status. Ideally, this should involve qualitative research. Although there is no single magic bullet to a successful relaunch, increasing perceptions of differentiation is always critical. Sometimes this comes through emphasizing existing product differences or innovation, but more often differentiation is achieved by making the brand seem more contemporary and appealing to the intended target audience.

The brands in the upper-left quadrant have high potential but tend to be more volatile than the brands on the right-hand side of the map. Many do gain share, but a fair number decline. The brands in this region run the risk that as they work to grow their footprint, they may move away from the branding formula that made them successful. These brands are also vulnerable to competitive actions, such as aggressive pricing and the introduction of "me-too" product offerings. It is important for the brand team to have a good understanding of what has driven the success of the brand to that point. Any decision to deviate from that formula should be examined very carefully. All too often, an individual, opportunistic action may seem low risk, but a series of such actions takes the brand away from the origins of its success. As we shall see in Chapter 10, this is precisely what has happened to Starbucks in the United States.

The brands in the lower left-hand corner, which have both low presence and low Voltage 2.0, face a relatively high failure rate. Many of these brands are new and face strong competition from incumbent brands. The key questions facing marketers responsible for these brands are: How do I disrupt the status quo? What strengths can I play to, and how do I raise the saliency of my brand with my target audience?

It is important to emphasize that, while the numbers shown in Figure 3.2 represent the average performance of each group of brands, there were exceptions in each quadrant. Therefore, while presence and Voltage 2.0 may describe a brand's potential, they do not dictate its future. A number of factors, including some that are beyond the influence of marketers, affect a brand's performance.

But where marketing does have influence, it can play a pivotal role in improving a brand's prospects. For example, consider the venerable British retailer Marks & Spencer (M&S). The chain was suffering from declining sales as shoppers deserted it in favor of trendier alternatives. Management recognized the need to refresh the stores and revitalize product lines, but also realized that M&S enjoyed a substantial reservoir of consumer goodwill. The campaign *Your M&S*, which received an IPA award from the Institute of Practitioners in Advertising, tapped into that goodwill, reminding people of what they loved about the store and drawing shoppers back. Customer visits increased by 19 million over the previous year. Food and general merchandise sales rose by 10 percent. As a result, the share price of M&S rose more than 60 percent, confounding experts who had predicted it would never rise again.

Commanding a Price Premium

Brands that are already widely known need to find other ways to grow. In today's highly competitive product and service categories, most marketers focus on trying to increase their volume share, either by convincing existing customers to buy more or by enticing new customers away from competitors. But strong brands that offer benefits that are not matched by other brands in the category can also increase profits by commanding a price premium.

Although these benefits may be of an emotional nature, more often they are functional aspects of product performance, the result of a successful innovation program. But the superior ingredients, technology, and systems that provide competitive advantages also add cost. This fact presents companies with a tough question: How can they recover that investment?

Colgate faced just such a dilemma with the introduction of the product that was to become Colgate Total. The new product contained the antibacterial ingredient triclosan, which has been clinically proven to help prevent the accumulation of plaque (which, if allowed to build up, can lead to gingivitis). The patented combination with the copolymer PVM/MA (polyvinylmethyl ether maleic acid) allows clinical efficacy to be maintained between brushings.

Even though the new formula seemed to offer a compelling proposition, management decided that to maximize the return for this breakthrough technology, it should be introduced as a stand-alone subbrand. The new subbrand, Colgate Total, was priced at a 15 percent premium over the product in the red box. Thus every person who traded up to Total from the base brand generated incremental revenue for the company.

Marketers would do well to remember that not all prospective buyers are of equal value. In every category, there are people who are more interested in a good price than in getting the "right" brand. While consumers in this group are easy to sway with promotional pricing, they may not be worth the effort, because they will also be easily persuaded to switch away by some other brand.

An alternative strategy is to identify and target the customers who pay attention to brands and perceive real differences among them. This group is likely to pay a premium price for a brand if they think it is better than others. A recent analysis of 209 consumer packaged goods brands in the United States found that consumer esteem was the key underpinning of a brand's ability to command a price premium. Respondents were asked to associate brands with a number of general attributes, and brands that scored especially well on the statement "I have a higher opinion of it than others" commanded a median price advantage of 11 percent.

The dimensions of esteem will vary from brand to brand and category to category, but the net effect will be the same. Consumers who care about getting the right brand will pay more for a brand if they can be convinced that it offers key advantages over others.

Implications for Marketers

All of the analysis presented here serves to illustrate the financial advantages provided by strong brands. Brands do add value. But to maximize that value, marketers must navigate through an increasingly complex maze of brand-building activities. No one route will be right for all brands; the most effective actions will differ for each brand according to its category and context. However, marketers seeking to maximize the value of their brands should start by considering three fundamental points:

1. The underlying equities of their brands
2. Performance on business basics
3. The profitability of the target

Understand Underlying Equities

The route to any destination depends on the starting point. Brands in different areas of the brand equity map need different types of support to thrive and grow. An understanding of the brand's strengths and weaknesses will help inform decisions on strategy and tactics by which to grow brand value.

Check Business Basics

In most product and service categories, there exists a close relationship between brand strength and market share. When a brand deviates from the basic category relationship, selling more or less than its equity might suggest, a structural issue may deserve more investigation. Pricing might be out of sync with buyer expectations, for example, or distribution may be limiting sales.

Focus on Profitable Customers

Segmenting potential customers on the basis of their predisposition toward brands can guide the targeting of customer acquisition strategies. In some categories, price promotion may be a viable tactic, but when overused, such a strategy will not only attract price-sensitive shoppers to your brand but also train your current loyal customers to buy the brand on deal. A far safer and ultimately more profitable strategy would be to focus on less price-sensitive shoppers who can be convinced that your brand is better than others and worth paying more for.

Key Points to Take Away

- The stages by which consumers develop relationships with brands are the same across brands, categories, and countries and can be measured in a quantitative survey.
- You need to understand where your brand stands and what its strengths and weaknesses are in order to realize its full value.

Questions to Consider

1. Do you have any idea what your brand's pyramid might look like?
2. Do you know the strength of your brand? Is it primed for market-share growth or decline? If you don't like the answer, do you know how to change the situation?
3. Is your brand able to sustain a price premium? If not, do you know why people don't believe it is worth it?

For more information related to these questions, visit theglobalbrandonline.com.

Chapter 4

The Most Successful Global Brands

In this chapter, we focus in on those brands that have the power to form a strong connection with consumers across different countries and cultures. Here we present a ranking of the most powerful global brands and then explore the sources of their brand strength. That exploration demonstrates that a strong, scalable business model is the platform on which strong brands are built and that continuing innovation is required to keep them successful. But on their own, these characteristics cannot create a strong brand. Strong consumer relationships depend on five additional factors: a great brand experience, clarity of positioning, a projected sense of dynamism, authenticity, and a strong corporate culture.

Both the brand ranking presented here and the BrandZ™ Top 100 Ranking described in Chapter 5 are based on data collected for BrandZ. BrandZ is a quantitative brand equity study, based on the BrandDynamics brand equity framework that has been conducted annually by Millward Brown on behalf of WPP since 1998.

The Most Powerful Global Brands

Table 4.1 shows the top 25 global brands ranked according to our Global Brand Power Score, a measure of how well brands form strong relationships across countries.[1]

The Global Brand Power Score is a combination of two measures. The first measure is the average percentage of people bonded to the brand across all the countries where the brand was studied. For instance, on average, over 40 percent of mobile phone buyers across 30 countries are bonded to Nokia in the mobile phone product category. By contrast, less than 1 percent of people are bonded to Philips.

The second measure is a multiplier that describes a brand's ability to create a strong relationship with category consumers in multiple countries. The brand qualifies as having a "strong" relationship if its bonding score is among the top

Table 4.1 Global Brand Power Scores

Ranking	Brand	Global Brand Power Score
1	Pampers	42.8
2	Nokia	37.5
3	Microsoft	33.0
4	Colgate	31.9
5	Coca-Cola	29.6
6	Nike	27.8
7	Sony	27.6
8	McDonald's	20.8
9	Adidas	17.0
10	IBM	16.4
11	Nescafé	14.3
12	Visa	12.4
13	Philips	9.4
14	Yahoo!	9.0
15	Pantene Pro-V	8.9
16	Axe	8.8
17	Dove	8.3
18	Carrefour	8.1
19	Nivea	8.1
20	Oil of Olay	7.7
21	Toyota	7.5
22	HP (Hewlett-Packard)	7.1
23	Vodafone	7.0
24	Chanel	6.5
25	Marlboro	6.3

33 percent of bonding scores in the category. For example, Coca-Cola achieved strong bonding scores with soft drink consumers in 30 out of 31 countries, yielding a multiplier of 0.97 (30/31). By contrast, 7-Up has a far lower multiplier. It achieves a strong brand relationship in only 1 country out of the 25 in which it was measured. The Global Brand Power Score is the product of the average bonding level across countries and the multiplier just described.

Some well-known brands that might be considered global, such as BMW and Louis Vuitton, did not make the list because they compete in luxury categories that are accessible to only to a relatively small segment of the population. While the ranking focuses on mass-market brands, it does provide us with some interesting insights into the sort of brands that have the power to compete on the global stage.

Brand Strength Is Not Guaranteed Everywhere

Although these 25 brands are some of the strongest (and by definition biggest) brands in the world, the ranking drives home the fact that no one brand is dominant everywhere. Coca-Cola places well up the ranking, with a stronger-than-average relationship with consumers in every country where it has been measured. However, although Coke is viewed with affection by many around the world, it is not the preeminent soft drink in every country. The percentage of soft drink buyers in each country bonded to Coke varies from a low of 6 percent in India to a high of 56 percent in South Africa. In India and Thailand, more people bond with Pepsi. Even in the United States, the homeland of both Coke and Pepsi, the two brands are locked in a battle for people's hearts, minds, and wallets that has yet to be won convincingly by either one.

The story of why Coca-Cola is not stronger in India is an interesting one. In 1977, India's first non-Congress Party government appointed a firebrand trade union leader, George Fernandes, as minister for industry. Drawing on rarely invoked laws, he asked Coca-Cola and IBM to dilute their equity in their Indian operations to 40 percent or leave. Coca-Cola was also asked to reveal its secret formula. Both companies chose to leave rather than comply.[2]

The government's subsequent attempt to launch its own cola failed, leaving the Parle Group's brand, Thums Up, to fill the void and become the leading cola brand. Coca-Cola acquired that brand shortly after reentering the country in 1993, and Thums Up remains a strong brand in India today. Quoted in the *Hindu Business Line* in November 2007, Coca-Cola's president and chief operating officer Muhtar Kent said that it was because of "historical reasons" that Thums Up still sells more in India than the trademark Coca-Cola brand."[3]

But a long absence from the Indian market is not the only reason that Coca-Cola struggled to regain share. When the company reentered the market, its marketing approach for the Coca-Cola megabrand was similar to that adopted elsewhere in the world, and it failed to resonate with local consumers. It was not until 2001, when Douglas Daft, then the chief executive officer, shifted the company to a "think local, act local" philosophy that Coke India set about developing more local campaigns. These not only spoke more directly to Indians but also recognized the deep divide between urban and rural consumers.

The rural-focused *Thanda matlab Coca-Cola* campaign that launched in 2002 featured Bollywood star Aamir Khan. He portrayed a variety of distinctive characters, all of whom equated *thanda* (generic for a cold beverage) with Coca-Cola. The highly successful campaign won many awards and spawned regionally focused offspring. In 2005, the first ad in the *Cool drink Na Coca-Cola* series featuring Tamil movie star Vikram (Chiya) appeared on TV. In this ad, Vikram appears as a "Chennai Rowdy" who comes to the rescue of two innocent women being conned by a shop assistant. Coke's experience points up one basic lesson for global brands: It can be difficult to trade on international heritage or cultural origin alone. The more a brand has the ability to embed itself in many different local cultures, the more successful it will be.

Coca-Cola is not alone in having variable levels of success around the globe. Few brands achieve a dominant position in every country in which they are distributed. In fact, most brands fail to scale beyond their country of origin. Since 1998, BrandZ has been used to measure the equity of over 10,000 brands across 31 countries. Only 329 brands—3 percent—made the cut for our global brand analysis, which required being measured in seven or more countries. (This can hardly be considered an aggressive cutoff, given there are 192 countries in the world.) Only 16 percent of the brands in our database were measured in two or more countries, leaving 8,690 brands that were measured in only one. This does not reflect a deficiency of the database; it reflects a reality of our brand world. A few brands make it big in multiple countries, but most remain strong only in their country of origin.

If few brands succeed in creating strong relationships with consumers on a truly global scale, what, then, gives a brand the power to transcend its local origins?

Build a Strong, Scalable Business Model

Unless a product or service can be produced, distributed, and sold efficiently, it stands little chance of building a strong relationship with masses of consumers around the world. But a strong scalable business model does not automatically create a strong brand. It is the platform on which strong brands are built. Efficient production systems, good supply chain management, competitive trading practices, and stringent financial controls will allow any product or service to be sold at a good price. You only need to stop by your local hardware store and look at the vast range of screws, nails, and tacks sold for cents each to know this is true. But try remembering which company made those goods a few hours later. Nothing coherent is going to come to mind. Given the choice between two similar packs of wood screws, you will pick the cheapest. And why not? There is little risk attached to your choice. But as the risk associated with your choice increases, so does the need for reassurance that you are making the "right" choice. This is where a brand comes into play. A brand creates a reason to choose one product over another, and, ideally, consumers will pay a price premium for the privilege of doing so. The more intangible differentiation a brand can create, the more valuable it becomes to the buyer and, in turn, the owner.

In her book *Warriors on the High Wire*, Fiona Gilmore reports that among the chief executives and key decision makers she surveyed, the majority would place the brand at the center of business in an ideal organization. Referring to this hypothetical organization, she states, "The marketing department is no longer there in the sense that everybody has a responsibility for the brand."[4] In this way, all the different aspects of the business work toward meeting customer needs and the realization of a strong brand.

It is a lovely idea but one that is far from the reality of most companies today. The marketing department is still needed to represent the views of customers and consumers and to organize, persuade, or cajole colleagues in other departments to act in the best interests of the brand. Doing this is a difficult process at the best of times, and it is incredibly challenging when the organization and its brand or brands are global in scope.

Business Models Must Be Adapted to Meet Varied Needs

Our top-ranked brands draw on a variety of business models, which have all been adapted to serve the needs of the local consumer, the local retail infrastructure, and the business economy. Without these varying platforms, the brands would not be able to deliver on people's expectations, the fundamental requirement of any brand.

Eighth-ranked brand McDonald's is a classic example of how a business model helped to create an entire service category. From the start, the focus of the company has been on selling high volumes of a limited number of items as efficiently as possible. This approach makes it easy to leverage economies of scale and control quality effectively. In fast-food establishments, customers do a lot of the work traditionally done by employees of more traditional restaurants. Standardized processes allow the staff to function with relatively little training or remuneration. This does not mean McDonald's is inflexible; it adapts its menu in different regions while offering meals of consistent quality at low prices. But the fast-food titan also draws on other aspects of its business model to extend its offer from one country to the next. While McDonald's is mainly a franchise operation, and still trains its franchisees at the Hamburger University in Oak Brook, Illinois, in most countries the company also owns the franchise sites. Thus the company collects rent from franchisees as well as the normal revenue from fees and the sale of supplies.

The Toyota production control system is legendary. The IBM Global Business Services report, *Changing Lanes for Success*,[5] finds innovation and a flexible business model to be the key drivers of automotive company profit improvement. The report highlights Toyota's ability to anticipate and respond quickly to changing customer needs because of the way it can adapt its production systems while maintaining product reliability. The Prius is an example of an innovative product, developed to meet specific needs, and made using a "lean" manufacturing process that drives down engineering and production costs and eliminates waste. This approach is applied to every vehicle, allowing Toyota to build strong brands like Scion, Toyota, and Lexus, assured that they will meet people's needs and deliver on their expectations.

These examples also help us draw out the distinction between a global business and a global brand. Gasoline companies like Shell and BP have outlets in many countries around the world. They are successful global companies, but by comparison to McDonald's, Toyota, and the other brands listed, they are relatively weak brands. The average proportion of people bonded to any gasoline brand is less than 6 percent. In most countries, people base their fuel-purchasing decisions more on location and price than on brand. Well-known companies may fare better than lesser-known ones, but the influence of "brand" on the purchase decision is relatively weak.

Whatever the category, and however strong the role of the brand in influencing the purchase decision, companies need to understand which aspects of their business directly impact their customer's brand experience. If they do, they will be far less likely to undermine that experience through shortsighted cost savings. On a global scale, they will be better able to judge where they might realize efficiencies across countries. Aligning the whole organization to support a brand may not be feasible, but companies should make sure that they understand how their business decisions affect their brand.

Like business models, the way innovation is managed and the degree to which marketing is involved varies from company to company. Many high-tech companies are led by innovation. Engineers and developers take the lead in defining the product to meet a technical set of needs. Once the product is defined, they hand it off to the marketers. By contrast, consumers often lead innovation at packaged goods companies. The marketing team may play an integral role in identifying new needs and developing a product to meet them. Either way, innovation is critical to the future of companies and brands alike.

The Importance of Innovation and the "First-Mover Advantage" Myth

Innovation is critical to brand success, but that does not mean you have to be first to create a new product in order to succeed. One of the biggest marketing myths is that of the so-called first-mover advantage—the theory that the first firm to market with an innovative product will have an insurmountable lead over the competition. By being the first to gain distribution, create brand awareness, and satisfy consumer needs, the first mover is thought to gain a commanding advantage over the latecomers. Extensive research reported by Gerald Tellis and Peter Golder in their book *Will and Vision: How Latecomers Grow to Dominate Markets* suggests that the truth is completely different. Citing examples like Gillette in razors, Hewlett-Packard in laser printers, and Apple in personal computers, Tellis and Golder demonstrate that these companies became successful by taking advantage of the deficiencies of the first mover's product or business model. They reveal that pioneers fail in 64 percent of all industries studied.[6] Even though first movers dominated their product category before it became a true mass market, the average market share they held once the dust settled was only 6 percent.[7]

The key conclusion that Tellis and Golder reach from their analysis is: "The real causes of enduring market leadership are vision and will. Enduring market leaders have a revolutionary and inspiring vision of the mass market, and they exhibit an indomitable will to realize that vision. They persist under adversity, innovate relentlessly, commit financial resources and leverage assets to realize their vision."[8]

As we shall see, the first-mover advantage *is* an advantage when moving a successful brand into new geographies, but innovation alone cannot guarantee success for a brand. All too often the leading edge becomes the bleeding edge.

How Vision and Will Changed Nokia's Fortunes

Today more people own a mobile phone than a computer, and there is a good chance that that phone is made by Nokia. Because innovation has been at the core of Nokia's success, the company provides a great example of how vision can transform a company's fortunes.

Most of us have become emotionally dependent on the personal connectivity that mobile phones provide, and we cannot bear to switch them off. Witness the people who continue talking into their phones long after the flight attendant has announced they must be turned off, or the men I have observed carrying on conversations as they relieve themselves in public restrooms. Nokia's ability to exceed people's expectations through the sale of innovative new phones has helped it leverage this dependency worldwide to rank number two in our Global Brand Power standings. Nokia has strong relationships with consumers in many countries (average bonding score: 40 percent), with the notable but not surprising exceptions being Japan and Korea. Nokia's history confirms the premise of Tellis and Golder: You do not need to be the first in a category (Motorola is widely attributed with creating the first mobile phone[9]), but you do need the vision and will to make tough decisions and stick with them.

The global giant that is Nokia today could not be further removed from its origins. Established in 1865 as a wood-pulp mill by Knut Fredrik Idestam, the company derived its name from the town in Finland where the business came to be based. Nokia Wood Mills was bought by Finnish Rubber Works after World War I, and the current Nokia Corporation was formed in 1967, when Finnish Rubber Works merged with Nokia Wood Mills and Finnish Cable Works, a producer of telephone and telegraph cables. Nokia began focusing its energies on becoming an international communications company but continued to make paper products, tires, and a wide variety of electronics products. In 1984, Nokia launched the Mobira Talkman, its first portable phone, and in 1987, it launched the Mobira Cityman, its first handheld Nordic Mobile Telephone (NMT) standard phone.

In the early 1990s, a deep recession sparked by the demise of the Soviet Union and heavy losses at its television manufacturing division forced the company to change both its management team and its business strategy. In 1992, Jorma Ollila, then just 41, was appointed CEO after having successfully run the company's mobile phone division. Ollila would provide the vision and will to change the company's fortunes and set it on the path to becoming a global brand.

Ollila was convinced of the need to focus the company's efforts solely on mobile phones and to leverage the emerging Global System for Mobile (GSM) communications standard on a global basis. Nokia launched its first GSM cell phone, the Nokia 1011, the same year, and later rode the success of the GSM network as it expanded around the world. Meanwhile the company divested itself of its noncore operations. The paper, rubber, and consumer electronics operations were spun off into different companies so that Nokia could focus single-mindedly on the telecommunications arena.

Key to the company's global success was its continued commitment to innovation. Committing itself to an ever-faster design cycle, by late 1998 Nokia was pumping out new models every 35 days. An easy-to-use operating system, a stream of new features, and a recognizable design aesthetic created a competitive advantage, while amortization of the costs across models and countries allowed the company to improve profitability. Nokia steers a fine line between the two worlds of technology-led innovation and consumer-led innovation. Over the years, the company has produced a string of technology firsts: the first mobile phone to feature text messaging, the first to access Internet-based information services, and the first to include an integrated camera. At the same time, it has evolved to meet changing consumer needs and desires. The company focused on leading-edge consumers in cultural hot spots in order to anticipate the next big thing. Naqi Jaffery, a wireless industry analyst for Dataquest, said: "Nokia's advantage is that it has been involved with all of these technologies from the beginning. It is all over the world; it learns what's good in every culture it works in, and combines it all."[10]

Innovation remains the linchpin of Nokia's success today. But reliance on innovation can be a double-edged sword. A company that depends on innovation must stay in touch with the latest trends and keep the innovation pipeline full. In the first quarter of 2004, Nokia's share of the mobile handset market dipped below 30 percent as a result of competitive brand introductions featuring a clamshell design. While slow to spot the emerging consumer preference for this design, Nokia eventually responded with a series of product introductions that helped it regain its pole position in the market.

Innovation and Branding: A Powerful Combination

Innovation alone is not always enough to achieve business success. But add world-class branding and you have a combination that is tough to beat. Procter & Gamble has always adhered to Tellis and Golder's belief that successful companies "persist under adversity, innovate relentlessly, commit financial resources and leverage assets to realize their vision."[11] Innovation is central to the success of P&G, which has two of its brands among our top 10, including the top brand overall, Pampers. Pampers now dominates the disposable diaper market (or "nappy," to the British) with global sales exceeding $7 billion.

Today Pampers is the number-one baby care brand in the world and tops our list for good reason. Pampers satisfies a basic need and addresses a desire shared by mothers around the world: for their babies to be dry and comfortable. Pampers may not have been the first disposable diaper—Johnson & Johnson's Chux diapers were on the market in 1932—but when it was introduced in 1961, the brand offered a better and more convenient solution than the existing alternatives. Since then, the brand's growth has been driven by continuing innovation and effective marketing, resulting in today's successful products, such as Pampers Baby Stages of Development, and the brand's expansion into the developing markets of India and China.

The brand's success in China demonstrates the combined power of innovation and brand building. In 1998, the disposable diaper category in China was in its infancy and few consumers knew much about Pampers. Only 3 percent were bonded to the brand. By 2006, the brand had achieved a presence score of 99 percent in the top three markets (Shanghai, Beijing, and Guangzhou), and 53 percent of mothers with babies were bonded to the brand. The second-largest brand in terms of bonding is Mamy Poba with 13 percent. Pampers' value share in China is now approaching 60 percent, and volume is reported to be rocketing as the brand extends out beyond the major cities.

By contrast, India poses a far more difficult challenge. As in China, the disposable diaper market in India is fairly new, but it is expected to grow by 15 to 20 percent a year. However, Huggies, not Pampers, is the market leader, with a 70 percent share. In such a situation, innovation can help a challenger brand make its mark. In December 2006, P&G launched a made-for-India diaper with a bikini design that makes the diapers more comfortable for babies in the country's hot and humid weather. P&G reports that Pampers sales have jumped 65 percent since the introduction.

Build a Great Global Brand

An efficient and scalable business model combined with innovation is necessary to stay ahead of the competition. But on its own, it is not sufficient to make a successful global brand. Five further overlapping components are required:

1. A great brand experience
2. Clear and consistent positioning
3. A sense of dynamism
4. A sense of authenticity
5. A strong corporate culture

We examine the role of each of these components in the remainder of this chapter.

A Great Brand Experience

You would think that providing a great brand experience would come naturally to service companies. After all, customer service is the primary aim of banks, airlines, and rental car companies. But all too often, business logistics undermine the consumer experience rather than enhance it. Nothing weakens customer loyalty faster than a system that, while clearly designed to be cost-efficient for the company, doesn't address the service needs of the customer. Anyone who has become lost in the labyrinthine "automated" customer service systems of major banks, airlines, or phone service providers will know what I mean. "Our customers don't want to pay for service, so we might as well make it cheap" seems to be their philosophy. How wrong they are. Successful brands align their logistics to deliver a great experience efficiently and, as a result, deliver added value that customers are happy to pay for. Truly great brands then stretch their brand and business model to find new ways of delivering a great brand experience. Toyota's Lexus, for instance, has created a new and better customer experience. Customers pay more for the car and the service but stay loyal to the brand because they love the service.

A couple of years ago, an accident left me with a six-inch gash in my new Arc'Teryx ski jacket. I sent it to the company for repair only to receive a brand-new replacement jacket, unsolicited and free of charge. That action not only made me feel a sense of connection with Arc'Teryx, but it has also created additional value for them. I now own another one of their jackets, and so does my wife. Furthermore, I tell everyone about my experience with the company. From discussing this experience with others, it is apparent that outdoor sports companies have made good use of exemplary customer service and replacement guarantees to generate business and advocacy. Nike, however, demonstrates how a global brand has found other innovative ways to make the brand experience personal again.

◾ Nike: From Exercise to Experience

While acknowledged to be the clear leader in the global sportswear market, Nike is strongest in its home market, the United States. It was not until 2003 that sales from the rest of the world exceeded sales at home.[12] Nearly one in two U.S. sports goods purchasers is bonded to the brand, and the average in other countries is high enough to carry the brand to seventh position in our Global Power ranking. The brand is less strong in the fragmented sports apparel category but still manages to attract a loyal following, particularly in Russia and China.

Endorsement from sports celebrities helped to build the Nike brand almost from the start. Oregon University athlete Phil Knight and his coach Bill Bowerman were already in business together when in 1962 they began importing running shoes manufactured by the Japanese company Onitsuka Tiger (now Asics). Aided by Bowerman's book, *Jogging*, which inspired many to take up running, the business, named Blue Ribbon Sports (BRS), Inc., took off. In 1971, however, when Onitsuka Tiger was seeking to regain control of the U.S. market, the two decided to design and manufacture their own shoes. Their first model, named Nike in honor of the Greek goddess of victory, was launched in February 1972 at the U.S. Olympic trials, where it was endorsed by two of the fastest runners there. In 1978, BRS, Inc. officially renamed itself Nike, Inc. Today the company sponsorships range far beyond the company's heartland of basketball and running to include Serena Williams, Tiger Woods, Wayne Rooney, Roger Federer, and skateboarder Paul Rodriguez, among many others.

You could argue that sports gear is all about experience (even if many of us never actually use the gear for its intended purpose), but Nike has found additional ways to engage people with its brand and products through NIKETOWN, NIKEiD and Nike+.

It was not until the late 1980s that Nike started advertising on TV and the "Just Do It" slogan was born. But Nike did not just rely on Weiden & Kennedy's blockbuster ads to promote its brand. In 1990, the first NIKETOWN was launched in Portland, Oregon. Today many different companies are using the retail environment to offer consumers a more engaging experience; back then, however, it was a bold new approach. NIKETOWN provided Nike with a place to showcase its products, elevating them to the status of art by its use of gallery-style presentation. But more than that, NIKETOWN sought to involve visitors in the drama of the setting, engaging their senses through ambient sound, video, and interactive displays. A trip to NIKETOWN immerses the visitor in a branded experience. NIKEiD then helps to personalize that experience.

NIKEiD is both an online service that allows visitors to customize products from running shoes to backpacks and a dedicated element of the revamped

NIKETOWN. The physical entity is a much more immersive experience and takes a leaf out of Apple's Genius Bar. It consists of two zones: the ID Bar, which has information on its sneaker customization process and sample shoes in eight styles exclusive to NIKEiD, plus the iD Studio, where visitors can have a 45-minute, one-to-one session with a "design consultant" trained to guide customers in creating their own footwear. An article in *Design Week* magazine reports that the emphasis here is on interaction with knowledgeable staff, not the "shock and awe" of the "brand palace." The article goes on to say "NIKEiD's store design is refined rather than spectacular, within walnut worktops, upholstered seating and formal display tables with a glass cube. What is more memorable is the personal service."[13] Not content with personalizing the brand experience, Nike's latest venture extends the depth of that experience and creates a sense of community.

Nike+, launched in the United States in July 2006, takes the whole concept of customer experience a step further (if you will excuse the pun) by bringing together two of the coolest brands out there to deliver an added-value experience. A small sensor embedded in their shoes allows runners to track their progress on an Apple iPod Nano. After each run, the iPod downloads data on distance, speed, and calories burned to the computer, and the details are posted on the Nike+Web site.

As *AdAge* reports, Nike+is more than a running shoe:

> Nike Plus epitomizes the increasing convergence of ideas and utility. It's a user-friendly product, and it's selling like ice cream on the French Riviera because it enhances the experience of running by allowing runners to measure and compare performances over time and with others . . . . Oh, yes, and it's made Nike a content player, a media owner operating the biggest running club in the world via a social network. There, people buy music to run to and share their running experiences, whether by challenging and chatting with friends on the site, mapping their runs for others to see and use, or simply trash-talking.[14]

In short, it is a great brand experience that is helping transform perceptions of Nike. It is also another factor in reducing the proportion of Nike's budget that goes to above-the-line ad spend. As reported by the *New York Times*, in 2006, Nike spent just 33 percent of its $678 million U.S. advertising budget on ads with television networks and other traditional media companies.[15] That is a 3 percent increase compared to 2003, but it's dwarfed by the 33 percent increase in nonmedia ad spending. The *Times* article reports Trevor Edwards, Nike's corporate vice president for global brand and category management, as saying, "We're not in the business of keeping the media companies alive, we're in the business of connecting with consumers."

Clear and Consistent Positioning

Marketers have long believed that brands with strong, differentiated positioning are more likely to be successful than poorly differentiated offerings. Innovation not only ensures a positive brand experience but can drive perceptions of differentiation. Gillette has consistently used product innovation to keep ahead of the competition on a global basis, but that has not kept it from heralding each new razor with a fanfare of advertising confirming its positioning as "the best a man can get." This combination of innovation with single-minded positioning has resulted in high loyalty toward Gillette and allowed it to enjoy high market shares even though it charges a high price premium wherever it is sold.

Procter & Gamble's Pantene Pro-V is a classic example of a brand that has maintained a very clear and consistent positioning around the world. The focus of that well-known positioning is healthy, shining hair. What may not be so well known is how that positioning came to be. The brand was the first globally successful P&G brand to be created outside the United States.

The global hair-care market has always been characterized by incredible brand proliferation. In every country, there are a plethora of brands on offer: value brands, mass-market offerings, prestige brands, and salon brands. The pace of innovation has typically meant that the life cycle of a hair-care brand is relatively short. Pantene Pro-V is one of few brands that have been able to stand the pace of change for more than a decade. Out of 26 countries where we have measured the brand's equity, it achieves a strong connection to consumers in 20. It is particularly strong in Thailand and China, something that, even 17 years later, may derive from its 1990 restage in Taiwan.

Rising Tide: Lessons from 165 Years of Brand Building at Procter & Gamble by Davis Dyer, Frederick Dalzell, and Rowena Olegario details the restage of Pantene in full.[16] I repeat the salient points here because it introduces several approaches now considered best practice for global branding today.

P&G acquired the Pantene shampoo brand when it bought Richardson-Vicks in 1985. Until then, Pantene had been sold as a prestige brand, but had limited distribution and an unexploited product story: Its name was derived from the ingredient panthenol, the pro-vitamin of B5, which penetrates the hair cuticle to strengthen the hair and make it more elastic and shiny.

Pantene might have remained a niche beauty brand had not Durk Jaeger, who was in charge of the Asian region at the time, directed the Taiwanese team to develop a new brand for Taiwan and recommended they try Pantene. With limited resources, the team had to shortcut the innovation process by combining existing assets to create something new.

With two functional brands already in the Taiwanese market, the local team wanted to position Pantene as a beauty brand. A habits-and-practices study revealed that "shiny hair and healthy hair" was a strong proposition. What they needed was a product formulation to support that proposition. Based on his experience working with laundry brands in the United States, James Wei, a young brand manager, recommended they use an existing technology adapted to the brand's specific equity needs.

The technology was the two-in-one shampoo and conditioner code named BC-18. The result of years of research and development, BC-18 had helped rejuvenate Pert in the United States, taking it from a failing brand at the beginning of the 1980s to the number-one brand on a value basis by the early 1990s. Combined with the existing pro-vitamin formula, BC-18 gave the Taiwanese team a new product without lengthy R&D.

Adopting an existing product technology is now an accepted practice for global brands; so too is "search and reapply." As *Rising Tide* reveals, the lack of local resource also forced the Taiwanese team to appropriate elements from Pantene positioning elsewhere to create a new one. They appropriated the "beauty-through-health" positioning from the United States and combined it with the "shine-outside/strength-inside" positioning from France to create the health-on-the-inside, shine-on-the-outside positioning. The bottle was redesigned as an oval but adopted the U.S. "rainbow" color scheme to denote different versions. The launch ads were also repurposed from the United States, featuring fashion models with permed hair who urged, "Don't hate me because I'm beautiful."

The ads, however, fell short in two key respects:

1. They did not highlight the shine that the brand promised.
2. They did not fit the sensitivities of the Taiwanese culture.

Not until the team used ads from Japan featuring women with straight hair did the campaign take off. (Straight hair shows off the shine far better than permed hair.)

Within six months of its launch in Taiwan, Pantene Pro-V more than doubled its original first-year target. The brand rapidly expanded throughout Asia, and the same "for hair so healthy it shines" platform was adopted in the United States, even before the relaunch there, in order to stave off a competitive introduction from Helene Curtis (now part of Unilever). Since then, the new Pro-V brand has become a megabrand. The basic positioning is still serving the brand well, having evolved through several restages to today's "let yourself shine."

A Sense of Dynamism

People like winners, and they tend to judge the success of brands by how many other people they see using them. They like to be part of the latest fashion.

Ideally a brand creates perceptions of leadership not just by producing trend-setting products, but also by acting and communicating like a leader. By doing so, a brand can create a sense of dynamism that attracts and holds people to it, making them less likely to chase off after the next new thing.

According to Unilever's Web site, Dove is the world's number-one cleansing brand, with sales of over €2.5 billion a year (US $3.9 billion) in over 80 countries. The brand, which started as a humble bar of soap in the 1950s, now spans a broad range of categories including shampoo, antiperspirant, and antiaging moisturizers. Our Global Power ranking demonstrates that the brand has the ability to span countries as well as categories. One consistent idea, "moisturizing care for naturally beautiful skin," has provided the clarity of positioning that underpins all of Dove's lineup. With the new *Campaign for Real Beauty*, however, Dove is going a step further. By taking on the beauty industry, Dove is taking a leadership stance.

One of the early parts of the *Campaign for Real Beauty* was the *Real Curves* campaign used to launch Dove's firming lotion in 2004. That campaign, which was successful in both the United States and the United Kingdom, was noteworthy because it featured not impossibly slim models but "real" women with real curves. In 2006, the Real Beauty campaign went viral when the Cannes Award-winning ad *Evolution* was put on YouTube.

Evolution portrayed the transformation of a model from an ordinary-looking woman to a physically and digitally enhanced icon of female beauty. *Evolution*'s message was loud and clear: What you see on billboards and in magazines is not real but fake. The ad, which reminded viewers of the Dove Self-Esteem Fund and exhorted them to participate in the Dove Real Beauty Workshops for Girls, struck a chord across a broad cross-section of women. Survey results on the Dove Web site reported that only 2 percent of women considered themselves beautiful, and 68 percent strongly agreed that the media sets an unrealistic standard of beauty. To date, *Evolution* has been viewed over 15 million times online—not bad for a film that was never intended for broadcast.

Following up on the critical success of *Evolution*, Dove released a new ad online, *Onslaught*. *Onslaught* opens by showing us a straightforward shot of a young girl smiling confidently at the camera, accompanied by the song "La Breeze" from U.K. group Simian. This image is in view for a long time— 15 seconds or more—seemingly to establish a sense of tranquility, before it cuts to a barrage of traditional beauty industry images, perhaps intended to approximate the number of exposures the girl is likely to receive in the coming year. A sequence of presenters intones: "You will look . . . younger . . . smaller . . . lighter . . . firmer . . . tighter . . . thinner . . . softer" before the ad closes with the tagline: "Talk to your daughter before the beauty industry does."

In taking a stand against the image of the "ideal woman," Dove seems to be taking a leaf out of Douglas Holt's playbook for the iconic brand.[17] Dove conveys that it is not simply an advertised product but a brand that stands for something, an entity that people can really connect with. Quoted in *AdAge* in 2007, Kathy O'Brien, marketing director for Dove skin care in the United States, said that *Onslaught* "does show our commitment to our mission, and we think it does have a positive effect on the brand. We feel a responsibility as a billion-dollar brand in the beauty industry . . . to change the way the beauty industry communicates with young girls."

In planning marketing campaigns, most companies ask: "How can we make people buy more?" But the people behind the Dove campaign asked a different kind of question: "What can we do to make life better for people?" They thought about the needs and desires women have expressed and set out to make a difference. So far the campaign has succeeded well, particularly in English-speaking cultures, such as the United States, Canada, the United Kingdom and Australia. Its success elsewhere is reported to be mixed, and we shall return to consider the possible reasons for this in the next section.

A Sense of Authenticity

In examining the brands that have become successful on the global stage, we are struck by the numbers that have stories spanning many decades. Whether publicized or not, the origins of these brands are original and compelling. In today's world of pirate copies of clothes, music, and identities, people are attracted to brands that are true to their origins. A strong heritage is not only a sign of authenticity but also a sign of success. People recognize and respect an authentic brand that was created by a specific person or persons and has stood the test of time.

Like Jack Daniel's, Levi's, Hewlett-Packard, and Ford, Chanel is a great example of a brand that has successfully leveraged its authenticity to become a global brand. However, before considering the origins of that brand's success, it is worth taking a moment to consider the market in which the brand competes. Although very different from more mundane product categories, Chanel is facing many of the same challenges.

At the ESOMAR Fragrance 2007 conference in Paris, Diana Dodson of business intelligence provider Euromonitor International provided a comprehensive review of the global fragrance market that highlighted these points:

- The $35 billion fragrance market is growing fastest in the BRICs (Brazil, Russia, India, and China).
- By contrast to these fast-growing markets, Western Europe and North America are growing more slowly, with markets characterized by high churn rates, a proliferation

of brands, and stagnating prices. The typical fragrance brand has a two-year life span.

- The mass market is growing, and retail marketing is blurring the line between fine fragrances and the cheaper end of the market. As premium brands are increasingly placed alongside the mass brands in pharmacies and mass merchandisers (and discounted along with them), this trend may be tough to reverse.
- Celebrity fragrances, which have proven successful at attracting new, younger consumers, add to the instability of the market. As the celebrity goes, so too does the fragrance. The brand Shh . . . from Jade Goody suffered as its namesake fell from public favor; the brand was withdrawn long before its two years were up.

In her presentation, Diana suggested that consumers are getting fed up with the frivolities of the rich and famous and that a backlash against celebrity brands might be on the horizon. David Cousino, global category director at Unilever and chair of the session, suggested that these celebrity brands, which are focused on image and not the "juice," were "dumbing down" the market for fragrance in general. In effect, the presence of cheaper brands that smell OK is training younger consumers to judge brands on price, not scent.

For my part, I doubt very much that people will lose their fascination with celebrities any time soon. And if the fragrance houses don't want their consumers to become scent illiterate, they must break their addiction to volume sales and find compelling propositions that justify a price premium. In other words, they need to take a page out of Chanel's playbook and grow truly strong brands.

It is tough to maintain a strong bond to significant numbers of people in a competitive, fashion-driven, fragmented market. Yet in all the turmoil of the fragrance market, twice as many people bond with Chanel than is normal for the category, and the brand maintains a strong relationship in over 90 percent of the countries in which it has been measured.

Chanel is, of course, named after a real person. Born in 1883, Gabrielle Bonheur Chanel was orphaned at a young age and was raised by her aunts in the province of Auvergne, France. They nicknamed her "Coco," or "little pet," and taught her to sew. She used this skill, combined with her talent as a designer, to get her start in the fashion business as a milliner. Her hats were worn by famous French actresses who helped establish her reputation. From there she moved on to design haute couture clothing, offering simple designs that contrasted with the frillier garments of the time. She created the tricot sailor dress, turtleneck sweaters, introduced pants for women, and her "Chanel suit" met with phenomenal success in the United States.

The single element that most insured Chanel's fame, however, was her most famous fragrance, Chanel No. 5, in its 1923 Art Deco bottle. It was the first perfume to bear a designer's name. Today there are hundreds.

Over the years, the brand's TV and print advertising has helped it reach iconic status. Like many of the enduring brands featured in this chapter, Chanel is not shy about pushing the boundaries of brand building. In 2004, the company pushed financial boundaries by spending a reported $40 million to produce *No 5: The Film*, the world's most expensive commercial. Starring Nicole Kidman and Rodrigo Santoro and directed by Baz Luhrmann of *Moulin Rouge!* fame, this fairy-tale extravaganza lasts precisely three minutes. While billed as a movie, and sharing a movie's production values, the branding is fairly blatant, featuring an enormous rooftop installation and a diamond pendant in the shape of the famous double-C logo.

Strong Corporate Culture

In their book *Uncommon Practice: People Who Deliver a Great Brand Experience*, Andy Milligan and Shaun Smith provide a series of case studies to justify their premise that some companies succeed because "their cultures are uniquely developed to meet the needs of their customers in a distinctive way. Critical to the development of that culture is a genuine belief in, and commitment to, the people in the business that has engendered a loyalty uncommon amongst many organizations. This loyalty translates onto a genuine passion for their customers."[18]

Many of the companies that made it to our Global Brand Power Top 25 have very strong global corporate cultures: Nokia and P&G are just two examples.

The Nokia Way

As well as being instrumental in the company's focus on mobile telecommunications in the early 1990s, Jorma Ollila also expressed what were to become Nokia's basic values. The values—customer satisfaction, respect for the individual, achievement, and continuous learning—were to become known later as the "Nokia Way." Talking about the Nokia Way, Sari Baldauf, president of Nokia Networks, said: "The value base makes it possible to communicate fast and transparently globally and if that is missing, I wouldn't say that there is any chance of success."[19] After an extensive process involving staff from all around the company, Nokia's values have been restated in this way on the company Web site:

Engaging You, Achieved Together, Passion for Innovation and Very Human[20]

Procter & Gamble's Values

P&G has long focused on aligning and binding together the interests of company and staff. It introduced profit sharing as early as 1887 and an employee stock purchase plan in 1892. Today P&G's values are summed up succinctly as leadership, ownership, integrity, and a passion for winning and trust, and they run throughout the organization. The belief that P&G staff has in the company and their desire to see it succeed has been very apparent at meetings I've attended. Whether they are seeking to understand the latest approaches to return on investment measurement or examining a different approach to brand equity research, P&G staff members have been open-minded and focused on the company's best interests.

Values written down on paper or on a Web site can seem dispassionate and soulless. It is all too easy to dismiss them as meaningless. As Milligan and Smith suggest, it is up to a company's leaders to find ways to bring values to life and "walk the talk" if they want the company culture to motivate employees and delight customers. A few companies, such as Nokia and P&G, have managed to accomplish this, and as a result, they enjoy a real competitive advantage.

The success factors outlined here lie behind the success of all brands, global and local. Without them, to use a baseball analogy, an aspiring global brand will not get past first base. As I demonstrate in the rest of the book, other challenges exist, not the least of which is the competition provided by strong local brands.

In the next chapter, Joanna Seddon, who heads up Millward Brown's brand valuation practice, examines how a strong brand helps deliver strong financial returns.

Key Points to Take Away

- There are very few strong global brands.
- To be successful on the global stage, a brand must combine a strong, scalable business model, innovation, and great brand-building skills.

Questions to Consider

1. Which global brands offer a good role model for you? What were the keys that unlocked their global growth?
2. Is your business model set up to scale globally?
3. Is your innovation pipeline full? Is it consumer-led or technology-led?
4. Are you working to build your brand across the five dimensions of experience, clear positioning, dynamism, authenticity, and corporate culture?

For more information related to these questions, visit theglobalbrandonline.com.

Chapter 5

How Strong Global Brands Create Lasting Value

Joanna Seddon
Millward Brown Optimor

In Chapter 4, Nigel showed how a strong relationship with a brand makes customers more likely to buy its products than those of competitors, stimulating volume and share growth. This chapter picks up where that one left off, by explaining how we can trace the impact of brand right through to the bottom line. I explain how Millward Brown Optimor created the BrandZ Top 100 Most Valuable Brands ranking, and, drawing on examples from the ranking, I demonstrate that companies with strong brands enjoy greater sales, profits, and long-term business value.

We believe that it is extremely important to make this link between brand strength and financial value. The only way that you will ever get chief executive officers, chief financial officers, and boards truly to take brands seriously is to show that by doing so they will make more money. Talk about branding has to be translated into the language of the finance director, the analyst, and the accountant.

Fortunately, creating this bridge between marketing and finance is easier than you might think. The financial community has already got most of the way there. They are painfully aware that the tangible assets they are used to measuring, such as property and equipment, now constitute only a small part of the value of companies. They know that the majority of company value consists in "intangibles," assets that clearly exist and have value but can't be touched, and they realize that one of these intangibles is brand value.

Why Does Brand Value Matter?

Brand value matters because by investing in brands, a company can create a sustainable financial advantage. The most successful companies are those that

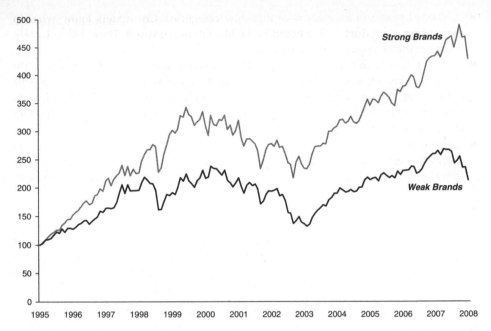

Figure 5.1 Indexed Share Price of Companies with Strong and Weak Brands

Source: Proprietary WPP BrandZ™ brand strength data

recognize that their brands are assets to be carefully crafted, nurtured, and developed. They manage their brands like any other assets: They invest in them, put them to work to generate value and expect to get a good return on their investment. Our analysis, which forms the basis for the BrandZ Top 100 ranking, shows that companies that understand this and have invested to develop strong brands create more business value and command higher share prices. Figure 5.1 compares the share price performance of strong versus weak brands and shows that, over time, a strong brand generates an average 20 percent share price premium over its weak brand competitors.

A strong brand can impact the financial results of the business in these ways:

- A strong brand can drive sales growth by increasing the ability of a business to attract new customers and to retain existing customers. More customers equal more sales.
- A strong brand can increase margins by commanding a price premium over competitors. Examples include Starbucks and China Mobile.
- A strong brand can provide a competitive advantage. Brands with strong bonds to consumers create barriers for entry to competitors; consumers will be reluctant to switch to new players, even when their products and services are of equal or higher quality.

- A strong brand can ease entrance into new categories. Consumers know what to expect from a product with a brand name like GE or Samsung. They will recognize and trust the brand name in a new context.
- A strong brand can help a company reduce working capital costs. Companies with strong brands are able to hire employees more easily and suffer lower employee turnover rates than companies with weaker brands. Suppliers are more willing to work with companies that have a strong brand reputation; governments and regulators are more likely to grant favorable terms.
- Companies with strong brands have the option to minimize investment costs and risks when extending into new areas by licensing the brand to a third party and getting royalties in return—pure profit. An example is The Gap, whose rapid expansion of stores has been entirely due to brand licensing.
- A strong brand can protect against downturns. Brand loyalists are more likely to stay with them through tough times. Fidelity has managed to retain investors through times when its funds were underperforming. Strong brands are resilient in times of crisis. The reputations of brands such as Coca-Cola and Johnson & Johnson's Tylenol enabled those companies to recover quickly from adverse publicity.

Taken together, these factors give companies with strong brands greater certainty of future growth than companies that do not have strong brands.

How Does a Brand Create Value?

A brand is created and managed through the customer experience—the points at which products and services touch customers and potential customers. Through these touch points—which include not only marketing activities but also all the operations of the business—a brand creates preference and loyalty among its customers. Thus a brand forges a pact with its customers, which guarantees a flow of future sales and profits.

Brand value is a direct result of the strength of the customer relationship. This idea has to lie at the heart of any valid brand valuation methodology. The BrandZ Top 100 Most Valuable Brands ranking constitutes a robust, reliable, and comprehensive ranking of brands. The results deserve serious consideration and analysis. In the following sections, I outline the advantages of the methodology we have developed and explain how we do it.

The BrandZ Top 100: A Better Approach to Valuation

The BrandZ Top 100 valuation differs from earlier rankings in six key ways:

1. It is grounded in a quantitative measure of consumer allegiance. We believe no valuation of brands can have validity if it doesn't draw on consumer attitudes as a key input.

2. It takes a "market-facing" approach, valuing consumer-facing brands such as Dove instead of corporate brands such as Unilever. This makes sense because, after all, it is the Dove brand that is the object of consumer preference and loyalty, not the corporate entity called Unilever. In doing so, the BrandZ Top 100 makes a major departure from other rankings.
3. It is grounded in BrandZ, the world's largest brand equity database. BrandZ provides an incredibly rich reserve of data on the strength and growth of the brand relationship for almost all of the world's major brands, tracked over 10 years.
4. The BrandZ ranking is comprehensive. It values strong local brands as well as global ones, without requiring brands to be present in multiple markets or in a particular country. It includes brands not included in other rankings, such as retailers, and, the BrandZ ranking is able to provide comprehensive value rankings by category.
5. The BrandZ approach is forward looking; it can be used to predict financial performance, not just provide an estimate of current value. Millward Brown's analysis, based on 10 years of data, has already shown through a combination of brand metrics that we can identify businesses that will outperform the Standard & Poor's 500 index.
6. It provides actionable information for marketing, finance, and business professionals. The ranking gives insight into not just how much value has been created but *how* this value has been created.

BrandZ

- The BrandZ brand equity study has been conducted annually by Millward Brown for WPP since 1998.
- BrandZ has collected information on more than 10,000 brands across 31 countries, including both developed and emerging markets.
- Over 200 separate product categories have been studied.
- Buyers or users of each product category are asked about brands in the competitive framework of that specific category.
- More than 1 million consumers and business customers have been included in the study.

Table 5.1 shows the top 25 brands from the BrandZ Top 100 Most Valuable Brands Ranking for 2008. (To see the full list of 100 brands, see Appendix A.)

Table 5.1 BrandZ™ Top 100 Most Valuable Brands Ranking 2008

Position	Brand	Brand Value $M	% Change in Brand Value (vs. 2007)
1	Google	86,057	30%
2	GE (General Electric)	71,379	15%
3	Microsoft	70,887	29%
4	Coca-Cola[1]	58,208	17%
5	China Mobile	57,225	39%
6	IBM	55,335	65%
7	Apple	55,206	123%
8	McDonald's	49,499	49%
9	Nokia	43,975	39%
10	Marlboro	37,324	−5%
11	Vodafone	36,962	75%
12	Toyota	35,134	5%
13	Wal-Mart	34,547	−6%
14	Bank of America	33,092	15%
15	Citi	30,318	−10%
16	HP	29,278	17%
17	BMW	28,015	9%
18	ICBC	28,004	70%
19	Louis Vuitton	25,739	13%
20	American Express	24,816	7%
21	Wells Fargo	24,739	2%
22	Cisco	24,101	28%
23	Disney	23,705	5%
24	UPS	23,610	−4%
25	Tesco	23,208	39%

(1) Coke's value includes both Coke and Diet Coke

Three Steps to Valuing a Brand

Our approach to valuing brands is similar to that used by financial analysts and accountants for valuing businesses. We employ an "economic use" approach, in which we calculate the present value of future earnings. We forecast the proportion of sales and profit growth that is expected in the future. But where an analyst would include the whole business in the calculation, we are only interested in the portion of the sales and profits that are generated by the brand.

There are three key steps in the brand valuation approach used in the BrandZ ranking.

1. Identify and allocate out intangible earnings to brands.

A company's assets can be divided into two classes: tangible assets, such as property and equipment, and intangible assets, which include brand and other types of intellectual property. It is essential that we set aside the earnings generated by tangible assets, to avoid inflating the importance of brand.

We allocate the total value of intangibles out to each brand owned by the company. (For companies such as Starbucks, where there is only one brand and its name is the same as the company, we can skip this step.)

Then we divide up each brand's intangible earnings by each country of operation. It is important to do the valuation "bottom up," at the country level, since the strength of a brand's relationship with consumers may vary a great deal from market to market. For example, in the credit card business, Visa is the strongest brand in Asia, while MasterCard is stronger in Europe.

2. Determine the brand contribution.

The process through which we identify the brand contribution—the extent to which a consumer's decision to purchase a brand is underpinned by factors that are emotional rather than functional—lies at the heart of our rigorous valuation.

The brand contribution used for the BrandZ Top 100 Ranking is derived from the brand equity data collected in the BrandZ research. Using the BrandDynamics Pyramid described in Chapter 3, we observe the degree to which each brand derives sales from people who have a strong emotional relationship with it. Thus the number of people at the bonding level is a crucial ingredient of the valuation of each brand.

Additional analysis takes into account the degree to which the category in question is driven by brand versus price. Brands drive less value in categories where low price is an important driver of choice.

We also include a third factor in the determination of the brand contribution. This is a measure of the "structural" factors that create barriers to switching. Sales and profits from lines of business where the buyer has no real choice, or where the market exhibits high degrees of inertia, are excluded from the brand value. So, for example, we do not include any sales and profits from Microsoft's operating system business, because Windows is a near monopoly.

Using these three factors, we calculate the brand contribution—the percentage of intangible earnings that can be attributed to the impact of brand, as opposed to everything else that happens in the business (product, price, distribution, customer service, etc.).

3. Discount future earnings back to net present value,
   including a measurement of brand risk.

The final step in our brand valuation process is the determination of an appropriate risk rate and multiple to use in calculating the brand's value. Figure 5.2

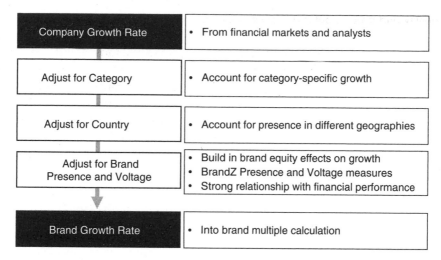

Company Growth Rate	• From financial markets and analysts
Adjust for Category	• Account for category-specific growth
Adjust for Country	• Account for presence in different geographies
Adjust for Brand Presence and Voltage	• Build in brand equity effects on growth • BrandZ Presence and Voltage measures • Strong relationship with financial performance
Brand Growth Rate	• Into brand multiple calculation

Figure 5.2 Process by Which Brand Momentum Is Calculated

summarizes this process. We look at the brand's financials, its sector, and the BrandZ data to forecast its short-term future performance. In addition to the factors that financial analysts take into consideration when valuing the business (such as company, sector, and country risk), we also add a factor to reflect the brand's consumer risk profile and growth potential.

The Voltage metric from the BrandZ data, which describes a brand's efficiency at converting people from presence to bonding, is used to adjust the discount rates. Getting more people bonded to your brand means you will have more loyalists.

The result is a brand risk or discount rate and corresponding multiple, expressed in an index we call *brand momentum*. Brand momentum is an index of a brand's short-term growth rate relative to the average short-term growth rate of the brands with which it competes.

The output from the brand valuation gives us three ways of looking at how strong brands create value:

1. Financial value: the total "dollar" value created by a brand
2. Brand contribution: the impact of brand equity on the customer purchase decision
3. Brand momentum: a brand's future growth potential

We have defined the world's most valuable brands as those that score highly on all three metrics. However, they achieve their success in many different ways, as the wide variety of brands in the BrandZ Top 100 testifies. We'll take a look at some of these.

Valuable Brands Can Be Old or New

There are no hard and fast rules about how long it takes to build a strong brand. The world's most valuable brands include some that have existed for more than a century (American Express, Louis Vuitton, and Hermès) and some that have existed for less than a decade (Google, Accenture, China Mobile, and Amazon). The brands that have built value very fast have been helped along by some extraordinary circumstances, such as world-transforming technology (Google and Amazon), government assistance (China Mobile), or massive investment (Accenture). For brands that are developing under more ordinary conditions, the BrandZ data suggests that a period of 25 to 30 years is a more reasonable time frame to build value. Starbucks, for example, established its first coffee shop in 1971; Apple launched its first computer in 1976.

Brands Can Build Value with or without Advertising

The world's most valuable brands create value in many different ways. Most of them invest heavily in marketing. However, the number-one brand in both 2007 and 2008 is Google, a business that does almost no paid advertising. How does Google do it? In part, the brand doesn't need much advertising; it creates awareness through ubiquitous distribution and positive word of mouth.

More interestingly, Google's story highlights a factor common to many of the world's best brands. Google's two founders, Larry Page and Sergey Brin, don't spend their time thinking about branding. They spend their time thinking about the customer experience. Their objective is to create an ever easier and more user-friendly search experience for their users. This focus on what Chief Executive Eric Schmidt referred to as "end-user happiness"[1] has enabled Google to create a strong emotional bond with its users. The strength of this emotional connection creates a barrier that competitors will have difficulty breaking through for as long as Google continues to deliver on its brand promise of the best customer experience on the web.

If you look at some of the other brands that have built the most value in the last few years, you can again see the customer experience factor at work. Retail brands such as Best Buy and Marks & Spencer owe their growth in value first to investing to improve the customer experience and, second, to communicating this.

Brands Can Build Value in Consumer and in B2B Businesses

Almost any business in almost any industry has the ability to build a brand and to reap the resulting financial advantages. The BrandZ Top 100 shows this quite clearly. The world's most valuable brands include not only Coca-Cola and Pepsi, Louis Vuitton and Chanel, Gillette and L'Oréal, but also Citi and HSBC, Microsoft and Samsung, Wal-Mart and Tesco, Shell and BP. All of these businesses have created competitive advantage for their products through brand building.

Branding is not something that applies only to consumer brands. Some of the world's most valuable brands, including financial brands such as Goldman Sachs, technology brands such as Cisco, and professional service brands such as Accenture, are pure business-to-business (B2B) firms that don't sell to consumers at all. Other top-scoring brands like IBM, Citi, and GE have a large B2B component in their business mix.

The example of Goldman Sachs shows how a strong global brand can be built without even paying lip service to the external trappings of branding. Because the Goldman Sachs culture is sales oriented, not brand oriented, its people have little desire to spend money on their "brand." Consequently, the firm does no advertising. And yet, Goldman Sachs is all about reputation. It is the stellar reputation of Goldman Sachs that enables it to hire the top graduates from business schools and that makes the firm the first choice in merger and acquisition deals. No CEO or CFO ever got into trouble with his board for hiring Goldman Sachs.

Other companies have taken the opposite tack from Goldman Sachs and built valuable B2B brands by consciously applying consumer branding practices to B2B situations. The professional service brand Accenture is a case in point. Recognizing that a strong brand name was critical to its future success after its forced divorce from the accounting firm Arthur Andersen, the consulting firm very deliberately set out to create one.

The new brand launch in 1999 was a massive global implementation, which employed 50 teams to execute the changes across 137 offices worldwide. Using traditional consumer marketing techniques, the new brand reached out to B2B customers in 46 countries. Approximately $1.8 billion was spent on advertising in the three years following the launch.

Accenture has continued its strategy of brand building through advertising, investing around $500 million a year ever since. Everyone who travels by air is familiar with Accenture's airport billboards featuring Tiger Woods.

Accenture has built its brand by marketing directly to its business clients. Other B2B companies have succeeded by reaching past their business customers to the ultimate end users of their products. Intel pioneered this tactic by calling out the presence of its chip through computer stickers and retail point-of-sale and consumer advertising. The "Intel Inside" idea of branding a component has now been widely adopted. Similar ingredient brands have been launched by numerous technology companies, several of which—Cisco, Visa, IBM, HP—have made it into the world's most valuable list.

The Most Valuable Brands May Be Global or Local

As you would expect, an analysis of the world's most valuable brands identifies many global brands. While a good number have American origins (Coca-Cola, Microsoft, Apple, GE, McDonald's, Starbucks), brands from Germany (Mercedes and Lidl), France (Louis Vuitton and Chanel), Japan (Toyota and Sony), Korea (Samsung), and Sweden (IKEA) all make it to the Top 100 on the basis of their global presence.

However, not all of the world's most valuable brands are *global* brands. The BrandZ Top 100 also includes brands that are in only one market. There in the Top 10 is China Mobile, whose presence is, as yet, limited almost entirely to China and Hong Kong. Other local or regional brands that have most of their value concentrated in one country include Target, Marks & Spencer, Bank of America, Wells Fargo, and Verizon.

China Mobile has created more brand value in one country than its partner Vodafone has created in 25 markets. Granted, the company has a built-in advantage (the size and growth of the Chinese market), but the rise of China Mobile is due not only to economics but also to its understanding of branding power. China Mobile deliberately set out to develop a strong brand by investing heavily in brand image, identity, customer service, and advertising. And it succeeded in building a brand that resonates very well with consumers and has won accolades from Chinese and western marketers alike. Even allowing for the less competitive nature of the Chinese market, China Mobile's customers have far higher levels of bonding or loyalty to the brand than customers of global players such as Vodafone.

Its success in building brand equity has enabled China Mobile to tap into the huge potential of the Chinese market, while charging a price premium over competitors. The result is not only tremendous growth but tremendously *profitable* growth. As of last count, China Mobile had 370 million subscribers in China, compared to 250 million for Vodafone globally. Its profit margins were 55 percent compared to 33 percent for China Unicom, its main domestic competitor, and 30 percent for Vodafone globally.

Brands Can Build Value in One Category and in Many Categories

The world's most valuable brands include brands that are confined to one category and brands that have successfully built value across a number of categories. Not surprisingly, there are far fewer of the latter—it is difficult to preserve a brand's strength and integrity when it is extended broadly.

Two brands in the BrandZ Top 100 have been outstandingly successful at building value across a number of categories: GE and Samsung. Each brand is based on simple principles, which can be applied to many businesses.

While he was chairman of GE, Jack Welch famously declared that he was going to make GE "the most competitive company on earth" and pursued a policy of divesting businesses that were not number one or two in their categories. As a result of his consistent implementation of this strategy, the GE brand came to symbolize excellence and leadership, whether applied to light bulbs and consumer appliances, financial services, nuclear reactors, medical equipment, or, most recently, entertainment. Under his successor, Jeff Immelt, the expression of the brand has evolved. The long-lived slogan "We bring good things to light" has changed to "Imagination at Work," and new emphasis has been placed on sensitivity to the environment. The brand, however, retains its strength and position as one of the global top 10 most valuable.

In 1996, in the midst of the Asian economic crisis, Kun-Hee Lee, the chairman of Samsung, decided that the revival of the company depended not on making products but on building a single strong brand. As a result, Samsung moved to a master-brand strategy, doing away with subbrands such as Plano, Tantus, Yepp, and Wiseview. The Samsung brand is now attached to B2B and consumer-facing businesses ranging from computer chips and storage equipment to TVs, cameras, and mobile phones. Following the chairman's declaration that "an enterprise's most vital assets lie in its design and creative capabilities,"[2] Samsung has put money behind its words, investing in 17 design centers in major cities around the world. This has enabled Samsung to succeed in developing products that truly embody innovation and design excellence and to build one of the world's leading brands within a five-year period.

Many of the Most Valuable Brands Come from Single-Brand Companies

One of the most striking things about the world's most valuable brands is how few of them are consumer packaged goods (CPG) products. Only two CPG brands make it to the Top 10 most valuable brands: Coca-Cola and Marlboro. Some additional CPG brands are represented in the rest of the Global Top 100, including Gillette, L'Oréal, Budweiser, Pampers, Pepsi, and Colgate. However, there are surprisingly few of them.

The majority of the world's most valuable brands belong to single-brand companies—companies in which the brand and company share the same name. These include Google, McDonald's, and Nokia, companies that started with one brand and built value in that brand name (in the case of Google, very rapidly).

There are also many brands like HSBC and Vodafone, which have grown by acquiring and absorbing (i.e., renaming) other brands. The current HSBC brand has been created from an amalgam of many individual bank brands. In 2003, Vodafone completed the largest brand migration in history, transitioning more than 15 different brands, serving 65 million customers from around the world, over to the Vodafone brand.

The lack of consumer products brands among the BrandZ Top 100 becomes even more surprising when we consider that these brands are among the best at creating strong relationships with their consumers. Brands such as Pampers, Dove, Pantene, and Axe achieve strong Global Power Scores but don't create enough total value to be counted in the Top 100.

There seem to be three main reasons for the comparative lack of consumer products brands among the Global Top 100: brand fragmentation, organizational structure, and distribution strategy.

Companies such as Unilever and Procter & Gamble don't typically feature their company names on their products. Rather, they are "Houses of Brands," owning huge portfolios of different brands. P&G, for example, has sales of almost $80 billion, but these sales come from about 300 brands in 140 countries. The company owns 23 brands with over $1 billion in sales, but even Gillette, one of the largest brands, brings in no more than $6 billion.

By its very nature, the structure of a House of Brands company places obstacles in the way of creating powerful brands. The consumer product giants are organized to achieve synergies across brands and categories. Many functions are shared by different brands, including research and development, procurement and purchasing, manufacturing, recruiting and human resources. Although marketing is for the most part carried out on a brand-by-brand basis, the brand managers are company employees rather than brand employees— they move from brand to brand as they progress in their careers, often staying only a couple of years with one product. While generating efficiencies, this approach makes it much more difficult for the organization to "live the brand" in the way that the best single-brand companies do.

In addition, the mass-distribution channels used by the CPG giants compound the difficulty of creating and maintaining a consistent brand experience. Unilever and P&G have much less control over the retailers that sell their products than a Toyota, McDonald's, or Starbucks, which own or franchise the majority of their distribution outlets.

The use of third-party distribution channels also means that a large part of the value created by CPG brands goes unrecognized. Only part of the sales and profits generated by brands such as Dove or Pampers goes back to their brand owners. As manufacturers, Unilever and P&G benefit only from the trade price sales they make to wholesalers and retail stores. The vast amount of additional value that the brands create through sales to consumers, at much higher retail prices, benefits the Wal-Marts, Targets and Tescos of this world and is not captured in any valuation.

Given all this, the consumer products brands have done extraordinarily well on a brand-by-brand basis. They bring into relief the fact that brand value is a composite of three things: total business value, brand contribution, and future momentum. All three are needed to qualify among the most valuable brands. That's how Wal-Mart makes it. The sheer amount of business value realized by Wal-Mart creates a large amount of brand value, even though brand accounts for a relatively small percentage of total value and Wal-Mart's momentum lags that of many other brands.

The consumer products brands are at the opposite extreme. They have traded off total brand value for individual brand strength. Add up the individual brands of a Procter & Gamble, Unilever, and Nestlé, not to mention Coca-Cola, to see a more impressive picture of value creation.

Conclusion

Brand is one of the most valuable assets of any company—whether old or new, consumer facing or B2B. Brand plays an important part in creating value across all categories, from consumer products to finance, and across all geographies, from established to emerging markets. The huge amount of value driven by brands today means that brand valuation is a tool that all companies should be using. Just as companies measure the returns on their other investments, they should be measuring and demonstrating the sales, profits, and business value generated by investment in brand. Brand needs to be put on the same level as other assets of the company in terms of accountability.

But that's just the start. The examples given here provide sufficient evidence that brand valuation is about much more than just a number. Brand value can be created in many different situations, through many different strategies. The true value of brand valuation lies in its diagnostic capabilities. It should be used to understand how branding drives value for the business and to identify the brand strategy and investments that will do most to grow this value in future. It's not about the *what*, it's about the *how!*

Key Points to Take Away

- Strong brands create greater profits, a more stable revenue stream, and improve shareholder returns.
- Brand value is an intangible but quantifiable asset. If it is to be managed, it must be measured.

Questions to Consider

1. Do you know the business value of your brand? Is that value well recognized by your company?
2. Do you understand which elements of your brand strategy will do the most to grow future brand value?

For more information related to these questions, visit theglobalbrandonline.com.

Part Two

Building Strong Global
Brands Is Challenging

Building a strong global brand is not easy. The aspiring global marketer faces an intimidating array of divergent consumer needs and desires. Complexity is presented by different cultures as well as by the gap in economic status between developed and developing countries. In order to create strong relationships with consumers across countries and cultures, global brands need to take these differences into account.

Then they need to take on the local brands that people have grown up with. Our research confirms that local brands enjoy a home-field advantage by being a familiar part of the local culture. Global brands must find ways to make themselves relevant and create an advantage. They can do so by leveraging their advantages of scale to introduce better-quality brands with a strong heritage from abroad. To be competitive in the local arena, they may need to adapt their offer to meet local needs and budgets as well as change the way they communicate.

There is no such thing as a global consumer. The vast majority of people live their lives locally, and people's needs, values, and desires differ dramatically from one country to the next. In large countries, especially developing ones such as Brazil, Russia, India, and China (the BRICs), there are important differences across regions and between urban and rural dwellers. In Chapter 6, I review the key socioeconomic and cultural differences between developed and developing countries and provide brief portraits of the BRIC markets.

Analysis of the BrandZ database and the Global Brand Survey confirms that, on average, local brands are stronger than global ones. In Chapter 7, I demonstrate that strong national brands, when embedded in the local community and culture, can make formidable adversaries.

Chapter 8 is written by my South African colleagues Judith Kapanga and Matthew Angus and focuses on the challenges of marketing in Africa.

Following the BRICs, Africa is the next big frontier for global brands. This chapter highlights the complexities the continent presents to marketers.

In Chapter 9, I draw on case studies from the BRICs to illustrate how global brands can enter new markets successfully. In the past, good-quality products and a strong international heritage were enough to ensure success. Today global brands must leverage their advantages of scale and adapt their offering to ensure local relevance. Once a global brand is established in a country, it needs to work to become part of the local culture; otherwise it leaves itself open to renewed local competition.

A big challenge facing global brands is to reap the advantages of scale rather than getting lost in them. Operating on a global scale magnifies the issues faced by any operation, and in Chapter 10, I highlight four issues that can undermine global brand strength.

Chapter 6

A Global Economy, Local Consumers

There are vast differences in the ways people live in developed and developing markets. A global brand must adapt to these differences—in living standards, attitudes, and customs—if it is to be successful. Living as we do in a global economy and working in international business, it is too easy for us to lose sight of the fundamental differences that influence brand success. In this chapter, I highlight some of the socioeconomic and cultural differences that have important implications for global marketers and provide brief portraits of the BRIC countries (Brazil, Russia, India, and China), which promise vast growth potential for brands that can successfully adapt to meet their varied local needs.

We May Have a Global Economy . . .

It was the first run on a U.K. bank in over a century. In September 2007, hundreds of customers lined up outside the branches of Northern Rock, patiently waiting for a chance to withdraw their funds. The U.S. subprime meltdown and the ensuing global credit squeeze—in other words, the forces of our global economy—had brought the U.K. mortgage lender to this crisis.

Northern Rock had been searching for a buyer since August. Rival banks that were interested in acquiring the lender were unable to do so because of the difficulty of borrowing money. Then Northern Rock was forced to issue a profit warning and request emergency funding from the Bank of England.

In a matter of days, savers withdrew over $4 billion. Northern Rock's share price plummeted, the overnight rate at which British banks lend each other money soared, and financial institutions in Europe and the United States experienced weakening share prices.

On November 29, a consortium led by Richard Branson's Virgin Group won the endorsement of the Bank of England for a takeover bid. If it had been successful, the takeover would have proven once again that Virgin—famous for its planes, trains, and record stores—was one of the most "stretchable" brands in the world. But, after protracted negotiations, the U.K. government decided to nationalize Northern Rock. The Northern Rock crisis brought home to many that events on one side of the world can have repercussions for those who live far, far away. While most people don't think about it in the course of their everyday lives, the global economy has awesome reach and power.

But We Are Not Yet a Global Village

In the course of conducting interviews for this book, a few people directly challenged the notion of the global village. Tony Palmer, chief marketing officer at Kimberly-Clark, stated, "There's no such thing as a global consumer. Ultimately people buy locally."

The world has, in some ways, shrunk. As a result of globalization and advancements in technology, people today are exposed to more international news and goods than ever before. In terms of their daily lives, however, their frame of reference is still local, very local. People care about their friends and neighbors. They shop in the local stores. They support the local team, visit the local bar, listen to local radio stations, and read the local newspaper. The vast majority of things they engage with are local. They may buy goods that come from elsewhere—for example, many products sold in the United States say "Made in China" in small print at the bottom of the label—but the act of buying imported products rarely disturbs their very local focus. Eric Salama, chairman and CEO of Kantar, the market research division of WPP, puts it this way: "Companies may espouse the 'think global, act local' mantra, but the vast majority of consumers still get their cultural cues from events, discussions, and behaviors that are primarily local."

Those of us who work for global companies are all too quick to overlook regional and cultural differences. Whether we are at home or abroad, we tend to spend our time in environments that are affluent, urban, high tech, cosmopolitan. Wherever you are in the world, the look and feel of the airports, hotels, and corporate offices is eerily similar. The culture of international business dominates that of the individual countries we visit and disguises the vast differences that still exist between East and West, developed and developing, urban and rural.

And yet, even in the context of international business, we can see cultural differences if we look. For example, at Millward Brown global management meetings, the Latin American contingent wants to go dancing each evening, the Europeans would rather settle down for a good meal, while the Anglo contingent heads straight for the nearest bar.

Major Differences Still Exist

Back in 1989, when I first started work in the United States, I was dismayed when a very senior manager at a client company asked me why we could not just treat Europe as one country. I had to explain that the differences between Greece and Germany were rather important if you were trying to position and market something like toilet cleaner. (At that time, you were still more likely to find a hole in the floor in much of Greece rather than a porcelain toilet.)

Things have changed since then. I doubt you would find many people asking the same question out of ignorance. Instead, managers are struggling to cluster countries together, trying to achieve economies of scale, while recognizing that by doing so, they might be dumbing down their marketing effectiveness. I return to this topic in chapter 11, identifying commonalities and differences, but for now I believe it is worth reminding ourselves just how different people's lives are around the world. It might seem self-evident, but we marketers have a wonderful way of judging the world on the basis of our own experience, and for many of us that experience is limited to the developed western world.

Economic Differences

Much attention is currently being given to the developing economies of the BRICs. With gross domestic products rising far faster than western economies and expanding populations, they promise untold riches for brand marketers now and in the years to come.

However, the economic differences between the developed and the developing worlds are enormous. The data on gross domestic product (GDP) per capita shown in Table 6.1 highlights the differences between some well-developed western economies and developing ones like Mexico and the BRICs.

Table 6.1 GDP per Capita at Purchasing Power Parity

Country	U.S.	Mexico	Brazil	U.K.	Germany	Russia	India	China
$'000	46	12.5	9.7	35.3	34.4	14.6	2.7	5.3

Source: *The World Factbook*, estimates for 2007.

Purchasing power parity (PPP), the measure most economists prefer to use to compare living conditions or use of resources across countries, values all goods and services produced in a country at prices prevailing in the United States. While this measure is sometimes difficult to calculate (what is the equivalent value of a motorized rickshaw or an ox cart?), it is useful because it takes into account the systematic inequalities inherent in the cost of producing goods and services in different countries.

Clearly the data in Table 6.1 suggest that, GDP growth rates notwithstanding, most people in India and China are not going to be buying global brands anytime soon. The daunting challenge for owners of mass-market brands is to gain penetration among the vast numbers of urban and rural poor. The hope is that economic growth will gradually raise the standard of living for all and present global brands with millions of new consumers, but that day may be further away than expected.

A yawning gap exists between rich and poor in many parts of the world, and in some developing nations, this gap seems to be growing. In 2007, *The Economist* reported that China's Gini coefficient (a measure of the gap between rich and poor, where a score of 0 would be perfect equality) rose from 0.41 in 1993 to 0.47 in 2004.[1] While this gave China the distinction of having more income inequality than the United States (Gini coefficient 0.46), the Latin American countries of Argentina, Brazil, Chile, and Mexico all have even higher coefficients.

At the end of 2007, the World Bank issued a revised estimate of the size of the Chinese economy based on up-to-date PPP estimates. By this reckoning, the number of Chinese who live below the World Bank's poverty line of a dollar a day is 300 million, not 100 million as had been previous estimated.[2]

The main cause of the increased inequality, especially in China, is that productivity and income are growing much more slowly in agriculture than in manufacturing or services. The result is a growing gap between the urban and rural areas that is exacerbated by the limited options for those without skills. While this gap constitutes an obvious humanitarian concern, the growing disparity might also presage social unrest in China and other countries that would make them less fertile ground for multinational corporations. Attractive GDP growth rates do not necessarily signify long-term stability, and the real incomes of many people will need to rise a lot further before they can afford to buy more than the occasional imported brand.

Demographic Differences

The distribution of population across age groups is one of the most obvious and striking demographic differences across countries. The figures in Table 6.2 highlight these variations across some developed and developing nations.

Table 6.2 Age by Country

Country	U.S.	Mexico	Brazil	U.K.	Germany	Russia	India	China
Median Age	36.6	25.6	28.6	39.6	43	38.2	24.8	33.2
% Over 65	12.6	5.9	6.3	15.8	19.8	14.4	5.1	7.9

Source: *The World Factbook*, estimates for 2007.

In India, the population is very young and growing at a rate of 1.6 percent per annum. In Germany, the population is aging and in decline. Compared to the aging markets of Europe, the relatively young and growing populations of the developing countries present different opportunities and challenges for financial services, health care, and entertainment brands. But, that said, it is important not to get hung up on stereotypes associated with age groups. While the vast "boomer" market represents a real opportunity in Europe and the United States, it seems to be an opportunity that many fail to really understand.

In 2006, a collaboration among ad agency JWT, media agency Mindshare, and Millward Brown on behalf of a major global client led us to review ads from around the world that were aimed at the "over 50s." Our investigation turned up two key concerns. First, props such as false teeth, canes, and eyeglasses were apparently considered to be acceptable visual signals to the audience. And second, the ad copy seemed to reflect a belief that older people wanted facts, not emotion. This led to lots of boring text in print ads and some pretty mundane TV executions. The main point we took away was that even among the marketers who are trying to communicate with this important group of consumers, very few are doing so in a relevant and empathetic way. The essential call to action of our analysis was "back to basics." If you want to communicate effectively with any group of people—old or young, rich or poor, American or Chinese, urban or rural—set your stereotyped images aside and seek to truly understand the needs, desires, and aspirations of your target audience.

Cultural Differences

While economic and demographic differences between markets have obvious ramifications for business, it is culture that really affects the way that brands need to be developed and marketed. Culture—the history, beliefs, customs, habits, values, and social behavior of a group of people—determines the way people will think, behave, and react to the world around them. Therefore, culture has a massive effect on the acceptability and appeal of brands and their marketing communication, from broadcast advertising to direct mail. For many global marketers, this quote from Geert Hofstede, Emeritus Professor at Maastricht University, The Netherlands, is all too appropriate: "Culture is more often a source of conflict than of synergy. Cultural differences are a nuisance at best and often a disaster."[3]

From 1967 to 1973, while Hofstede was working at IBM as a psychologist, he collected and analyzed data from over 100,000 individuals from 50 countries in 3 regions. Based on these initial results and later additions, Hofstede developed a model that identifies five primary dimensions that can be used to describe and differentiate cultures.[4] The strength of these factors varies enormously by country, and the extremes are shown in Table 6.3.

These dimensions combine and interact to exert significant influence on consumer behavior, brand preferences, and communication. In a chapter in Hofstede's 1998 book, *Masculinity and Femininity: The Taboo Dimension of National Cultures*, his colleague Marieke de Mooij highlights some important implications for product purchasing.[5] According to de Mooij, people in individualistic cultures tend to prefer living in separate houses with private gardens, while those in collectivist cultures tend to prefer apartments. This has obvious ramifications in terms of the types of products and services that will be bought as well as the size and scale of items such as household appliances. For example, the vacuum cleaner brand Dyson had to create a new line of compact cleaners to compete successfully in the Japanese market.

Table 6.3 Hofstede's Cultural Dimensions

Low	Dimension	High
Nordic	**Power Distance** Runs from collectivist societies (low) to ones that accept that power is distributed unevenly (high).	Russia
Pakistan	**Individualism** Runs from societies composed of tight-knit groups (low) to individualistic (high).	United States
Nordic	**Masculinity** Runs from societies with very similar male/female values (low) to ones where male values differ strongly and are more competitive and assertive (high).	Japan
Jamaica	**Uncertainty Avoidance** Runs from societies comfortable with ambiguity (low) to those that find a need for clarity and rules of behavior (high).	Greece
West Africa	**Long-term Orientation** Low values are reflected in respect for tradition and fulfilling social obligations. Values associated with high long-term orientation are thrift and perseverance.	China

Another example cited by de Mooij is that people from cultures that rank high on uncertainty avoidance prefer new cars over used. (And we might hypothesize that as they shop for a car, they will pay more attention to reliability reports and warranties.) In countries that score low on Masculinity, a major purchase such as a car is likely to be a decision discussed by a husband and wife, but in strongly masculine cultures, the decision of which car to buy is far less likely to be shared with a spouse. Two countries that are close together geographically, such as Belgium and the Netherlands, can be far apart on the masculinity scale. (Belgium is highly masculine; the Netherlands, less so.) Therefore, different car-buying styles exist on either side of the border.

Culture and Advertising

According to de Mooij, different types of cultures respond to advertising in different ways. She hypothesizes that importing male-oriented advertising from the United States may be acceptable in other masculine markets, such as the United Kingdom and Germany, but less acceptable in countries that index lower on masculinity.

We have seen this theory come to life in advertising we have evaluated. At Millward Brown's London seminar on global advertising, Jaroslav Cír, Unilever's global consumer and market insight director for the Rexona brand, described the reactions to Rexona's *Love and Hate* campaign. Developed in Argentina and intended for use in western Europe and Latin America, the campaign featured scenes of women reacting to things they hate. One ad showed a woman jumping onto a soccer field to steal the ball, so her man cannot watch the game.

When the ads were tested in Brazil, the campaign performed very well. Female Brazilians found it true to life and related strongly to the frustrations expressed by the women in the ads. But when the campaign was tested in Europe and the United States, the reactions were less than positive.

"Some of the comments we got really took us back," said Cír. "Women were saying 'How dare you present us with these clichés? This is so old-fashioned. It is out of touch with my life.'"

Differences Do Matter

There is no getting around it: Differences matter. Socioeconomic and cultural differences, if not noted and accounted for, can make life difficult for local marketers. The potential influence of local culture on the success of global brands is enormous and cannot be underestimated.

As packaged goods manufacturers seek to market to a broader cross-section of consumers, they will experience the full brunt of both socioeconomic and cultural factors. Marketers of infrequently purchased, high-tech or high-ticket brands may think they will encounter fewer problems, because their target is the small proportion of affluent consumers in each market and on the surface these consumers appear to behave similarly to their western counterparts.

This perception is misleading, however. An analysis of Global Target Group Index data suggests that the values of the richest 30 percent of consumers in a society are remarkably consistent with those of the population as a whole, though we observe bigger differences between people who have traveled abroad and those who haven't. Like people involved in global business, people who travel have been exposed to other cultures and seem to have a more worldly outlook. For example, they are more likely to say that they enjoy eating foreign foods. These "internationalists" are also more likely to buy western brands like Nike, Apple, and Johnnie Walker than their stay-at-home peers. You might hypothesize that as the quality and status of local brands improve, they may be better able to appeal to the richer stay-at-homes, leaving western brands to market to the internationalists.

In the remainder of this chapter, I provide brief portraits of the BRICs, highlighting socioeconomic and cultural differences and some of the implications for marketers.

An Introduction to the BRICs

Investment bank Goldman Sachs is convinced that when it comes to countries that offer future growth potential, it is a one-horse race. In a recent report, the company considered whether any of China's biggest rivals, the other BRICs—Brazil, Russia, and India—could give China a run for its money. Goldman Sachs also compiled a list of the "Next 11" (N11) countries that it believes might have the potential to challenge the BRICs: Bangladesh, Egypt, Indonesia, Iran, South Korea, Mexico, Nigeria, Pakistan, the Philippines, Turkey, and Vietnam. Over the last three years, economic growth across the N11 averaged 5.9 percent, the strongest in 15 years and more than double the 2.3 percent average growth of Old Europe. While all these markets offer incredible potential, the strongest by far is China.

Most brand marketers agree that China is the number-one priority. Their approach shares a whatever-it-takes-to-win mentality, throwing money and resources into the battle for future revenue and profits. But although China is the primary focus for most marketers, the other BRICs do represent sizable—but distinct—opportunities. Talking about the four countries as a unit—that is, lumping them together as "the BRICs"—seems to suggest that they have much in common. But this acronym really obscures the fact that these four countries have little in common aside from their rapidly developing economies and tremendous growth potential. The portraits that follow demonstrate this fact.

China

The People's Republic of China ranks first in the world by population with over 1.3 billion people. Over the last 25 years, China's economy has evolved from a centrally planned system, largely closed to international trade, to a more market-oriented economy. Gross domestic product growth has averaged more than 8 percent per year. Measured on a PPP basis, China was the second-largest economy in the world (after the United States) in 2007.

It should be obvious, then, why everyone wants a piece of the action in China. Multinational corporations (MNCs) have poured in billions to buy up local companies, set up factories and research and development centers, and market their brands. But so far their results have been mixed.

To build brands in a land as vast and complex as China, marketers must recognize the prodigious array of physical, emotional, and cultural needs presented across its regions. China is not one single enormous market, but rather a loose confederation of several very large markets, more akin to Europe than the United States. It has been said that so many languages and dialects were spoken in China that even Chairman Mao needed a translator. Overall, the Chinese are differentiated from western countries by a belief in duty to others, but across the country, local values interact with economic status to create a complex web of differing needs and attitudes.

Western marketers, however, have typically ignored these cultural differences, thinking they can focus their efforts according to economics. They divide China up into "tiers": tier one cities such as Beijing, Shanghai, and Guangzhou; tier two cities such as Chongqing, Harbin, Wuhan; tier three cities, which include Lanzhou, Zibo, Hefei; and the rural areas. Until the last few years, marketers tended to focus on the upper-class population in tier one cities. Today, however, as competition in these markets has heated up, the focus has necessarily shifted to the lower-tier cities and growing urban middle classes. McKinsey expects that by 2010, the urban lower-middle class will number 290 million people, representing 44 percent of the urban population.[6]

Now that the purchasing power of the lower tiers has attracted the attention of MNCs, they face a challenge in competing in those markets. While the MNCs were focusing on affluent tier one urbanites, regional Chinese manufacturers were stepping in to serve the massive lower-income market, marketing their cheaper products with a noisy barrage of junk advertising. Noise alone is not enough to create strong brands, but the local brands often enjoy solid grassroots support along with the advantages of lower distribution and marketing costs. These factors contribute to a price differential between local and MNC brands that is hard for cash-strapped consumers to overlook, even if they want to buy a premium brand. Thus the makers of premium brands face an uphill battle when they seek to extend their reach beyond the middle class.

A recent study by Ogilvy Discovery and Mindshare Insights reveals some striking differences among the urban middle class across the three tiers of cities. For a start, those living in the lower tiers are much less likely to buy foreign brands than their tier one peers. Tier one consumers favor Sony, Nokia, and Motorola, while tier three shoppers are partial to TCL, Lenovo, Changhong, and Konka. Among sportswear brands, Nike and Adidas are more popular in tier one, Li Ning prevails in tier two, and Anta, Jeanswest, and Double Star are preferred in tier three. Tier three consumers are thrifty and less willing to pay a premium for well-known brands.

In tier one, the focus is on replacing and upgrading items. For example, conventional TV sets are being replaced with plasma or LCD sets. Tier three consumers lag behind those from higher tiers on the consumption curve; they are just now buying computers and digital cameras for the first time.

MNCs need to ensure that the appeal of their brands is strong enough to overcome local loyalties. Overall, our BrandZ data, based on tier one cities, suggests that perceived product performance remains a major weakness for Chinese companies—although increasingly this may be a perception among Chinese consumers that no longer has a basis in reality.

But the BrandZ database also suggests that Chinese brands are beginning to build deeper relationships with consumers. Back in 1998, Chinese consumers bonded to Chinese brands for one major reason: price. That reliance on price is declining over time. Chinese brands developed better products and stronger branding credentials, and in the 2006 data, we see bonding based more on rational affinity (i.e., perceptions of product quality, leadership, and setting trends). And as the factors underlying bonding are shifting, the overall proportion of people attitudinally bonded to Chinese brands has also increased.

India

Like the other BRICs, India is enjoying a rapid increase in general standard of living, although its lower-per-capita GDP reflects itself in even stronger demand for "value" goods and services. Lacking China's "one-child" policy, however, the Indian population is set to overtake China's by 2050.[7] This combination of economic and population growth means that the retail market is expected to grow from some $300 billion today to $637 billion by 2015.[8]

Economic reforms begun in 1991 have cut extreme poverty in India by half. Even people living in rural areas have benefited from the improvement in standards of living. (This is not the case in other developing countries.) It is reported that over half of consumer packaged and durable goods are now sold to people living outside the major cities.[9] The retail trade that fulfills that demand, however, is still very traditional. Modern retail outlets are less common in India than in the other BRICs, but heavy investment in the retail sector is likely to result in a rapid increase in the number of supermarkets and modern store formats.

The country's sheer size and diversity, however, means that marketers can no more treat India as one country than they can China. In her 2006 ESOMAR paper titled *Unravelling the Diversity of the Indian Market*,[10] Sangeeta Gupta speaks to the cultural diversity of India. History has left India with 17 major languages, 844 different dialects, and 8 religions. Gupta's paper makes the case for a geographic segmentation of the country based on the characteristics observed across consumers in the North, South, East and West:

- For the North Indian, societal approval is a pivotal value. That means demonstrating status. Big is beautiful. Larger cars, package sizes, and household appliances sell well in the North.
- The South Indian seeks strong sensory stimulation. This urge manifests itself in the color of their saris and lungis (a wrap worn by both men and women), the spiciness of their cuisine, and in their higher-than-average consumption of incense sticks, shampoo, talcum powder, and filter coffee.
- Looking east, Gupta describes the Bengalis as "hypochondriacal in their practices and beliefs regarding health," making them a good target market for over-the-counter drugs and remedies.
- The West Indians are best characterized by the Maharashtrian principle of *"Sadhi rahuni ani uccha vichar,"* which translates as "simple living and high thinking." Their consumption patterns demonstrate no clear biases to one product category or another.

These generalizations, broad though they may be, help to highlight the complexity of this enormous country.

A substantial difference between India and China is the legacy left by India's colonial past. Many brands familiar to the British are just as familiar to Indians. Cadbury's, Lux, Will's, Surf, and Horlicks have almost lost their "foreign" identities and are seen more as Indian brands. Gupta reports that an analysis of

ACNielsen's Retail Store Audit data for 21 consumer packaged goods categories found few truly pan-India market leaders. Most of the brands that achieved that status are foreign-originated brands (though they may not be viewed as such by Indians): Colgate Dental Cream, Pond's Dreamflower Talc, Cadbury's Dairy Milk, Stayfree, and Axe. As a result of the assimilation of brands into the local culture, when compared to China and especially to Russia, there is less inclination in India to regard a foreign brand as something much better than the local ones.

Russia

Russia was the largest republic of the centrally planned Union of Soviet Socialist Republics. Although Russia was designated a market economy by the United States and the European Union in 2002, the government continues to play a big role in the country's economy and social institutions. The economy has grown strongly for eight years, increasing by just under 7 percent in 2006 and just over 7 percent in 2007.

My colleague Dominic Twose just spent the winter holiday season in Moscow. The freezing cold meant it was not a popular time to visit, which perhaps accounts for the fact that Lenin's Tomb was virtually unattended while the boutiques on the other side of Red Square (in the old GUM department store) were packed with local shoppers. Russians are avid consumers of luxury. By 2009, it is predicted that they will account for 7 percent of global luxury goods sales, which would make Russia the fastest-growing emerging market for such goods.[11] Commenting on this trait, the editor of the Russian edition of *Cosmopolitan*, Elena Myasnikova, says, "Russians, you know, being dressy and liking to look nice . . . tend to spend a much higher percentage of their income on make-up and clothes."[12] And while both economic growth and wealth creation are increasing at a fast rate, Russians are still not inclined to put anything away. In fact, Merrill Lynch calls Russia "a young consumption economy unwilling to save."

Among Russians, 56 percent agree that money is the best measure of success.[13] This is more than double the average agreement in Europe, and is matched among the BRICs only by the Chinese. Russians express a strong interest in shopping and buying the latest gadgets. Prices have been pushed up by readily available consumer credit.

Russian consumers tend to segment into two groups: those who grew up during the Soviet era and those who came of age after the breakup of the U.S.S.R. Members of the older group are used to traditional products from traditional Russian companies, many of which are now subsidiaries of multinationals. Members of the younger group, particularly those who are well off, strongly favor well-known international brands. The preferences of these two groups have caused three types of brands to develop: the traditional, the "à la Russie," and the "international" or "innovative" brands.

Brands in the first group, the "traditionals," have Russian names and are known from Soviet times. These brands have packaging that, in spite of being modernized and renovated, still has a recognizable "Soviet" style. These brands are targeted at older people of low social status who miss the old communist regime or others who might remember the brands from childhood. Examples are Jubilee biscuits (now owned by Kraft) and a range of chocolates from century-old confectionaries, such as Red October or Babayevsky.

The "à la Russie" brand is specially crafted to cater to the mysterious Russian soul. These brands are usually positioned around values thought of as traditionally Russian by marketers (such as the Russians' love of their country *dachas*, or their predisposition toward lengthy kitchen-table conversations with neighbors). Usually these brands use some Russian character in their ads, such as a *Domovoy* (brownie) or a talking and dancing washstand made famous by a children's poet early in the twentieth century. Examples are Beseda, a tea brand from Unilever, and Mif, a detergent from Procter & Gamble.

The third group of brands consists of those considered "international" or "innovative." These are typically brands that are promoted internationally and targeted at the mass market. While not positioned as exclusive products in Russia, they are often aimed at the upper part of the mass segment. Examples are Lipton (another tea brand from Unilever) and Tide from P&G (a detergent in the same category as Mif).Although the three types of brands appeal to very different groups of consumers, some experts suggest that it is too costly to maintain both the traditional and "à la Russie" brands. Consumers are not willing to pay a premium for these brands but expect them to be high quality. This situation obviously poses a serious challenge for marketers, especially with the cost of production climbing faster than inflation. Russians also believe that Russian goods made for export are better than those sold inside the country. Some brands add "for export" to their labels to cash in on this belief. Conversely, Russians are sure that if someone starts producing an international brand locally, the quality will inevitably fall and that these brands should cost 10 to 15 percent less than their foreign equivalent. Therefore, while in China, the availability of cheap labor makes local production highly desirable, in Russia, the people's doubts about the quality of locally produced goods make it a less desirable option. It may be more profitable for a brand to remain a premium import with lower volume than to try to offer lower prices with domestic production.

As elsewhere in the BRICs, modern trade in Russia is growing rapidly but still accounts for a minority of all retail sales. Pyaterochka, founded in 1999 in St. Petersburg, is one of the pioneers of modern grocery retailing in Russia.

Pyaterochka's format of neighborhood "soft" discount stores that offer a competitive alternative to open markets and Soviet-era outlets has been well received by Russian consumers. These stores are conveniently located, open seven days a week from 9 am to 10 pm, and offer up to 3,500 items. This format helped Pyaterochka become the largest grocery retailer in Russia in terms of sales, a lead that was further reinforced when it and Perekrestok (another large chain) merged their operations in 2006.

Store formats tailored to the Russian lifestyle have been a big success for Pyaterochka, but when it comes to grocery shopping, Russians appear to be among the least convinced of the quality and value of private-label products. While these are increasingly found on the shelves of Russian supermarket chains, a Global Online Consumer Survey by AC Nielsen reports that Russians tend to attribute the notable price difference between retailer and manufacturer brands to the poorer quality of the former.

Brazil

Brazil, the world's eighth largest economy, is home to 184 million people. Like India, Brazil is a youthful society, with 26 percent of the population under age 14 and only 6 percent over 65. Around 80 percent of the population resides in cities. São Paulo, with a population in excess of 20 million, is not only the largest city in South America but the third-largest city in the world.

Like many of its South American neighbors (e.g., Argentina and Chile) and its BRIC rival China, Brazil is a country with a vastly unequal distribution of wealth. The richest 1 percent of the population controls more wealth—14 percent—than the 50 percent with incomes below the median.

Affluent Brazilians, who tend to display westernized buying behavior, particularly enjoy luxury brands. Looking good is important; 80 percent of people believe that it is important to be attractive to the opposite sex. As a result, plastic surgery is very popular. Celebrities talk openly in the media about their latest surgery on *barrigas* (bellies) or *bundas* (buttocks), all in the name of looking good on the beach. Several glossy magazines dedicated to the topic appear on newspaper stands across the country.

Fun is also important to Brazilians. Key aspects of local culture include the beach, samba, carnival, and soccer. The samba "schools," such as Mangueira, Portela, and Vila Isabel, are important brands in their own right that increasingly attract corporate sponsorship as more and more people flock to see the annual carnival celebrations.

National pride is an obvious feature of the Brazilian spirit. Two supermarket chains boldly claim they are "Proud to Be Brazilian," as does the local airline, TAM. Millions wear Havaianas (a Brazilian brand of flip-flops) decorated with the Brazilian flag. Brazilians who prize their local food traditions flock to the locally run fast-food joints that provide popular alternatives to the American chains.

In the retail segment, we find big local brands: Pão de Açúcar (competitor of Wal-Mart and Carrefour), Casas Bahia, and Magazine Luiza. Global retailers are buying their way into the country, but to date the local retailers have proved to be tough competition. In spite of a huge trend toward low-priced brands in the last five years, store brands are still relatively new to Brazil and have yet to take off. Brazilians trust name brands and have yet to develop the same affinity for retailers. Therefore, it may be some time before store brands become popular.

A big difference divides developed and developing economies

Many of the needs of people with lower disposable incomes are common across developing markets—not the least of which is a strong demand for value goods and services—but, as we see in looking at the individual BRIC countries, context and culture impel people to attempt to satisfy these needs in different ways. Compared to western consumers, however, people in the BRICs have one attitude in common: They think it is more important to choose the right brand than to get the best price. The data from our Global Brand Survey, shown in Table 6.4, shows that the proportion of people who seek a specific brand is lowest in the United States, the United Kingdom, and Germany. The difference across markets is greatest for consumer packaged goods and lowest for fast food (reflecting the fact that most people patronize a variety of different fast food outlets).

These results may seem surprising and counterintuitive. After all, consumers in the West have more experience with branded products, more choices, and the means to try them out. Why should they be more price conscious than consumers in developing markets?

Table 6.4 Percent More Concerned with Getting a Specific Brand than the Best Price

Average Percentage across Five Product Categories							
Country	USA	Mexico	Brazil	UK	Germany	Russia	India	China
%	65	74	69	64	65	81	79	75

Source: The Millward Brown Global Brand Survey, January 2008.

The answer has to do with perceptions of trust and quality. In western markets, the vast majority of consumer goods are sold through modern trade. And although consumers who have never experienced any other form of shopping might not be consciously aware of it, they rely on retailers like Wal-Mart, Home Depot, and Mercadona to provide them with a selection of quality brands. As competitive brands in their own right, retailers have a stake in ensuring that shoppers can trust the brands they stock on their shelves. India, one of the most brand-loyal countries considered here, has the lowest proportion of modern trade stores among the BRICs.

Modern retail stores also facilitate comparison shopping. When consumers have a number of quality brands to choose from, price often becomes the most important differentiator. The influence of the retail environment extends way beyond packaged goods. In Russia, fewer than 25 percent of people place a higher emphasis on price than brand when shopping for a car. In the United States, where people have vastly higher disposable incomes and auto malls are popular, 50 percent agreed that they look for the best price. The challenge to marketers in developing countries is to avoid the mistakes made by U.S. and European marketers, who have allowed consumers to think all brands are the same. Consumers need to be trained to look not simply for the best price but the *best brand* at the *best price.*

In the next chapter, I examine how being seen as part of the local culture is an important asset for local brands and a desirable one for global brands.

Key Points to Take Away

- Although we are all subject to the forces of the global economy, the majority of people think, live, and act locally. There are major differences in standards of living, values, and culture between developed and developing countries and among the countries that make up the BRICs.
- Huge differences in standards of living exist both across and within developing countries. The differences between urban and rural consumers are particularly striking.
- Huge differences exist in the age of populations around the world. In the developing countries—except for China—the populations are relatively young and growing, while Europe and the United States are aging.
- A common approach to marketing is unlikely to result in a strong global brand unless you are appealing to an affluent and international target audience. Even then, cultural values and attitudes will differ from country to country.

Questions to Consider

1. How much will income disparities, both across and within countries, affect your brand?
2. How relevant is the age profile in each country to your brand and to its communications?
3. How much do you need to adapt your marketing across countries in order to take cultural sensitivities into account?

For more information related to these questions, visit theglobalbrandonline.com.

Chapter 7

The Power of Being Part of Local Culture

In Chapter 5, Joanna Seddon highlighted the value attached to the China Mobile brand. Already dominant in China and with a foothold in Pakistan, China Mobile is now eyeing other markets. But can that company successfully export its brand strength? Will it be able to create the same strong bonds with consumers outside of China? The evidence suggests that the chances are low.

In this chapter, I review findings from analysis of the BrandZ database as well as a proprietary survey conducted by Millward Brown for this volume. The results of our analysis clearly show that both global and local brands gain value by being considered part of the local culture. To drive sales, brands still need to create strong relationships with consumers (as outlined in Chapter 3), but strong local ties will increase people's propensity to purchase.

Brand Strength Is Hard to Stretch

Few brands establish dominant positions in multiple countries. Moreover, analysis based on the BrandZ database has shown that brands distributed across multiple countries tend to have weaker overall relationships with consumers than brands that stick close to home.

For the purposes of our analysis, we define a global brand as one that had been included in a BrandZ survey in seven or more countries between 2000 and 2007. Of the 10,000 brands in the database, only 3 percent satisfied this definition. A further 13 percent were measured in two to six countries. The remaining 84 percent of brands were measured in only one country. Included in this large group were brands like Life Insurance of India, Bombril (the Brazilian pan scourer), Pick n Pay (a South African-based hypermarket), Swisscom, and Malaysia Airlines. (Note: The fact that these brands were measured by BrandZ in only one country does not mean that they have no presence elsewhere in the

Table 7.1 Average Bonding across All Countries Measured

	Number of Countries Brands were Measured in:		
	1	2–6	7+
Average % bonded	6.5	5.7	4.8
Number of brands	4512	920	265

world but rather that in the other countries in which they compete, they are very small relative to other brands in the category.) To eliminate the confounding effect of very small local brands, we restricted our analysis further to include only brands that achieved at least 1 percent bonding wherever they were measured.

The data summarized in Table 7.1 suggests that brands that compete in more countries tend to have weaker bonding scores overall. This view of the database confirms that the 25 strong global brands listed in Chapter 4, which average 19 percent bonding, are truly exceptional in the way they deviate from the prevailing pattern.

For most brands, most of their strength and equity come from their original home markets. This should not be surprising, because few of today's global brands were originally designed to travel. Most originated long before the imperative to go global took hold. We can hypothesize that as a strong brand moves from its country of origin, it struggles to meet different consumer needs and desires in the new territory. No matter how strong a brand might be on its home turf, it can be tough to win over local customers who have grown up with their own well-loved brands.

The home-field advantage gives local brands an edge that makes them formidable adversaries, but it does not necessarily help them go global. China Mobile may well have an impregnable position of strength in China, but whether it can extend its geographic footprint is far less certain.

The Global Brand Survey

In order to explore the role of local culture on brand success, Millward Brown commissioned a survey to better understand the strength of global versus local brands. (The full details of this study can be found in Appendix B.) We wanted to answer these questions:

- What role do factors like heritage, culture, and local production have on people's likelihood to buy a brand?
- Is there a difference between global and local brands in terms of what motivates people to buy them?

The global brands we selected for study were McDonald's, KFC, Budweiser, Heineken, Toyota, Ford, Pantene Pro-V, Dove, Coca-Cola, and Pepsi. However, because truly global brands are scarce, in some countries we had to make substitutions for one or more of these brands. For example, in Russia we replaced Budweiser with Miller, and in Brazil, KFC with Pizza Hut. It is not that Budweiser is not present in Russia; rather, its presence there is too low for it to serve as a meaningful example of a global brand.

We selected local brands on a similar basis in each country. They had to be well known enough for the majority of people to have an opinion of them. Again, we had to make some adjustments for certain countries and categories. For example, because there are no major car brands that are truly "local" to Brazil, we selected two foreign-owned brands, Volkswagen and Fiat, that are regarded as local because they have been manufactured in the country for many years.

Our research findings clearly suggest that perceptions of heritage and associations with local or national culture affect the fortunes of global and local brands alike.

Factors Driving Purchase Probability for Global and Local Brands

The first two columns of Table 7.2 show the average percentage of people mentioning any global or local brand across the five product categories and eight countries studied.

Table 7.2 Average Percent Mentioning a Brand for Each Statement

	Average Percent Mentioning Any Global or Local Brand		Significant in Relation to Purchase	
	Global %	Local %	Global	Local
First choice or seriously considered for purchase	53	40		
Are very easy to recognize	63	56	*	
Have very distinctive identities	52	43	*	
Are very high-quality brands	48	39	*	*
Are brands that are setting the trends	42	27	*	*
Have a strong heritage	42	31	*	*
Are made in (country)	27	56		*
Are part of our (nationality) culture	21	42	*	*

Note: An asterisk (*) indicates that regression analysis (conducted separately for global and local brands) has identified a statistically significant relationship between the image statement and the probability of people purchasing a brand.

From these data, it is clear that the global brands chosen for the survey are stronger overall than the local ones. Survey respondents considered them more often for purchase, and the global brands receive higher scores on all statements, except those related to where they were made or whether they were part of the local or national culture.

Perceptions that a brand is part of the national culture are significantly related to purchase for both global and local brands. This confirms our hypothesis that brands that are identified with local culture will perform better than others (all other things being equal). While it has less impact on purchase probability than perceptions that a brand is high quality or setting trends, association with local culture is definitely a benefit.

Although global brands like Toyota, Heineken, McDonald's, Pantene Pro-V, and Coca-Cola can be associated with the local culture (e.g., 64 percent of people in Brazil agreed that Coca-Cola was part of their local culture), this association is less beneficial to global brands than it is to local ones. Our analysis suggests global brands rely more on the basic building blocks of successful brands.

Global brands lead local brands in being mentioned as "very easy to recognize" and having "very distinctive identities." These two elements are significantly related to purchase for global brands but not local ones. This fact suggests that global brands do a far better job than local brands creating brand saliency and identity through mass marketing. Not surprisingly, local brands rely more for purchase on the fact that people believe they are made locally. (This is not a significant factor for global brands.) Perceptions that a brand is high quality, is trend setting, or has a strong heritage work in favor of both global and local brands, but people are more likely to think these statements apply to global brands.

Local Brands Have the Home-Field Advantage

The research findings suggest that local brands have the home-field advantage, provided that they qualify as strong brands in their own right. The different ways in which a brand can be perceived as part of the local culture include:

- meeting unique local needs or tastes,
- nostalgia—being a brand people grew up with,
- local operational or logistical advantages,
- strong community ties,
- cultural identity.

In the remainder of this chapter, I provide examples of strong local brands that benefit from one or more of these factors.

Marmite: Nostalgia for a Local Jewel

Multinational corporations understand the value of strong local brands. Witness the fact that as Unilever winnowed its vast portfolio of 1600 brands down to a core of 400, many of those that remained were distinctly local.

Unilever refers to these brands as "local jewels." Some of these prized assets are more than 100 old, such as Marmite, a savory spread made from yeast extract that was established in 1902. The brand, which for many years was marketed under the tagline "The growing-up spread you'll never grow out of," is loved by many Brits who have fond memories of it from childhood. Such is the brand's appeal that adult expatriates, myself included, have been known to carry large jars of the stuff back from the United Kingdom for themselves and others.

Outside of the United Kingdom, few people appreciate the taste of Marmite, and whether the brand would have the same appeal to Brits if they were introduced to it as adults rather than children is a matter of speculation. Today Unilever markets the brand with the tagline "Love it or hate it," which reflects the fact that even in its country of origin, the brand's strong savory taste is polarizing.

Interestingly, the brand's taste is rejected even by those who eat something that appears, to outsiders at least, to be remarkably similar. During World War I, New Zealanders, many of whom were British expatriates, found themselves cut off from their supply of Marmite. To meet the unsatisfied demand, the Sanitarium Health Food Company obtained sole rights to manufacture the product in New Zealand and Australia. Over the years, the recipe for Sanitarium's product diverged from the original, and though the brand in the Pacific region is still called Marmite, its taste differs enough from original Marmite that people who have grown up with either spread are likely to reject the taste of the other.

While Sanitarium continues to market Marmite in Australia, another brand of yeast extract actually dominates that continent. Vegemite, now owned by Kraft Foods, was created in response to the same Marmite shortage that provided Sanitarium's opportunity. Vegemite is now firmly entrenched in Aussie culture, present in many homes, and celebrated in songs and sayings.

The fact that each of these three countries maintains a strong and virtually exclusive loyalty to one of three similar products testifies to the power of a local brand. Although they seem to meet the same need—a nutritious spread for bread or toast—they are not considered substitutable, even in three related cultures. The unique taste of each, entrenched as it is in childhood memories and reinforced in the local culture, presents an insurmountable barrier to competing brands.

◗ MINI: Empowered by Its Origins

My first car was a battered orange Mark IV Mini 850. It was tiny, it hopped out of second gear, and it often failed to start. But when I think of my days at Lancaster University, what do I remember? I remember the sense of freedom I felt when I drove away from campus in the Mini, and the camaraderie I enjoyed with my friends as we motored through the beautiful Lancashire countryside. My fond memories of that car can't help but shape my attitude toward the new BMW MINI. The fact that the new MINI is bigger, great to drive, and far less temperamental than the one I owned merely adds to its attraction. Given the choice, I often rent one of the new MINIs when I return to England, and twice I've found myself at the local dealer in the States asking to test drive one.

Most people who own today's MINIs didn't have experience driving the original version. They didn't buy the car because it rekindled happy personal memories. But I believe that many of them did buy because they bought into the iconic status of the brand. In our Global Brand Survey, we found that people in the United Kingdom who would consider a MINI as their next car believe it is easy to recognize (77 percent), has a distinctive identity (74 percent), and is part of British culture (70 percent).

Today the new MINI is also a popular choice in the United States. Rather than being limited by the British origins of its predecessor from the 1960s, today's MINI is empowered by them. Its size and ingenious design aid in its recognition, but the car owes its enduring appeal to its association with British popular culture. The car's launch in 1959 predated the British Invasion, and when the Beatles, the Rolling Stones, and Petula Clark crashed the *Billboard* charts in the United States, they carried the Mini with them. The car appeared in a number of movies, including the Beatles' *Magical Mystery Tour* and the original *Italian Job*.

Though BMW's reinterpretation of the Mini is a far cry from its tiny predecessor in terms of size, the German carmaker has successfully tapped the Mini heritage in both design and marketing. It projects the brand's fun-loving, British image through color combinations, styling details, and smart, tongue-in-cheek advertising. In our survey, a majority of Brits said they thought of the new BMW MINI as an English brand. Whether it is spelled Mini or MINI, the status of the tiny icon seems assured for years to come.

Amul Ice Cream: Building a Brand with Local Appeal

When the Gujarat Cooperative Milk Marketing Federation (GCMMF) set up shop in 1946, a year before Indian independence, its goal was to help a few dozen dairy farmers make a living. Today it is a multimillion-dollar business that makes it possible for millions of Indians to earn a living wage.

Originally GCMMF sold only milk, under the brand name Amul, but in 1996, the Indian Market Research Bureau (IMRB) conducted a consumer survey to learn what other dairy products consumers wanted. Based on the findings, the GCMMF decided to launch Amul products in a number of dairy categories, including ice cream. Amul's 1997 entry into the ice cream market brought it into direct conflict with Hindustan Lever (51 percent owned by Unilever) and its Kwality Wall's brand. After a hard-fought battle, Amul captured a significant portion of the bigger company's share. Between 2001 and 2006, Amul's volume sales almost doubled, and by the end of the five-year period, it claimed a 36 percent market share (a claim Hindustan Lever contests).[1]

Amul's growth has been fueled by expanding production and distribution to new regions within India. Five factors lie behind the brand's success:

1. A focus on ensuring availability. Amul ice cream can be found in a wide variety of outlets, from its own parlors to pushcarts and snack kiosks.
2. Lower prices, in part the result of its specialization in dairy-related products.
3. A "real ice cream" positioning based in Amul's dairy heritage.
4. A stream of new products designed to appeal to local tastes.
5. Its local status as "A Taste of India." R.S. Sodhi, Amul's general manager for marketing, was quoted in the *New York Times* in 2002 as saying "All our competitors in food products are multinationals. We hope to strike a patriotic chord among consumers."[2]

In the same article, a representative of Hindustan Lever states that that company is more concerned with earnings than volume sales. If so, then both companies may be satisfied with how things have proceeded since 2002. Early in 2007, the Hindustan *Business Line*'s report on volume sales and revenues for the two companies clearly indicates that while Hindustan Lever's volumes have dropped precipitously in favor of Amul, its revenues have stabilized and recently shown signs of growth.[3] The article also reports that GCMMF recently launched "pro-biotic ice creams that have live beneficial culture that confer beneficial health effects such as improving immunity and digestion and strengthening bones." The threat to Hindustan Lever is that by focusing on profits alone, it may cede the mass market to GCMMF, which may then launch its own premium brand.

Typically, however, multinational corporations like Unilever succeed because they have genuinely better products and significantly stronger marketing skills or because they buy up the local competition, as Unilever did with Ben & Jerry's ice cream in the United States. The example of Amul is unusual because it managed to leverage its home-field advantage to become a strong brand in a relatively short time. More often, however, global brands find that the competition is well established and may even own the same positioning that they do in other parts of the world.

Efes Pilsen: Strong Community Ties Help Create Turkey's Beer of Choice

The Efes Beer operation has a unique history. Beer production in Turkey did not begin until 1890, when a brewery was founded in Istanbul by two Swiss entrepreneurs. This brewery was later nationalized, and for a time, Tekel, a state enterprise, was the only beer producer in Turkey. In 1969, a change in the regulations opened the market to private enterprise. During that year the Efes company established its first two breweries in the cities of Istanbul and Izmir, while its local competitor Tuborg started producing beer in Izmir.

Today Efes controls around 80 percent of the Turkish beer market, while Tuborg's share is around 15 percent. Other foreign brands, so successful in other countries, have made little progress in Turkey.

One of the most notable things about Efes is the degree to which the company is involved in the local Turkish community. This is the result of a deliberate effort by the company to improve the quality of life in Turkey, a goal expressed in the Efes mission statement. As part of this effort, the company has established a tradition of local sponsorship across a broad range of areas, from theater to archaeology. Sports sponsorship took a more prominent role for the brand in 1976 when Efes bought a local basketball team and renamed it Efes Pilsen. The team became successful and now enjoys support from towns all over the country.

Efes has also undertaken projects to address two major problems in Turkish society: education and unemployment. Efes now funds almost 70 percent of the Anatolia Education and Social Assistance Foundation, dedicated to building schools and hospitals and providing scholarships.

Recognizing that tourism can be a source of jobs in Turkey, Efes is also working with the United Nations Development Programme on the Tourism Project. The objective is to train local people to serve the tourist trade, teaching them how to act as guides, run pensions out of their homes, and grow organic vegetables. Efes's partnership with Bosphorus University in creating a one-month tourism certificate program has proven to be quite successful and is being expanded in 2008.

The strong presence established by Efes through its integration into local culture helps explain why foreign imports have much smaller shares in Turkey than elsewhere. Dilek Dölek Başarir, the marketing director of Efes's Turkey Beer Operations, explains: "In contrast to Russia, where any outside brand is seen worthy, the competition is much tougher in Turkey because of Efes Pilsen's well-established quality and its appeal to a broad cross-section of people. People who could afford to buy a foreign import justify their loyalty by asking 'Why pay more for the same quality? And besides, it is from my country.'"[4]

Efes is a compelling example of a domestic brand that has become successful and beaten off multinational competition by becoming an integral part of its home culture. The company's early use of sponsorship has helped ensure that people readily recognize the brand and love it. When faced with such a strong local brand, the conclusions are self-evident: Unless you have a truly compelling advantage, either steer clear or consider partnering with the incumbent to benefit from its strength. (Miller Genuine Draft, the only imported beer in Turkey that enjoys any significant volume, used this approach, allowing Efes to brew and distribute the brand under license.)

Cola Turka: Powered by Cultural Identity

Brands need to stand for something. But global brands rarely adopt a partisan positioning; typically they tap into needs and desires that cross cultures. This creates an opening for local competitors to take a stand against them. Recently the two global powerhouses in the soft-drink category, Coke and Pepsi, have faced some tough local competition in places where admiration for the United States has waned, such as the Middle East, Central America, and Turkey.

Cola Turka was launched in July 2003 by Ulker, a large food and drink producer in Turkey. With Coca-Cola the market leader, followed by Pepsi and Fanta, Ulker needed to find a way to make Cola Turka stand out against the global brands. Ulker's ad agency Y&R came up with a three-minute execution that did just that. Set in New York, the ad portrays the "very strange day" of Chevy Chase, when everyone he meets speaks to him in Turkish.

Not content with simply creating an ad that played to Turkish pride, Y&R also took special pains to ensure that as many people as possible saw the ad. One day prior to the launch, ads in national newspapers exhorted readers to watch TV on Friday at 20:00. No additional information was given. Intrigued, people wondered which TV channel to watch. Those who had their TVs on at the appointed time found out that it didn't matter. Cola Turka had "road-blocked" Turkish TV, buying space on every channel at that hour. Tracking research found that nearly 90 percent of people claimed to recognize the ad, which was very positively received. As one research respondent put it, the ad "made me feel proud to be a Turk." The discussion that followed this dramatic launch boosted the impact of the brand's paid communications, enabling Cola Turka to leapfrog past competitors to the number-two position in the market.

Cola Turka's strategy of appealing to national pride was very effective, but the brand couldn't hold the ground it gained. After successfully using the concept "Show off the great Turkishness inside of you" to launch the brand, Ulker veered away to a less jingoistic approach. Perhaps influenced by political turbulence prior to the elections in 2007, when the country was divided over the influence of religion in a secular state, Cola Turka now relies on the concept "We are all together, we live all together and every walk of life drinks Turkey's local Cola." However, the new campaign lacks the emotional charge of the launch campaign, and the brand's market share has gradually declined. At the time of writing, the brand's share was 13 percent, down from 20 percent at its peak, making it the third player in the market.

Cola Turka succeeded against well-known global brands precisely because it was seen to be local. This strategy has been adopted by brands in diverse categories in countries from Australia to Colombia. Global brands may get a head start in countries where local brands are considered inferior, but that advantage is not insurmountable. Local brands that adequately meet the needs of consumers and effectively tap into partisan feelings can make significant inroads against the international competition.

Key Points to Take Away

- As brands move beyond their countries of origin, it is more difficult for them to create a strong relationship with consumers in new countries.
- Local brands can be formidable adversaries because being part of the local culture is a positive influence on purchase.

Questions to Consider

1. To what degree is your brand's global appeal limited because its strength lies in factors related to local culture?
2. Does your brand have strong quality and heritage credentials that will allow it to compete effectively on a global basis?
3. Do you have the budget necessary to ensure your brand is easy to recognize, has a distinctive identity, and will be seen as setting the trends?

For more information related to these questions, visit theglobalbrandonline.com.

Chapter 8

Light on the Dark Continent

Matthew Angus and Judith Kapanga
Millward Brown South Africa

Ex Africa semper aliquid novi

More than 2000 years ago, Roman scholar Pliny the Elder noted "something new always comes out of Africa." Yet ever since that time, westerners have misunderstood the African continent. The Romans, who recognized Africa as the narrow Mediterranean strip from Morocco to Egypt, believed it was a place where fearsome and fantastical monsters prowled, terrorizing and devouring the wretched primitives who lived there. They knew nothing of the prosperous and powerful kingdom of the Nubians, or the exquisite terra-cotta figurines crafted by the people of the Nok kingdom.

As it was in Roman times, so it is now. We still lack the knowledge and perspective to understand Africa on its own terms. Modernity, progress, and culture, when judged from a western perspective, all seem to be lacking in Africa. There can be no doubt that from the 1950s to the 1990s, many parts of Africa earned their grim reputations, but in recent years, peaceful resolution of tense situations has become the norm rather than the exception. Political and social reform has been accompanied by economic growth; in the last decade, Africa has experienced its highest growth and lowest inflation in the past 30 years.[1]

The International Monetary Fund predicts a 6.8 percent increase in gross domestic product for sub-Saharan Africa[2] for 2008 (8 percent in oil-exporting countries). This rate of growth is far higher than the global average. Although Africa's growth still lags behind that of the BRIC (Brazil, Russia, India, and China) economies, it is speeding up while BRIC growth is slowing down. Therefore, Africa represents a tremendous opportunity for businesses prepared to take advantage of it. But an unbiased mind-set is needed to do this, and that mind-set must be based on constructive and open-minded engagement with local cultures.

The Opportunity that Is Africa

Most talk of Africa's potential has revolved around its abundant natural resources. But another gigantic opportunity exists, and that is the opportunity to provide Africa's people with goods and services. While most African citizens remain poor by western standards, the sheer economic and political force of millions of hardworking and resourceful people in India and China is already being felt. The African continent has roughly the same number of people. While it is complex and multifaceted, it is probably no more challenging to marketers than India or China.

Enterprises that can serve the African consumer base by meeting a basic functional need can realize fantastic returns while also helping society progress and advance. For example, before the cellular industry arrived in Nigeria in 2003, that country of 143 million people had only 2 million land telephone lines. By September 2006, MTN Nigeria had 9.6 million mobile subscribers; Globacom had 9.5 million. Many Nigerians now have two or more phones and see the cellular industry as the best thing to have happened in the country since independence.[3]

The growing presence of food and drink companies also benefits local society. In Uganda, SABMiller—the world's second largest brewer, and one of the first African-originated companies to emerge as a global business—is scaling up its Eagle Lager project. Eagle Lager is brewed from sorghum, a local grass crop, and is the second largest pan-African brand. The brand's success is of substantial benefit to over 10,000 small-scale farmers in Uganda and Zambia who grow the sorghum.[4] Cases like these indicate that commercial success in Africa can have a far greater impact on local standards of living than pure philanthropy could ever have.

So global business, while being an agent of change, can also share in the rewards. We at Millward Brown have seen the business coming through our South African offices from north of the border grow to such an extent that we have founded ventures in Kenya and Nigeria.

But we confront major challenges when we go into new markets where little or no research has ever been conducted. How do you know what messages will resonate with consumers? How do you know what your product or service needs to do to succeed?

Because Africa encompasses 53 countries and at least 1,000 different ethnic groups, there are no simple answers to these questions. However, our on-the-ground experience in sub-Saharan Africa has allowed us to identify some of the key factors that drive brand growth. While a number of these elements are common to developing nations around the world, other key considerations are firmly rooted in unique aspects of African culture.

Marketing Basics

The most basic elements of marketing are the same around the world. Issues of price, value, quality, distribution, and packaging must be addressed wherever you do business. However, these fundamentals must be approached differently in developing countries, where new consumers have relatively low incomes and have not been exposed to a wide variety of brands and products. Marketers in Africa share these challenges with those in other developing regions.

Price

Many of Africa's most successful brands over the years have placed low price above all other considerations, because making ends meet is a daily challenge to many Africans. A large number of consumers lack access to even moderate savings and thus can spend only as much cash as they can gather on a particular day. If a product's price is higher than they expect, they may not be able to make the purchase. When a group of consumers were asked what they thought of before purchasing a product (in this case washing powder), the response was: "The first thing is that you think that you do not have the washing powder and you need one. So at that time you will find that you have only R5.00 and you are short of R0.80c and then you think of going to a friend to lend that R0.80c in order to go and buy your washing powder."

A matter of 80 South African cents (around 12 U.S. cents) makes or breaks millions of transactions in Africa every day. Prices vary widely and fluctuate over time, both because the import and manufacturing infrastructure is often unreliable and because the traders who sell the goods get different deals at different times. A trusted brand name has an important role to play in maintaining a sense of order and trust in all this. As one consumer said: "One cannot rely on the price because prices changes every day. What is important is that the washing powder can remove the dirt and stains in your clothes and also keep the clothes that are white, white."

Consumers often have to switch brands if their first choice is so expensive that they will not be able to afford other important purchases: "[You switch when] you think that the R5.00 extra that you were going to spend on your washing powder you can save it and use it to buy your kids some bananas or oranges."

Pack size can make a huge difference in making brands accessible to people at affordable prices. In Nigeria, Close-Up toothpaste is sold in pack sizes as small as 5 milliliters (0.17 ounces, or about 1 teaspoon). In Kenya, Weetabix cereal has brought out a 37-gram (1.3 ounce) twin pack, while potato chips, peanuts, and popcorn are now sold in small packs containing just a handful of product.[5]

Quality

The equation linking price to quality is quite tenuous in Africa. Consumers think of quality as something independent of price, so a low-priced product is not automatically associated with poor quality. As one consumer told us: "I like my washing powder because firstly it is cheap. It has too much foam [a positive] and makes my things look bright."

Truly popular African brands deliver quality as well as price. Sunlight Washing Powder is a classic brand that has delivered value and quality to South Africans for years. "Yes, Sunlight is less when it comes to price. . . . When I soak my clothes with it for five minutes, by the time I do my washing, dirt is no longer there. And another thing is that is has foam and when I rinse my clothes I normally do not use fabric softener because my clothes do not need that."

During a qualitative research project, consumers were asked to do a "brand sort" in which they were given several brands and asked to place them in groups or categories as they saw fit, discussing this classification within the group until a consensus was reached. Respondents grouped health products together, then products that conveyed status, and finally, the cheaper brands. But the "cheaper" brands were not so much the price-fighters as the ones that had a key benefit that made them a good value for the price paid. An example is Geisha, a very popular soap that comes in a large bar. Other more pricy soaps last for only three days or so, while Geisha, which lasts much longer, also performs well and can be used by the whole family. As a large solid bar, it withstands frequent use without disintegrating and thus delivers value to its consumers.

The separation of anti-bacterial soaps into a group at the start of the process touched on an aspect that is intrinsic to a brand's value: the functional benefit. While low price is a benefit in itself, and may be enough to drive brand success, consumers have no problem with higher price points for products that provide a concrete, understandable justification of the price.

Value

The concept of a product being so cheap that its quality is dubious *does* exist, but in Africa, in many cases the cheapest product is actually the best. The lesson here is that local businesses, shabby as they may seem, should not be underestimated. They may have brands that, while not backed by global resources, have enough to beat many global brands on business basics as consumers are convinced both of their superior quality and their value.

The Value of Status
Although the association of price with quality may be cloudy, the association of high price with high status is clear. Thus there is potential for premium brands

to gain a foothold. One Malawian respondent related an amusing tale of her communal washing days: "I buy the little packet of Surf—it is expensive—and [also] the laundry bars. When I am washing I put the open Surf on the top so that people think I am using it and meanwhile wash the clothes in a basin so that people don't see me rubbing the laundry bar. They assume I am using Surf."

Surf was regarded as a high-priced product, good for showing off, but the higher price did not mean that the product itself was any better than the laundry bar she was using. In fact, the respondent went to the extra expense of buying a laundry bar to get the job done, even though she had already paid a premium price for the washing powder.

In many ways, the status associated with a brand is linked far more with the price paid for the product than the quality of the product itself. Expensive packaging conveys status even though the product inside may be identical to what everyone else is consuming: "In our countries people still drink cold drinks from the [glass] bottles because they have a return value. If you are seen carrying a can you are seen to have money as cans are expensive, mostly imported, so if you see someone drinking from a can you are like wow he has money."

The Value of Versatility

In developing markets, where people have little money and limited retail options, they are not accustomed to using many specialized products. Often one product is used for a number of related purposes (such as washing or cleaning). Versatility, then, is a very important factor in a market where people face budget constraints. It is a facet of value. And because resourceful Africans find alternative uses for virtually everything they own—old tires become sandals, the back end of a pickup becomes a donkey cart, and paint cans are fashioned into lawnmowers—it is a facet that requires some attention.

Laundry bars set the benchmark for product versatility across the continent. William Lever's initial success came from the first wrapped and branded laundry soap, the legendary Sunlight. Introduced in the United Kingdom in 1885,[6] the brand was launched in South Africa in 1891. Across most of the rest of the world, the Sunlight brand, where it still exists, has evolved into more modern forms, but in southern Africa the name Sunlight is still synonymous with the classic green laundry soap. This soap, which is far cheaper than washing powders, is intended for bathing, dishwashing, and laundry applications, but over the years it has acquired a mind-numbing array of other functions, from sealing damaged fuel tanks to cleansing the bowels as an enema.

Sunlight is not the only soap brand with diverse uses. In the rural areas of Kenya, Lifebuoy is used as a toilet soap and a disinfectant for baby rashes. It is also smeared on the body after a bath as a lotion and used by teenagers to treat pimples. In the service sector, companies also try to tap into the African predilection for multipurpose products. For example, the Mzansi banking initiative in South Africa aimed to bring people with no bank accounts into the sector by providing multiple benefits: interest on low amounts, a certain number of free transactions per month, and free cell phone banking.

Availability

A brand cannot be sold if it is not on the shelves, but in Africa, poor infrastructure and operational shortcomings often make brands unavailable for purchase. Established and trusted brands may inspire enough loyalty in consumers that they will shop around for them or even buy a related product under the same brand name. As one respondent told us: "With me, if I do not get what I am looking for, which is a Sunlight washing powder, I do not buy something else. What I do is that I go for a Sunlight laundry bar."

But a consistent lack of availability ultimately is deadly for any brand, as it gives consumers an opportunity to discover alternatives.

Packaging

Where media in general and advertising in particular are young industries, packaging often fulfills the role played by advertising in more developed markets. Product packaging in Africa has historically been simple, with clear labels and brief details on the products inside. Consumers look to the packaging for clarity on what the product offers; we were told, for example: "Before I buy something, I make sure that I read the ingredients and the benefits of buying that thing, and for example with Rama [a brand of margarine] they are saying that it is rich with vitamins and is tasty."

To less-experienced consumers, the brand name alone sometimes can provide important information about the product benefits: "What would make me buy a brand is also in the name. For example, Jeba Hair Fertilizer is a turnoff to others but for me it would catch me. It's great because I need growth in my hair. So the name speaks to me."

Much of what has been covered up to now will be familiar to marketers working elsewhere in the developing world. Consumers in Africa, India, and China may have limited financial resources, but they are interested in learning about and trying brands, if they are available and accessible in terms of price. This presents marketers with an interesting challenge: How do you make your brand affordable in absolute terms without undermining your margin or brand status? Making the brand as cheap as possible—by, for example, using a simpler product formulation—may work for a while. But such tactics will also open the brand up to local competition. Selling a desirable brand in smaller pack sizes is one solution that works.

Africa has much in common with other developing regions. Yet anyone who has traveled to Africa is instantly aware that something here is different. In many ways—environmental, economic, and especially sociocultural—Africa is unique. This uniqueness plays out in forms of consumer behavior that are distinctly African.

Tradition and Identity

Africa is a continent of migrants. For thousands of years, groups of Africans have traveled across huge expanses of land in response to environmental, social, or economic pressures. This migration continues even today as populations increase and the need for resources becomes more intense. Millions of Africans flood into cities every day, looking for work, a place to live, and a new life. But most of these migrants retain connections to the village or town they originally came from, and those who go on to become successful in the modern African city develop a dual identity. They think of themselves as successful modern men or women who are proud of where they came from.

Advertising in emerging economic powerhouses like South Africa and Nigeria taps into this consciousness. A successful beer advertisement in South Africa features a businessman who abandons a key pitch to clients halfway through to go outside and help an elderly woman load a sack into a wheelbarrow. He wins the job, regardless, because his clients recognize him as a man who knows where he comes from.

When Africans journey from village to city, they often bring their brand loyalties with them. The African bush is not a branding vacuum; long-established brands have been hiding out there for decades. Broadly speaking, these well-established, successful brands can be classified into three groups: homegrown, naturalized, and global.

Homegrown Brands

Many of Africa's most powerful brands are homegrown. PZ Cussons, for example, the owner of Imperial Leather soap and now one of the world's largest soap manufacturers, began as a trading post in Sierra Leone in 1879. From there, the company expanded into Nigeria, then to the rest of Africa and beyond. Promasidor, owner of the massive Onga and Cowbell brands and now one of the world's largest food manufacturers, was founded in the Democratic Republic of the Congo (then Zaire) in 1979. Brands like Meikles and Tanganda in Zimbabwe, Tusker in Kenya, Windhoek in Namibia, and Club in Ghana date back to the colonial days of the early twentieth century and are integrally woven into the culture of their nations.

Naturalized Brands

Naturalized brands were introduced to Africa by foreign or global companies but were later cut off from their parent companies and left to fend for themselves. This situation was particularly prevalent in South Africa, when international companies disinvested due to antiapartheid pressure but often left their local operations and brands intact. These brands adapted to local conditions over time, often becoming market leaders, but with brand identities and strategies that were very different from the prevalent global branding. Toyota South Africa is a typical example. The Toyota Tazz, often the country's top-selling model in the monthly sales charts, is based on the Toyota Conquest (which made its debut in 1988) and is advertised using a campaign featuring a famous local comedian, David Kau.

Global Brands

Where global companies such as Nestlé have succeeded in establishing themselves strongly on the African continent, it has often been as a result of getting in early. Maggi (a brand of stock cubes) has been in West Africa for so long that its name has been corrupted to "Magic" over time; shoppers frequently ask for "Magic cubes." One characteristic of Nestlé's global marketing that certainly applies to its African powerhouse brands like Maggi and MILO (a chocolate malt beverage) is their use of advertising that is conceived and produced locally In contrast, Unilever, which has attained success in Africa with brands like Blue Band (margarine) and Royco (stock cubes), now follows a globalized branding and marketing strategy.

As archaic and outdated as some of these brands may seem to the sophisticated global marketer (naturalized brands often bear little resemblance to their global namesakes, as they are still using branding devices from several decades ago), to Africans these brands form an unchangeable bulwark that they can trust in a world where everything may seem unfamiliar and intimidating. A respondent told us: "I am now in SA [South Africa] but if you come to my cupboard I brought back products that I use to use at home (Uganda), natural foods which have taste. Whatever I used at home is absolutely what I learnt from home, it's all about what I learnt, what I grew up with."

Brands with heritage and a history often rely on this sense of trust and nostalgia. A Royco advertisement features Nigerian brothers who emigrated to the United Kingdom. They sit miserably by the window, looking at the rain and talking about how much they miss home. Then their sister walks in with a package from their mother in Nigeria. Opening it, they find brightly colored African fabrics, Nigerian football jerseys, and two packs of Royco cubes. The commercial ends with the smiling family dressed in their African attire sitting down to a meal cooked by the sister, using the Royco cubes.

This sense of tradition is closely tied in with African concepts of identity, which are complex and layered in line with the society. An African typically negotiates his or her identity at several levels: a family or clan level, an ethnic level, a linguistic level, a national level, a religious level, a political level, as well as a racial or continental level. Virtually every African has all these layers of identity, but the relative importance of the various layers, and the degree to which they are perceived by others, varies widely. For example, Nelson Mandela is of the Ixhiba clan of the Thembu people that are part of the Xhosa nation of the Eastern Cape region of South Africa, but this has played a relatively small part in his public identity, which is aligned more closely with his identity as a former freedom fighter, a South African as well as an African.

Many brands, especially in countries such as Ghana and South Africa, where a cohesive national identity has been formed, use patriotism in their brand identity. Kenyans are proud of their country and the relative success of their nation over the years, and as brands have grown with the country, they have intertwined themselves with the national identity. Tusker beer is a classic Kenyan example, as is Kenylon tomato paste. Most African countries have a de facto national beer, which the patriotic sports fan drinks to support his country: Star in Ghana, Three Horses in Madagascar, and Nile in Uganda.

Brands may also be imbued with other forms of identity. In Accra, Ghana, many shops and services have adopted religious names, such as "Jesus Is Lord Enterprises" or "Isaiah 21:12 Electricians." Glory Oil is one of Ghana's leading petroleum companies. For the global marketer, these branding strategies are difficult to compete with. Although Ghana's religious branding is evidently Christian, it is locally flavored with many subtleties; attempts by outsiders to play the same game are more likely to end in misunderstanding or offense than success.

Giving Back

Many African countries have witnessed the virtual collapse of sectors of the formal economy at some stage over the past 50 years. As a rule, across the continent there has been significant economic progress in recent years, but not so much that ingrained systems of coping are lost.

African economies (especially the informal sectors, which are often larger than their formal counterparts) operate within a framework of mutual assistance that is essential to societies across the continent. The act of helping others is hardwired into African culture. Custom dictates that a lone traveler, even a European, who arrives in a rural village must be given food and accommodation for the night, regardless of how little that village may have to spare. In

South Africa this convention is called *ubuntu*, a word that very roughly translates into "I am because you are, you are because we are." One South African respondent described *ubuntu* in this way: "If one has a problem, you go to neighbor for assistance and she will do likewise if she also has a problem. To give an example, if I do not have sugar, I go to her and she will give some and some other time if it is now her that has a problem, if I can assist I do assist with whatever that she wants. That is how we live."

A recent South African TV ad encapsulated this concept. A little boy is sent by his mother to go and ask for dishwashing liquid at the "neighbor's" house, which is in fact miles away. He runs the distance and is welcomed by the neighbor, who happily gives him a teaspoon of dishwashing liquid. Almost immediately after the boy has returned, there is a knock on the door. Another neighbor has sent her child to borrow some of the borrowed dishwashing liquid! This shows how your brand can travel hand to hand way beyond the households of those who first bought it. It also shows how intrinsic helping others is to a successful life in an African community.

Thus the successful African brand is part of the community it serves. Corporate social responsibility is not just an exercise to keep the government or shareholders happy but a crucial part of the brand's image and a make-or-break marketing tool, especially for new global brands without historic presence in the community. Brookside Dairy in Kenya has achieved strong grassroots support for its brand by donating milk to impoverished communities, sponsoring blood donations and testing, and sourcing 93 percent of its milk from small farmers.[7] Brookside's brand health, as reflected by Millward Brown data, is exceptional, more than strong enough to fend off global competitors.

The Power of Human Interaction

In cities such as London or New York, a trip to the shops is a quick, convenient, low-maintenance affair, requiring minimal face-to-face interaction with others. In those places, it is possible, even commonplace, to commute across the city on public transport, buy a load of groceries, and get a take-away meal on the way home without ever saying more than a few words to another human being.

Such a disconnect from the rest of humanity is anathema to African culture. Day-to-day life in African countries is an exceptionally social experience. In Africa, most shopping takes place in open markets seething with crowds of people, and the actual act of buying involves a spirited debate with the store owner about the virtues of the product in question and the price to be paid for it. Everything from eating meals to working and commuting is characterized by ongoing conversation and interaction that western travelers find exhausting. It is not at all uncommon for two strangers to pass on opposite sides of the street in Ouagadougou, pause for conversation with each other (without crossing the street), and still be there an hour later.

The incredible intensity of interpersonal interaction in Africa has a few environmental origins—for example, TV is generally very limited and of poor quality across the continent—but is also linked with *ubuntu*. It is incumbent upon all Africans to care about the people around them and do what they can to assist—but how can you know how to help someone without knowing them?

Word of Mouth

The simple act of getting to know people involves the exchange of ideas, views, and feelings. Knowledge of brands is one of many types of information that may be transferred. In discussing common problems and issues in daily life, people may offer or solicit information about products and brands they rely on.

The sharing culture also helps promote trial, which becomes a form of sampling. A product that worked well for a borrower is likely to be considered for purchase in the future. Brands might do well to keep this uniquely African method of product sampling in mind; one respondent we talked to was particularly fond of a specific brand of laundry bar because it already came in cut-out blocks, which made it easier for her to share with her neighbors.

In recent years, word-of-mouth communication has attracted increased attention from marketers around the world as they have recognized its power in driving brand growth. It has been argued that word of mouth contributes more to building brand equity than simple product satisfaction. Our evidence suggests that this is true in Africa, because of the value placed on personal interaction as well as the relative dearth of conventional advertising. Access to conventional media is limited, and many branded products still have novelty value; therefore, Africans are eager to talk about them.

Figure 8.1 illustrates that while westerners may express a willingness to recommend a brand, relatively few (50 percent on average, far lower for big brands) will actually follow up. The data shown are for the detergent market in Spain. For the top 10 brands surveyed, an average of 19 percent of respondents said they would recommend the brand. But barely half of that number—10 percent—had actually done so.

In Nigeria, however, levels of advocacy are far higher. Of the total willing to recommend a brand, on average, 82 percent turn this into actual brand

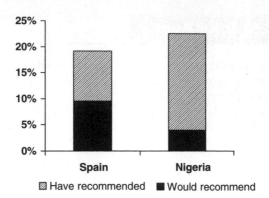

Figure 8.1 Degree of Personal Recommendation in the Detergent Category

Source: Millward Brown tracking studies.

recommendation (22 percent willing to recommend, with 18 percent having followed through).

Thus while word-of-mouth communication is important around the world, its role plays out differently according to culture. It is important for marketers to understand the consumers in their markets. In Africa, there is huge potential to capitalize on the opportunities presented by brand ambassadors and social interactions, whether in the formal settings of clubs or societies or in day-to-day conversations.

Conclusion

Many of the basic issues related to marketing brands to people with low disposable incomes and varied needs are shared across all developing countries. In the next chapter, Nigel looks at the ways global brand marketers meet these challenges in other countries. But to assume that the same strategies and tactics will work without adaptation in Africa is to ignore the rich and varied culture of its peoples. For brand marketers willing to embrace the challenge, Africa presents an incredible opportunity. To maximize their chances of success, marketers need to understand the psyche of the local people and develop strategies appropriate to the local culture.

Key Points to Take Away

- While the African continent represents a very diverse set of cultures, the rising standards of living across most of sub-Saharan Africa present the next big opportunity for marketers after the BRICs.
- Some common themes begin to emerge across the description of the BRICs and Africa, including the need to get the value equation right and the power of word of mouth.

Questions to Consider

1. Based on the description in this chapter, do you see an opportunity for your brand in the developing nations of Africa?
2. What challenges do you foresee trying to seize that opportunity?

For more information related to these questions, visit theglobalbrandonline.com.

Chapter 9

How Global Brands Have Met the Challenge of Going Local

The history of global brands is rich with stories of success and failure, often the result of trial and error as brands seek to establish themselves in new markets. As we have seen, local market conditions do differ dramatically, with local brands often enjoying the home-field advantage. In entering new markets, brands face challenges that may be hard to anticipate. Many of the more egregious failures have resulted from a misguided belief in the strength of the brand to overcome local obstacles: "It worked well back home, so it will work here too." Even when research is used to inform the process, marketers may have difficulty fully appreciating the extent to which they need to adjust their approach to the new circumstances.

To establish themselves, global brands usually need to find ways to disrupt the existing status quo. Until recently, multinational corporations could present the same brand and product that had worked elsewhere and feel confident that it would be perceived as superior to local goods and services. Increasingly, however, local companies are becoming effective adversaries. The Chinese company Huawei, which initially partnered with Cisco in China, is now seen to be a growing threat to Cisco's continued success on the global stage.

Brands that have extended globally and retained their equity inside and outside their home markets tend to be those built on an idea that appeals to some universal human need or desire. But if a well-entrenched local brand already owns that positioning, making headway as an outsider can be tough. The launch of the Milka chocolate brand in the United Kingdom failed because Cadbury's Dairy Milk owned the same full-cream milk positioning that had made Milka so successful in Germany. After Milka's owner, Jacobs Suchard, was acquired by Kraft, Milka met with far more success by heading east to central and eastern Europe, Russia and the Ukraine. Similarly, Wal-Mart was forced to withdraw from Germany because the established hard discounters proved tough opponents. Global brands entering developing markets, however, often have significant advantages over the local competition, not the least of which are scale and the experience of knowing what works in other countries.

Multinational Companies Have Advantages over Local Ones

Local brands are often owned by family-run businesses. In the United Kingdom, there is an old saying, "Clogs to clogs in three generations," meaning that small businesses rarely last two generations beyond that of the founder (clogs being a sign of poverty in nineteenth-century England). Business acumen does not necessarily breed true, and even when it does, there may be less incentive for sons and daughters to continue growing the business. Being acquired by a multinational company (MNC) may seem a more attractive alternative than trying to fight them off.

By contrast, a strong, scalable business model is a major advantage for MNCs. In addition, these companies have an extraordinary depth of management talent that allows them to outthink the competition and survive changes in leadership. They can draw on the best advice from their global media, advertising, and research agencies. Their global research and development capabilities provide a constant stream of innovations and can readily adapt existing products and services to meet new market needs. They have deep pockets and can afford to reach into them to establish their brands. From operating in multiple countries, they develop an understanding of what is likely to work in a new market. If their first attempt fails, they have the resources to try again, using research to understand where they went wrong and how they might do better.

MNC brands can disrupt the status quo and enter a new market by following five steps:

1. Adapting products and services to meet local needs and tastes
2. Solving the value equation through product and pricing strategies
3. Creating a strong presence and a distinctive identity
4. Adopting more aggressive point-of-purchase tactics
5. Keeping track of consumers' evolving relationship with brands

I consider each of these in turn before looking at a case study for Buick, one of the more unlikely U.S. brands to have made it big in China.

Adapting Products and Services to Meet Local Needs and Tastes

Many consumers in developing countries assume that western brands are of better quality than the local alternatives. In our global survey, we observed that, on average, global brands were over 20 percent more likely to be mentioned on this attribute than local ones. But even if a global brand does offer high quality, you cannot assume that it will meet local needs. This is particularly true for food. For many years, Pizza Hut met with limited success in Brazil because its thick-crust-style pizza was out of sync with local tastes. Far from regarding the American offering as better, Brazilians, used to their own style of thin-crust pizza brought over by Italian immigrants, treated it as a novelty, something to be eaten occasionally but not a replacement for what they were used to. Eventually Pizza Hut adapted its menu, offering a variety of crust styles, including a lighter Italian style and a stuffed crust with Brazilian cheese.

Incorporating local ingredients and flavors into international brands works well to ensure local acceptance, particularly in countries with distinct culinary styles or strong traditions of herbal medicine. In Russia, where cranberry flavor is popular, it is featured in Finlandia vodka and Schweppes soft drinks. Danone (the global food and beverage company which makes the U.S. brand Dannon) added bran and berry flavors to its yogurt line there, and Colgate offers an herbal Gum Control toothpaste that, according to one British marketer, "You would not want to put in your mouth." In China, Frito-Lay incorporated Chinese flavoring into the snack brand, Poca, a brand they introduced in Chinese packaging at a price point between flagship brand Lays and the local competition.[1]

Regional differences in eating habits are well known and well understood. Typically they are rooted in local history, conditions, and resources. For less obvious reasons, there are also cultural differences in the appreciation of fragrance. These differences affect not only the perfume market, but also diverse categories such as personal care and hotels. (The hospitality business often uses subtle fragrances to create ambience.)

In Brazil, fragrances are an essential part of people's lives. There even exists a strong market for scents designed for babies. Local fragrance houses maintain a high share of the market by creating fresh scents that cater to Brazilian preferences. Colgate-Palmolive's Fabric softener Suavitel (known as Soupline in France, Softlan in Germany, and Cuddly in Australia) is sold with the same fragrance as in the other countries, although it is used at a higher level to deliver a more powerful fragrance impact. Brazilians expect their clothes to smell good.

By contrast, in Japan people prefer more subtle fragrances, because it is considered impolite to impose a smell on others. Perhaps this is because the Japanese live in a small and crowded country. Or perhaps they are more sensitive than other groups to various forms of sensory stimuli. According to Karen Hamilton, Unilever's regional category vice president of deodorants and male grooming for Europe, the Japanese have a wide variety of ways of describing the feel of something on their skin.

I made a similar observation when I did work for Martin Lindstrom's book, *BRAND sense*. We discovered that across an identical set of brands, Japanese consumers were far better able to recall and comment on the sensory experience of using them. Whether this means that the Japanese are physically more sensitive to the world around them or simply are better able to vocalize their sensory experiences, it has important implications for marketers, who tend to focus on the visual appeal of their brands while ignoring the impact of the other four senses.

Solving the Value Equation through Product and Pricing Strategies

Balancing Product and Price to Establish Relevance

You have to offer the right product at the right price. That basic brand-building adage may seem like a cliché, but for developing markets, where so much emphasis is placed on value, its message is critical. Perceptions of value result from the interaction between perceived product performance and price. Understanding and solving the "value equation" for developing markets will be the key to success for any global brand.

If a brand is to form a relationship with consumers, it needs to establish a relevant and motivating promise. People need to understand both its functional benefits and its price point (value, mass, premium, or super-premium). If people believe that a brand will meet their specific needs, and if they are comfortable with what using that brand will say about them, their perceptions of price and value will determine whether they progress to trying or buying the brand.

A brand can be priced so low that people will doubt its quality. This is rarely a problem for global brands entering new markets. More often, a global brand will be judged desirable but too expensive for people's budgets. Particularly in developing countries, it is rare that a global brand can match local brand pricing. Local competitors have lower production and distribution costs, and often can sell goods at prices 40 to 60 percent lower than MNCs.

A number of basic strategies have been developed to address this issue.

The first is simply to make the product cheaper. The challenge is to reduce the brand's price point without undermining perceptions of quality. Marketing well-known brands in smaller portion sizes is now an accepted tactic for reaching lower-income and rural consumers in developing countries. In China, Nestlé has met with considerable success with its Chocolate Wafer, sold singly for 1 RMB (12 U.S. cents) and supported only by packaging and point-of-sale material featuring a shark, symbolizing the crunch of biting into the wafer. Nokia responded to the value challenge by introducing the 1600 phone, which retails for substantially less than the top-of-the-line cell phones, as a slim and simple option at a good price.

The second strategy is that the very largest brands sometimes can compete with the locals by lowering their unit price somewhat while at the same time raising their profile. In China, Coca-Cola managed to fend off a threat from Wahaha's Future Cola by increasing marketing spend while rolling out a small 200-milliliter (6.8 ounce) returnable bottle at a price of 1 RMB. It successfully pursued the same strategy in India by offering a 200-ml bottle to rural markets instead of its standard 300-ml (10.1 ounce) size and at the same time launching its *Thanda matlab Coca-Cola* campaign.

Focusing solely on lowering prices, however, can be a dangerous approach. As people's incomes improve, they may leave cheaper brands behind in favor of premium ones. A third strategy, which recognizes that people often progress through brands, requires expanding the brand portfolio.

According to Tom Doctoroff, Greater China chief executive officer of J. Walter Thompson and author of the book *Billions: Selling to the New Chinese Consumer*, Colgate achieved success using a "branding down" strategy.[2] First the company introduced Colgate Total, which offered 12-hour protection against cavities, gingivitis, and bad breath. Once that premium brand was established, subsequent introductions included the Colgate Strong and Colgate Herbal lines. Each variant sold at a different price point, but all were premium compared to direct competitors.

Procter & Gamble also chose to expand its brand footprint through a vertical brand strategy, offering different product formulations at different price points for brands such as Olay facial care, Tide detergent, and Whisper feminine protection. This approach allows consumers to grow into the premium brands as their standard of living improves. Olay, which markets its Regenerist Intensive Cell Care line at a 200 RMB price point, also offers at least 10 other brand variants, some selling for far less than Regenerist. Even with a minority of the volume, however, Regenerist gets more than its fair share of advertising support to maintain its status. Again, each variant is sold at a premium compared to direct competitors, reflecting the colossal status of the Olay brand in China.

There is one further strategy, but it can be considered only for the strongest brands. A brand may simply choose to maintain its price point and benefit from higher margins, confident that growing standards of living will provide substantial future sales growth. Gillette, a brand with good equity in many countries, looks to maintain the same available net selling price into the retail trade across developed countries, and keeps that price as similar as possible in developing countries. People either can afford Gillete's premium razors or they can't. One ex-employee likens it to selling luxury cars. "It's like a Ferrari," he said. "Everyone wants one but you don't sell many more by dropping the price by 10 percent." (Although in Gillette's case, if you cannot afford the very best razor, lower-priced alternatives are available that deliver lower standards of performance.)

Creating a Strong Presence and a Distinctive Identity

Building Presence

Companies like BASES, the new-product forecasting unit of AC Nielsen, know full well that the second most important factor in determining the success of a new product is brand awareness. The first is distribution. Distribution and awareness go hand in hand when it comes to establishing a new brand in any market. But for global brands entering new markets, the challenge of building presence may last longer than just the introductory phase. In frenetic marketplaces like India and China, it is all too easy to drop off the radar. If MNC brands hope to grow, they must remain visible amid the constant barrage of local brand advertising in order to maintain presence, clarity of positioning, and perceptions of dynamism.

Brands that have been successful in China typically have increased spending dramatically over time. Colgate increased its share of voice in the toothpaste category from 15 percent in 1998 to 26 percent in 2005 in order to hold its position as the biggest brand. Over the same period, Budweiser increased its share of spending and became the import beer with the strongest attitudinal loyalty in China.

But sometimes simply spending more is not enough. Through its established presence and leading share of voice in China, Pantene Pro-V had created a strong bond with consumers. But in 2006, when additional growth was proving hard to come by, research helped P&G understand why its TV advertising was not working as hard for the brand as it had previously.

Because the hair-care category was so competitive and heavily advertised, consumers found little that was differentiating in any brand's TV advertising. As a result, Pantene's TV advertising was not strengthening the brand's key equity measures related to inner confidence and beauty. To address this problem, P&G created a TV reality program that celebrated the transformation of a group of ordinary women through a series of makeovers. The nine-episode format was highly successful, and, crucially, focused on developing not only the external appearance but also the unique inner qualities of each contestant. Awareness of the show was promoted through auditions in major cities, public relations, print advertising, and a Web site. The top-rated show attracted 40 million viewers, registered 10 million page views on the Web site, and inspired 1 million blog posts. As a result of this new approach, Pantene grew sales and value share in China by 10 percent.

While heavy media presence does convey a sense of leadership and ubiquity, simply shouting louder is not the panacea to competition. A global brand must clearly convey what it stands for and what differentiates it from other options. Communication needs to vary for different markets according to their level of development, but the brand essence expressed must be consistent.

A strong, unifying brand proposition is needed to stretch across different levels of consumer sophistication.

Consumers in rural areas may understand brands primarily as a symbol of trust. The proposition for them is: "This is a big, safe brand to choose." But in the more sophisticated urban markets, consumers have more choices and look for the product best able to meet their needs. It is not easy to present the same image and personality to consumers over time in the face of a rapidly changing society and fierce local competition. To accomplish this, marketers must really understand their consumers and tap into the fundamental drivers of the category and brand.

Choosing the Appropriate Communication Channels

Much to the chagrin of global marketers who would like to explore the new media options used by their colleagues in the United States and Europe, TV is still the name of the game when it comes to reaching a mass audience in most developing economies. But that does not preclude an integrated approach to communication. In India, faced with the need to drive volume, Pepsi distributed Khufiya cards (spy cards) on its larger bottles. Each one contained a visually encrypted secret code that guaranteed a prize. When placed against the blue screen that appeared during Pepsi Khufiya ads, the prize, typically money off the next purchase, was revealed. Trailers, TV station announcers, and newspapers helped publicize the promotion, which attracted a great deal of interest, and resulted in strong sales and share growth.

While TV remains a mainstay, if you are targeting the middle- or upper-class consumer, the sheer size of the audience means that new media do offer good potential. In India, the Sunsilk hair-care brand launched the Web site www. sunsilkgangofgirls.com with the idea of building the largest community of girls online. The site has been a huge success, with over 200 million hits, and has transformed the brand's image from one that appealed to housewives and older working women to one for the young, fun-loving, and stylish. Sunsilkgangofgirls.com was actively promoted through radio and TV advertisements with the line "Girls just wanna have fun!"

Word of Mouth Is Even More Powerful in Developing Markets
For some time now I have been amused by the newfound recognition that word of mouth is an important—sometimes the most important—driver of sales. As Matthew and Judith demonstrated in chapter 8, word of mouth is not only ubiquitous in Africa, it is more powerful there than in developed countries. In the developed world, much of the interest in word of mouth centers on the Web as a forum for sharing information and advice. However, a recent U.S./U.K.

survey conducted by Millward Brown suggests that relatively few people use the informal sources of online information (chat rooms, blogs, etc.) to guide their purchase decisions; the majority of shoppers turn to friends, neighbors, and colleagues for advice, just as in Africa. In rural India, word of mouth is a huge motivator. Recognizing this fact, marketers have invested in a wide variety of tactics designed to create buzz, such as participation at community events like *melas* (village fairs) and *haats* (markets), and mobile-van campaigns.

Adopting More Aggressive Point-of-Purchase Tactics

Given the complexity of China and India, representing as they do a composite of very diverse local markets, an overall brand strategy is often best executed at the local level. Speaking at the 2006 CEO Summit, "Winning in China," sponsored by GroupM (the parent company of WPP's media agencies) and CCTV (a TV station in China), Richard Lee, vice president of Pepsi in Greater China, stated that at the local level, brands should pursue not different strategies but different tactics. He highlighted the need for a dedicated field marketing team to focus on activating brand sales at the point of purchase.[3] This is important for all brands but particularly so for premium brands that need to fight off low-priced, look-alike competitors.

As mentioned earlier, distribution is the first step on the path to brand success. If a brand is not available—because the rains have washed out the road or because stock checkers did not do their job—and people turn to an alternative, brand loyalty is potentially disrupted. Then, even when a product makes it to the shelf, if the packaging fails to cue recognition and reassurance, people will not buy the brand. In developing markets, brands face the additional challenge of penetrating the traditional trade outlets, a process that relies more on trust between salesperson and shopkeeper than on good marketing and listing incentives. A brand cannot rely on broadcast advertising alone to establish itself in new markets; to be successful, it must also adapt to the local retail environment.

The penetration of modern trade is growing rapidly in India and China. A visit to a Carrefour, Wal-Mart, or a Chinese department store in Beijing can leave you feeling that retail is the same the world over; the store layout, signage, and even the presence of in-store TV all seem very familiar. (TV and digital advertising is used much more in China's major cities than in the West. Screens are everywhere: on the streets, in stores, elevators, and even taxis.) But the culture of shopping in China and other countries is very different from that of the West, leading to an increased emphasis on swaying buyers at the point of sale.

In traditional shopping settings, such as local markets or bazaars, stallholders don't hold back from selling their wares. Likewise in modern retail settings in developing markets, armies of retail promoters pitch their case to potential buyers. This tactic is particularly prevalent in categories like health and beauty products and consumer electronics. In Latin America, Unilever uses *impulsadoras*, merchandising girls who try to get people to buy brands on impulse at the personal care fixture. The Spanish retailer Mercadona also uses this tactic, encouraging the sales staff to persuade shoppers to try its store brands. At the Winning in China summit, Michael Tatelman, corporate vice president and general manager of mobile devices for Motorola in North Asia, cited the launch of the pink V3 mobile phone, which featured not only TV, public relations, and point-of purchase materials, but also new uniforms for the sales promoters that were linked to the campaign theme.

Keeping Track of Consumers' Evolving Relationship with Brands

One of the dilemmas facing global marketers is that consumers are at different stages in their relationship with brands depending on income and country.

In an undeveloped market, where basic needs have yet to be satisfied, a brand needs only to make its presence known to succeed, provided it comes from a reputable manufacturer. Relevance and advantage seem guaranteed. (After all, to people accustomed to washing their hair with soap, any shampoo represents an improvement.) But as consumers are exposed to a number of different brands, all of which satisfy functional needs, they begin to distinguish among them based on the status they confer and then the emotional benefits they offer.

To compete effectively, brands need to establish both their emotional appeal and their functional promise. It is not a case of one thing or the other. Analysis of our Link advertising pretest database shows that the ads most likely to produce a sales effect combine both a rational and an emotional appeal. That finding is consistent across countries. We expect consumers to continue to develop their relationship with brands in developing markets, seeking out the best brands for their unique needs and, ultimately, bonding with the brands that connect with them emotionally.

Respect the Local Culture . . .

All of the strategies discussed must be executed while maintaining sensitivity to each individual country. No global brand, no matter how big and successful, can afford to trample on local sensibilities. Of course, no MNC would intentionally set out to offend, but what might appear, from global headquarters, to be an appropriate message or image might be viewed very differently by locals.

Toyota learned this firsthand in 2005, when two of its print ads generated an online backlash in China. The first ad, for the Toyota Land Cruiser, shows the

Toyota pulling a broken-down truck—apparently a Chinese military vehicle—up a rocky slope. The suggestion, according to critics, was that Japanese SUVs are more durable than China's military equipment. The second ad shows a stone lion, a traditional symbol of power in China, saluting one of Toyota's new Prado GX SUVs. The offense generated by this ad was evident from the consumer-generated ads created in response, which showed the same lion crushing the upstart SUV.

It is also all too easy, after a brief visit to Bangalore, Beijing, or São Paulo, where people flaunt foreign brands and fashion, to assume that local consumers will eventually become westernized in their attitudes and brand loyalty. Although similarities may emerge, China is no more likely to become westernized than Japan, which has had far longer to do so. While Chinese consumers may decide that it is easier to shop in a modern supermarket than to visit a diverse set of market stalls, they are unlikely to give up their local tastes, customs, and beliefs. Brazilians are unlikely to give up their local tastes for food, music, and dance. If anything, rising standards of living may cause these cultures to become even more distinct, a point I will return to in Chapter 16.

... and Become Part of It

One of the key findings from the Global Brand Survey, discussed in Chapter 7, is that being seen as a part of the national culture is important to driving purchase for both global and local brands. But local brands—not surprisingly—are twice as likely as global brands to be seen that way. This fact suggests that global brands, once they have established themselves in a market, should work hard to become part of the local scene.

Nestlé's Global Beverage Brand MILO

MILO is often assumed to be a local brand in Southeast Asia. Originally a powdered malt energy drink, popular as part of people's daily diet, the brand has been extended to ready-to-drink formats, ice cream, and chocolates. Its strong relationship with consumers in Asia is partly a result of its longevity there; it was first introduced to the region in the 1950s. But much of its current success derives from its local marketing.

MILO has a long heritage of sponsoring local sports events, such as Malaysia's annual Le Tour De Langkawi bike race, as well as involvement in such regional events as the SEA Games, Southeast Asia's largest sport tournament. In 2007, MILO invested 43.5 million baht (U.S. $1.2 million) to become the event's official health drink. As the official partner of the twenty-fourth SEA Games tournament, Nestlé (Thai) had the right to use the games' trademarks in its marketing campaigns, events, and public relations.[4]

The publicity generated by sponsorships like these provides an excellent opportunity for MILO to reinforce its local relevance and strengthen its image as an energy drink. Once established in a local market, other global brands might do well to find their own way to participate in local culture and downplay their global origins.

How General Motors Turned Buick into a Strong Brand in China

One of the most startling contrasts in our Global Brand Survey is the difference in perceptions of Buick in the United States and China. This difference points to the way a multinational company can leverage success in one part of the world to offset weaker performance elsewhere.

On my first visit to Shanghai a few years ago, I was amazed by the number of sleek, black Buicks I saw cruising the streets. Billboard ads for different Buick models were common along the major routes. And just last year, the driver who took me to the Great Wall near Beijing spoke longingly of his desire to replace his existing Chinese car with a Buick.

In the United States, Buick is not a brand that inspires such passionate desire. Along with other U.S. automotive brands, it has suffered from an undue reliance on "cash on the hood" to get people to buy. Our data, shown in Table 9.1, confirms the vast difference in perception between the two countries.

The success of Buick in China owes much to General Motors' decision to enter the market early, before demand took off, and then move fast when it did. GM has capitalized on its global capabilities but applied them to suit Chinese needs with local design and production.

Chinese law requires that foreign automobile manufacturers operate in China under a joint venture agreement with a local manufacturer. GM moved early to secure an agreement with Shanghai Automotive Industries Corp. (SAIC), China's largest auto manufacturer, which also partners with others, including Volkswagen. In 1998, GM sold about 61,000 Regals.[5] Today, China is Buick's biggest market. GM China sells five other brands—Cadillac, Chevrolet,

Table 9.1 Perceptions of Buick

	U.S.	China
Strong heritage	45%	38%
High quality	34%	56%
Setting the trends	15%	49%
Would consider buying	21%	64%

Source: Millward Brown, *Global Brand Study*, January 2008.

Opel, Saab and Wuling—and more than 30 models. Total GM sales in China exceeded 1 million vehicles in 2007,[6] making China the company's second-largest market after the United States.

Locally inspired design has been an important part of Buick's success. In 2005, GM's Pan Asia Technical Automotive Center, or PATAC, co-owned by GM and SAIC, turned the stodgy Buick LaCrosse into a glamorous, stylish sedan.[7] The new car featured an oversize, chrome-laden front grille, a modern interior, and large, clear taillights designed to appeal to China's status-conscious young buyers. A stretch version features a roomy, luxurious backseat for chauffeur-driven riders.

In our global survey, Chinese perceptions of Buick's quality match those of Toyota. The Chinese also gave Buick a slight edge over Toyota on setting the trends in the category. Like many successful global brands in China, Buick markets its subbrands to separate audiences. Regal targets the winners, the ones with "conquering spirit" who have made it to the top. Excelle goes after those who are on the move, applauding those who actively play the game.

And who is to say that success in China will not reinvigorate the Buick brand in its homeland? In January 2008, a dramatically styled Buick Riviera concept car made its North American debut. The new design, the combined work of GM's design teams in Shanghai and Michigan, represents a distinct departure from previous designs while still harking back to the brand's heritage. First revealed at the Shanghai auto show the previous year, the concept car is likely to morph into the new Buick LaCrosse. With new designs and its existing strong initial and long-term reliability ratings from J.D. Power and Associates, all Buick needs to do now is spread the word.[8] Our survey data suggests that consumers will be receptive to positive news from a brand that many believe is part of the U.S. national culture.

Multinationals Need to Use Their Muscle without Losing Agility

The five practices outlined here have helped many global brands find success in developing countries, but even so, local conditions and competition constantly challenge their ability to adapt. As consumers become increasingly sophisticated, marketers need to keep tabs on changing conditions in order to ensure that they continue to deliver relevant messages. At the same time, they need to maintain a clear brand positioning and resist the temptation to apply brand development strategies commonly used in mature markets, such as launching horizontal line extensions to block off competitors, vertical extensions to cover price points, or overreliance on price promotion. In developing markets, even more than elsewhere, these approaches run a strong risk of confusing consumers and therefore diluting brand equity.

The example of Buick demonstrates what happens when a MNC uses its global muscle quickly and effectively. Often criticized for being slow in the United States, General Motors China moved fast to seize the opportunity presented. Scale, however, can present challenges as well as opportunities. MNCs must avoid letting scale undermine their flexibility and effectiveness. In the next chapter I examine some common issues that undermine the ability of global organizations to leverage their scale effectively.

Key Points to Take Away

- MNCs must effectively leverage their scale and experience when seeking to enter new markets in order to establish local relevance and value perceptions.
- Some basic strategies have served global brands well when seeking to establish and grow brands in the BRICs, but they do need to be adapted in the light of local market conditions and culture.

Questions to Consider

1. How will you solve the value equation? Does your brand really meet local needs? Does it have the right balance between product quality and price?
2. Does your brand have a strong identity that is acceptable to the local culture?
3. Is your mass-market communication effectively aligned with your point-of-purchase activities? What more can you do to gain advantage at the point of purchase?

For more information related to these questions, visit theglobalbrandonline.com.

Chapter 10

Balancing Brand Strength and Business Efficiency

With all the thousands of products and services sold on a multinational basis, how is it that so few manage to succeed at creating universally strong bonds with consumers? Or perhaps the question should be: How have the few companies that have succeeded at forging strong bonds with consumers around the world managed to pull this off? It's tough enough to grow a business in one country; the difficulty is magnified a hundredfold on a global scale. In taking a brand global, a company faces two overriding challenges: balancing investment in the brand against short-term cost savings and balancing effective local marketing with economies of scale.

Companies must be prepared to wrestle with these challenges not just once but over and over again, because for most companies, going global doesn't happen overnight. With the obvious exception of Internet companies like Yahoo!, Google, and MySpace, companies approach geographic expansion on a step-by-step basis. They take a brand that's been successful in one market and roll it out gradually, starting with the low-hanging fruit—the markets that offer the best prospect of success and rapid recovery of investment. The scope and infrastructure of established multinational corporations (MNCs) allows them to roll brands out more quickly than local or regional companies, but even MNCs work to establish a brand in one region or cluster of markets before moving on to the next.

Business First

In the early days in any market, a business needs to be flexible, adapting to issues on the ground. The main focus must be on establishing a viable, profitable business around the company's core competency. This applies equally to small companies seeking to go global and global giants. Tony Palmer, chief marketing officer at Kimberly-Clark, is convinced that winning locally is the first step to global brand success because ultimately people buy locally.[1] He says you must garner the benefits of scale by delivering greater effectiveness or efficiency. Even at this stage, however, a company that has global aspirations for its products or services would do well to bear in mind the success factors common across markets and not allow unfettered local customization.

Many companies seek to jump-start the globalization process by acquiring local businesses. This practice usually allows a company to draw on established business infrastructures rather than having to create them from scratch. For example, purchasing a local drinks company allows a company to tap into existing relationships with the retail trade. Buying an existing telecom allows a company to use the spectrum that's already leased. Talking about Nestlé's acquisition of Gerber in the United States, Peter Brabeck, of Nestlé SA, states, "We would never have had the opportunity to build such a strong presence in the U.S. without the acquisition. It filled a regional weakness for us. But at this point it is pure speculation as to what might happen to it. You have to sit with acquisitions awhile, come to understand them, figure out how it will work."[2]

As Brabeck implies, buying a company is only the start. The real challenge is successfully integrating it with the existing business. This is never an easy task, particularly if the two companies have different cultures.

The need to put business first and establish a viable presence on the ground causes many companies to find that their brands are disjointed on a global basis. Aspiring global companies should always seek to maintain the equilibrium that promotes both brand health and profitable growth.

The Balancing Act

A public corporation has a duty to deliver profitable growth for shareholders. As we saw in Chapter 5, a strong brand is an important growth engine, yet a brand needs continued investment if it is to maintain, let alone increase, its value. A plane in flight uses the lift from its wings and the thrust from its engines to overcome gravity and gain altitude. Similarly a strong brand uses a great experience (its wings) and its marketing investments (engines) to fight off competition and gain share.

But there is an inherent tension between brand strength and business efficiency. What may be best for short-term profits may not be best for the brand, which is, after all, the long-term growth driver of the business. Undermining the brand leaves a company vulnerable to increased competition, a threat that is particularly insidious because its deleterious effects may not be immediately apparent. Strong brands do not suddenly fade or die; they can live off of previous investments and continue to hold substantial market share for years. The threat is that competitors will use innovation and savvy marketing to make their own brands more appealing. Should they succeed in doing so, the brand that has been living off its accumulated goodwill may suddenly find its market share eroding. To avoid this situation, companies must strike a balance between brand investment and profit taking. When this balance is achieved, the strength of the brand serves to multiply the returns that could be achieved by the business alone and helps to secure a stable future income stream.

Local Effectiveness versus Economies of Scale

Many companies seek to globalize in the hope that they will reap the benefits of scale not only by selling more but also by lowering their costs. They reason that economies of supply, production, and marketing ought to yield a better return on capital. But the benefits achieved through increased scale need to be balanced against the advantages of acting locally. Economies realized by adopting the same product, positioning, and communications around the world may result in less revenue growth overall if, at the local level, people do not connect with the brand. Given the power that being part of the local culture brings, a brand completely tailored to meet local needs and desires ought to be stronger than a one-size-fits-all global proposition. It is, however, almost impossible to demonstrate the value that such a brand would add to the business ahead of time. Nevertheless, you can prove how much money would be saved by *not* customizing product formulation, packaging and design, advertising and promotion. The question then becomes one of a trade-off. When does a unified approach start to seriously undermine local brand strength?

"Local Jewels"

Unilever well understands the value of existing strong local brands. As I discussed in Chapter 7, when the conglomerate reduced the size of its brand portfolio, it wasn't only the global brands that remained. Management recognized the value of a number of "local jewels," such as Marmite and the ice cream brand Ben & Jerry's. While these brands come from very different categories and cultures, they share one thing in common: Their relationship with Unilever is not actively promoted, possibly because doing so might undermine the strong local heritage that makes these brands so valuable.

A Brand Needs to Remain True to Its Promise

Whether growing a brand in one country or across continents, management needs to remain true to the brand's identity and values. When, in the pursuit of growth and business efficiency, a company veers away from the formula that originally made a brand successful, something essential to the brand may be lost. As the next example shows, when a brand loses touch with its soul, drastic action may be required to get back on track.

Starbucks Loses Its Way

In 2007, Starbucks was still a growing business abroad, but back home in the United States, those closest to the brand were voicing concerns that it was off track. In February of that year, the company's founder and chairman, Howard Schultz, wrote a memo to chief executive officer Jim Donald, expressing concerns that cost savings had eroded the Starbucks "brand experience." Jeremy Bullmore drew on this heavily publicized memo in the essay he contributed to the 2006 WPP Annual Report, in which he points out how difficult it is to prioritize investment in the "soul" of a brand over the promise of hard savings derived from efficient business practices.

Romance and Theatre

In February 2007, a remarkable memo appeared on the website starbucksgossip.com. It's been confirmed as authentic and was the text of a message sent by the founder and chairman of Starbucks Corp., Howard Schultz, to his top executives. He wrote: "Over the past 10 years, in order to achieve the growth, development, and scale necessary to go from less than 1,000 stores to 13,000 stores and beyond, we have had to make a series of decisions that, in retrospect, have led to the watering down of the Starbucks experience."

Originally, Starbucks had all its baristas pull espresso shots by hand. Then, in the interests of consistency and speed of service, they switched to automatic espresso machines. And in doing so, wrote Mr. Schultz, "We overlooked the fact that we would remove much of the romance and theatre."

Again in the interests of efficiency, they adopted flavor-locked packaging: no longer did they scoop fresh beans from bins and grind them in front of customers. Wrote Mr. Shultz: "We achieved fresh-roasted bagged coffee, but at what cost? The loss of aroma—perhaps the most powerful non-verbal signal we had in our stores."

With hindsight, he said, the outcome of these and many other well-intentioned changes was "stores that no longer have the soul of the past."

"Romance" . . . "theatre" . . . "soul": these are words that seldom appear in respectable, rigorous marketing documents. They sound flaky, subjective, and immeasurable.

The decisions that led to the loss of romance, theatre and soul at Starbucks were undoubtedly based on serious analysis. Economies of time and cost would have been scrupulously identified and numbers would have been attached. The bottom line would have been mentioned more than once. Had any underling, or outside adviser, voiced instinctive apprehension—and maybe even murmured about the potential loss of romance, theatre or soul—they would have been challenging hard fact with subjective, baseless sentiment. No chance. It took the courageous Mr. Schultz, founder and chairman, to concede the error; and even then, since the company had continued to grow and prosper, he was probably relying more on his instinctive sense of rightness than on any new data.

It wasn't, of course, a mistake for Starbucks to calculate the benefits the company could enjoy by switching to automated espresso delivery. But it was a one-dimensional, outside-in analysis—and it should have been checked against an inside-out understanding of the brand: its culture, its personality, its soul—all those dodgy, flaky words that we flinch from using in case we're thought to be impractical romantics.

Unfortunately, when conceiving, describing and recommending a desired brand character, such words have to be used. They will always seem feeble and inadequate; they will always be easy targets for the skeptical. The wise client will forgive their use because they're striving to do the impossible: to make mere words evoke a rich complexity of fact and feeling that can in the end be fully appreciated only when it's been fully realized. The rewards for such trust can be priceless.[3]

I repeat this piece here because, in his inimitable way, Bullmore throws the problem faced by Starbucks into sharp relief. While Bullmore called Schultz "courageous" for recognizing that something was amiss with the brand, just recognizing the problem was not enough to turn the situation around, as over the course of 2007, Starbucks' share price declined almost 50 percent. In the third quarter, the average number of transactions per store in the United States fell for the first time ever. In January 2008, CEO Jim Donald was fired, to be replaced by Schultz. In a letter posted on the Starbucks Web site, Schultz said he was returning to the role of CEO "to share with you my personal commitment to ensuring that every time you visit our stores you get the distinctive Starbucks Experience." Speaking to analysts in early January, Schultz alluded to the brand's missteps, saying "growth and size can hide mistakes." He promised to "revitalize the romance, theater and warmth of experience" that was at the heart of Starbucks's success.

The Soul of a Value Platform: Efficiency

The same week that Schultz once again took up the CEO mantle at Starbucks, U.S. fast-food giant McDonald's announced that it was bringing baristas and espresso machines to nearly 14,000 locations in the United States to provide customers with lattes, mochas, and other specialty drinks. In an amusing counterpoint to Schultz's promises, John Betts, McDonald's vice president of national beverage strategy, explained why the new espresso machines would be located on the counter instead of behind the scenes. "You create a little bit more of a theater there," he said.

But McDonald's does not really want to be in the entertainment business. The mammoth purveyor of fast food merely wants to serve coffee to its customers— millions and millions of them. Starbucks set out to introduce Americans to a better "coffee experience," and whether the company truly sold their customers on the "experience" or not, it certainly helped the masses acquire a taste for a variety of coffee roasts and espresso drinks. Now that the market for specialty coffee drinks has been supersized, McDonald's is only too happy to step in and serve it.

It probably makes more sense for McDonald's to offer trendy coffee drinks now than it ever did for Starbucks to start offering breakfast sandwiches. Food, especially mediocre food, became a distraction from the coffee. The smell of the breakfast sandwiches in particular detracted from the ambience that Starbucks had worked so hard to create in every shop. But for good or ill, Starbucks made the first move toward bringing the two companies together in terms of their "product." Now, when about 80 percent of the orders purchased at U.S. Starbucks outlets are consumed outside the store, McDonald's has boldly taken the next step.

Starbucks may have blundered unwittingly into a competition with fast-food joints, lured on by opportunities that in retrospect seem incompatible with its core positioning. In a head-to-head battle with McDonald's, it is tough to see how Starbucks can win. McDonald's, seemingly the company with more to gain, has a history of leveraging scale and business efficiency to great effect. Its equity in the United States is strong and continues to improve (the result of its six-year turnaround program).

McDonald's upgraded its basic coffee offering in 2006, when it rolled out a darker-roast arabica coffee line nationwide, replacing the 60 different blends that the chain used to brew.[4] Now, by offering an inexpensive line of specialty coffee drinks, it is going a step further. By adding an upscale coffee offering, McDonald's should be able to improve its per-customer transaction value and possibly attract more people to stop by outside regular meal hours. (Currently many McDonald's customers just stop in for a quick take-away meal.) In January 2008, the *Wall Street Journal* reported that internal McDonald's documents say the program, which will also add smoothies and bottled beverages to the menus, will add $1 billion to McDonald's annual sales of $21.6 billion.[5]

With 20/20 hindsight, it is easy to see how Starbucks and McDonald's came to compete so directly. Now that Starbucks is facing not only a loss of romance but also direct competition from McDonald's, can it satisfy both customers and stockholders by refocusing on the coffee experience? Time will tell.

Big Is Not an Advantage unless You Are Focused

Acquisition is an important strategy when going global, but it can be very difficult to pull off successfully. After all, you do not need to look at the global scene in order to find examples of acquisitions that failed because of differing cultures and lack of focus. Over the years, large companies have made a habit of buying up small, innovative brands only to snuff the life out of them (and, in the process, lose much of the value they invested). Quaker and Snapple, Pepsi and PJ's, Kraft and Celestial Seasonings: The list goes on. What is it that dooms these acquisitions to failure?

Warwick Nash, chief executive officer, Millward Brown U.K. and Ireland, suggests that it is the need to drive volume—the "winner's curse"—that lies behind failures like these. He suggests that when the winning bidder buys a company for an inflated price, the acquirer needs to justify the purchase price through revenue growth.

Failure to achieve the necessary growth is often blamed on the departure of the entrepreneurs who made the business successful. Nash thinks that's missing the real problem. "You would have thought that production, distribution, and management are repeatable processes and that the additional marketing firepower would help boost sales," he says. "Is it really the lack of the expertise/insight/skill set of the founders that undermines the success of these companies? Perhaps it is simply as mundane as the difference between being the sales force's primary responsibility and its twentieth."[6]

When growth is an imperative, it must be accomplished while maintaining focus on the brand. Starbucks started to go astray when it decided to compete for its customers' lunch money. Scale is not an advantage if it is fragmented and efforts are diluted across conflicting priorities.

Global Scale May Undermine Local Effectiveness

Commenting on the issues facing companies on a global stage, Eric Salama, chairman and chief executive officer of Kantar, WPP's Information, Insight and Consultancy Group, believes that too many companies confuse a global structure with a truly effective global *orientation*. He observes three mistakes commonly made by companies trying to become global:

1. They seek global efficiencies without considering the subsequent impact on local effectiveness.
2. They redirect funds from their local organizations into the center without considering the subsequent impact on their local businesses.
3. They appoint global agencies with the idea of creating global campaigns for their brands without considering whether this is really appropriate for the brand or the category.

In reference to the last point, Salama states: "The cost efficiencies of cross-border advertising do not necessarily outweigh the effectiveness of local engagement."[7] He hypothesizes that Vodafone's sponsorship of the McLaren Mercedes Formula One Team with Fernando Alonso (Spanish) and Louis Hamilton (British) as lead drivers might be just such an example. As a marketing deal, it must be hugely efficient: one deal, the same ads, great media coverage across Europe. But, asks Salama, how do people react in the different countries? People in Spain and the United Kingdom might respond well, but will the Italians forsake their traditional allegiance to Ferrari? And what do the

Germans think of these foreign drivers? A local approach might better engage people and be more effective at building the brand.

Global Companies Share Common Problems

Over the course of six months, I talked to many senior managers working with global brands. They all grapple with variations of the four basic problems I describe next. The first of these problems relates to the need to balance investment in brands versus the desire to reap profit from them, while the next three all relate to the need to balance global efficiency and local effectiveness.

1. The power of the budget
2. Not invented here
3. Losing touch with local needs
4. The hidden cost: loss of local talent

The Power of the Budget

An inherent tension is created when global brand teams are rewarded for generating a consistent global strategy while local country teams are rewarded for business results. Because sales come from individual customers in specific locations, the responsibility for achieving the budget resides with the local group. The global guys can provide all the advice they like, but at the end of the day it's the local team that has to make the numbers. Under pressure, they often ignore agreed-on plans and do what they think they need to do to hit their budget. Too often they slash marketing budgets and use price promotion to drive volume to the detriment of the brand.

The problem is, once a brand has made do with less and still achieved its budget, the typical budgeting process tends to ratchet costs down rather than set funds according to the task that needs to be achieved. If you made your numbers with less this year, the thinking goes, surely you can do it again next year. Without adequate monitoring of brand equity and a clear understanding of brand objectives and what it will take to achieve them, budgets become eroded and brands weaken.

Not Invented Here

"Issues can come from a multitude of places," says Del Levin, marketing director of Colgate-Palmolive South Africa, "but 'not invented here' is the biggest."[8]

When it comes to marketing, many companies encourage local brand teams to "search and redeploy"—that is, to adopt campaigns and ads that have been used effectively elsewhere in the world. This is clearly an efficient approach.

The local company does not waste time reinventing the wheel. But unless this behavior is actively rewarded, human nature gets in the way. As one person I talked to said, "You get more credit for coming up with a new idea than reusing an old one. Besides, there is more kudos and fun to coming up with something new."

Richard Swaab, executive vice chairman at AMV BBDO, suggests that there is a constant gravitational pull as local teams try to find reasons not to adopt globally sourced thinking. He says: "I spend much of my time—and truthfully I suspect many people in agency networks do the same—getting across to local colleagues that they should be looking for why they should buy in, not why they shouldn't! In particular, we ask them to seek out strategic common ground, which is a far more productive process than trying to enforce executional uniformity."[9] He goes on to suggest that even when there are local differences in category, brand, or advertising relationships, brands still may be built from the same DNA.

"Not invented here" is not a one-way street from local to global. It can operate the other way too, when the global business ignores the needs of the local one.

Losing Touch with Local Needs

Ralph Blessing, formerly with Unilever and Helene Curtis in the United States, and now with the Arbor Strategy Group in Chicago, believes there are definite advantages to operating global brands. "If you have 18 different formula bases and multiple suppliers for your brand, it makes it very tough to upgrade. It's much easier if you only have one or two." He remembers back to his Unilever days, when the company dealt with 11 different fragrance houses for the Suave brand alone. The company saved millions of dollars by reducing the number of fragrance houses.

While recognizing the advantages derived from a more consistent, globalized approach, Blessing also sees a couple of traps that must be avoided.

The most dangerous trap, according to Blessing, has to do with responsiveness to innovation opportunities, particularly to those he characterizes as Horizon 1 (in-category) innovations (see Table 10.1). If the global team is not in constant touch with the local team, they may miss important opportunities for in-category innovation. Often, even if they recognize a need, they may be slow to react.

One of the reasons that Blessing believes innovation slows when under the control of a central team is the need to get buy-in from the local companies and avoid the not-invented-here syndrome. This is particularly true of longer-term innovation (Horizons 2 and 3 in the table). Global teams are apt to focus on

Table 10.1 Innovation Horizons

	Horizon 1	Horizon 2	Horizon 3
Description	Innovation of existing technology, product and positioning	Category extension with new products	Completely new technology, category or audience
Problem	Global team may miss near-term, local opportunities	Innovation becomes slow, process-laden and appeals to the lowest common denominator	
Resolution	Let key local markets lead	Ensure a long pipeline	

large-scale projects with wide geographic potential. In order to avoid the not-invented-here syndrome, they then try to involve key market stakeholders. But coordinating meetings and action on a global scale is a logistical nightmare. Even with the best will in the world, timelines lengthen. Of course, tardy innovation is not the only problem with processes that seek buy-in from all concerned. Scale brings inertia and can allow nimbler competitors, closer to the action, to step in to seize an opportunity before the bigger organization can even agree that there is one.

The second trap is a natural consequence of close teamwork. "When you have just one team working on innovation, the lifeblood of any brand, it is too easy to get 'groupthink,'" says Blessing. Even though a global team's remit is to innovate globally, it can be tough for them not to be influenced by their own knowledge and their understanding of the organization's needs. For example, if the United States is the big, developed market making a far better return than developing markets with very low margins, it will be able to command more attention with the central team and senior management. The innovation agenda could become more driven by the U.S. agenda and less by that of the developing markets, even though the real growth opportunities lay with the latter.

The Hidden Cost: Loss of Local Talent

One further problem occurs in companies that have pursued an aggressive policy of centralization: an insidious downward spiral by which the entrepreneurial spirit leaches out of the company's local operations.

When strategy, product, and advertising innovation are handled on a global or regional basis, the local company is often left with little more than implementation and activation. Because these tasks are generally considered less creative and exciting, talented people are likely to desert the local offices, either leaving the company altogether or taking a job at one of its power centers. In the short term, their absence may not be noticed, but in the longer-term, if competition heats up or the company decides to reverse its trend to central control, they may be missed, and it may be difficult to replace them if the positions offered by the local company seem to offer little more than order-taking.

The first problem I've described is a variant of the traditional battle between marketing and sales; it is simply played out on a global scale. The second problem will be familiar to anyone trying to run a business divided across tasks and geographies. Even housing people in separate buildings on the same site can lead to a loss of purpose and a divergence in goals. Operating globally simply magnifies the problem. The third and fourth problems are, however, inherent in a global organization trying to leverage economies across countries and cultures. We return to the potential solutions to these problems in chapter 12, as we work our way through three steps to growing a successful global brand.

Key Points to Take Away

- Brands need to leverage their company's scale, not get lost in it.
- Chasing revenue without due consideration of what your brand stands for can undermine long-term value.
- Global companies face four common problems:

  1. The power of the budget
  2. Not invented here
  3. Losing touch with local needs
  4. The loss of local talent

Questions to Consider

1. Is the balance between brand building and cost efficiency right for your brand or are you jeopardizing its future growth?
2. Are the members of your global brand team aligned in their understanding of what your brand stands for?
3. Is the team motivated to share learning and quickly adopt ideas from elsewhere?

For more information related to these questions, visit theglobalbrandonline.com.

Part Three

Practices that Help Build Successful Global Brands

In this section of the book, I outline some of the key practices that can help build a successful global brand.

When thinking about the process of extending a brand to multiple countries, I think the analogy of the Rubik's Cube is a good one. Just as a Rubik's Cube can present a wide range of initial color combinations, so too every country presents a different combination of challenges. Just as a consistent set of moves will solve the puzzle, some general practices will help solve those local challenges. The end result may not be the same in every country, but a common approach will help in the process of creating a strong, valuable global brand.

As we saw in Part Two, there are many potential challenges to be overcome in going global. By applying due diligence, insight, and organizational skills, you can figure out what will work for your brand.

To reap the benefits of scale, there must be some degree of commonality to your brand offering across countries, but how much will be dictated by a variety of interlocking factors. Chapter 11 takes a step-by-step look at the factors that dictate whether you can build a consistent global brand or not. What commonalities can you build around? What differences must you take into account?

Most successful global brands are founded on a brand promise that appeals to consumers around the world. Typically this promise is built on a rational or emotional benefit, using a consistent approach wherever possible. Chapter 12 discusses how tapping into human motivations can facilitate this process.

Chapter 13 considers the issues involved in communicating your brand promise on a global basis. What barriers to engagement do you need to overcome? Which local communication channels will help achieve those objectives? Does your creativity have the power to travel?

Market research can play a huge role in helping to uncover the crucial insights that can help create a global brand. It is also an important means of tracking progress and identifying effective strategies and tactics. Chapter 14 suggests how to use research to best effect.

A successful global brand does not operate independently of the business to which it belongs. One of the biggest challenges faced in growing and maintaining a global brand is ensuring that the brand team is organized to realize the benefits of scale. Chapter 15 discusses the critical issues involved in aligning the brand team across borders.

The world is changing fast. Chapter 16 examines some of the macrotrends facing marketers today and considers the future implications for global brands. While many have assumed world culture will become more homogeneous, there are signs that increasing standards of living and the spread of communications technology are creating as much divergence as convergence. On the basis of the available evidence, I conclude that strong brands will have a strong future, but one-size-fits-all marketing will not.

Chapter 11

Understand Commonalities and Differences

In this chapter, I take a step-by-step look at the factors that dictate whether you can build a consistent global brand or not. What commonalities can you build around? What differences must you take into account?

Different Categories Force Different Degrees of Globalization

The driving force behind the global imperative differs across product and service categories; in some categories, a global presence is truly necessary for a brand to remain competitive, while in others, expanding globally is simply an attractive option for growth.

In the business-to-business arena (B2B), if you hope to serve companies with a global presence, you need to match their geographic reach. B2B companies like IBM, Cisco, and Millward Brown, for example, need to be able to match their capabilities to their customers' needs wherever they are in the world. Major global customers want to get consistent service across countries and may choose to consolidate business with one company as a result.

On the consumer side, companies that sell high-ticket items—cars, durable goods, and high-tech products—will also find themselves at a disadvantage if they remain local. These items have long innovation cycles, requiring major investment in research and development. A company that can sell the same product in many countries will recover its investment faster than one that is limited to a small number of markets.

Cars and durable goods such as home appliances do need to be modified to satisfy consumer needs in particular countries—for example, geography influences driving conditions, and small homes need correspondingly small appliances—but this has more to do with local conditions than local culture. Similarly, high-tech consumer goods are less susceptible to the impact of culture.

This is because these items often serve as channels for communication or content; they are not ends in themselves. You use your mobile phone to talk to friends and family, your MP3 player to listen to music, and your flat-screen TV to watch news, sports, and weather. Items designed with ease of use in mind will readily travel across countries, as the eye-hand coordination and manual dexterity of citizens don't vary across societies. Although what is considered to be "good" design may be subject to local opinions, today's high-tech companies aim to give their brands a common look and feel across countries, seeking to differentiate one brand from another rather than indulging local tastes.

At the other end of the spectrum are food, household cleaning, and personal care products. These products will almost always need to be localized because they are rooted in local taste, traditions, culture, and physical needs.

Food is a case in point. Many food brands are inescapably local. Simon Rothon, senior vice president of Unilever Marketing Services puts it this way, "Apart from language and traditions, food defines national identity more than anything I know."

"Our Knorr brand must be adapted to match the meal type," he explains. "Even so, there are some standard meal types around the world. For example, the combination of carbohydrate, protein, and sauce is almost universal. So Knorr can be adapted to offer a relevant flavoring to that three-part combination and production, supply chain, and marketing adapted to deliver the right mix for each country."[1]

When it comes to beverages to accompany a meal, however, Rothon sees more scope for a common offering. Beverages, after all, have a common base of water or milk, and serve a common purpose: to provide hydration and to wash down food. So Lipton Iced Tea represents a universal concept that can be presented the same way around the world.

Seeking Commonalities in Complexity

In Chapter 10, I suggested that the key to global success is winning locally while realizing the advantages offered by global scale. Speaking of the complexity of this task, Peter Brabeck, chairman and chief executive of Nestlé SA states: "There is no simple answer. The real challenge is to combine an understanding of the complexity of the situation with operational efficiency."[2] In other words, a global brand should aspire to be as consistent as possible *within* the constraints of local market conditions and culture.

Consumer insight—or market research—has a critical role to play in identifying the right point of balance between local needs and global consistency, but it has to be used appropriately. Market researchers are taught to look for differences: across demographic groups, across countries, and across time. We even apply statistical tests to help identify these differences. But the real trick lies in looking for commonalities, not differences. Where differences do exist across countries, the question should be "Are these differences important?" not "Are they statistically significant?"

Geographic Brand Stretch

Thus far in the book, I have played fast and loose with the definition of "local." I have used the term in reference to specific locations, countries, or regions. Now I need to get specific. Which local market needs really matter? Which ones can you safely ignore? How far will the different aspects of your brand stretch?

If you already have a brand that is distributed on an international basis, the factors dictating its success or failure in different countries should be obvious. It is a matter of classifying these factors and clustering the different markets into homogeneous groups. If you are a local brand contemplating going global, then you need to either embark on a journey of trial and error or use research to anticipate what will stretch successfully.

In both cases, it is critical to figure out what commonalities might serve globalization and what differences might impede it. In the case of toothpaste, for instance, there may be a common need for clean teeth around the world and a consistent approach to cleaning teeth, but beliefs about what makes teeth healthy differ. The focus in the United States is on clinical prevention; in China, the focus is dictated by traditions of herbal medicine. The same base formulation can be used across countries, but flavors and marketing should be adapted to suit local beliefs. In other categories, the product might be completely consistent, but differing market development dictates a different communication strategy.

Eight Dimensions that Need to Be Considered

Here I consider the eight factors likely to influence the approach a brand may take to going global:

1. Political and legal issues
2. Practical and logistical constraints
3. Socioeconomic factors
4. Physical needs
5. Local tastes, preferences, and customs
6. Competitive context
7. Local understanding of marketing and advertising
8. Brand status

In many cases, you probably can summarize the outcome of your analysis in a matrix of geographies and brand assets. Working through this Rubik's Cube will help define whether the brand can pursue a unified approach or not.

Political and Legal Issues

On the surface, it might seem that political and legal issues have more to do with the business than the brand. In many cases, however, these issues have a direct impact on the ability to market the brand effectively. The differences in laws across countries and regions not only have important ramifications for global businesses but also affect product composition and communication. Is the brand allowed to use specific ingredients? Are you allowed to advertise the category at all? For example, advertising for alcohol and tobacco is subject to a variety of different advertising standards around the world.

Practical and Logistical Constraints

In developing countries, you may need to overcome infrastructure issues simply to make sure your brand can get to market. Transportation in landlocked countries, such as Uganda, Zambia, and Zimbabwe, is very different from transportation in an archipelago, such as the Philippines, which is made up of over 7,000 islands. And what about local standards and living conditions? These might make your product category less relevant to consumers.

Logistical decisions often have consequences that impact the marketing of a brand. In an article in *Brand Packaging*, writer Randall Frost gives the example of Hewlett-Packard's need to find the right packaging to protect its consumer electronics products.[3] Frost quotes Randy Boeller, a manager on Hewlett-Packard's global packaging team, in reference to the need to localize packaging in terms of language: "When you increase the number of languages on a package, and reduce that real estate, the marketing guys have to be really good at communicating with the customer." The decision to produce centrally or locally is not just a matter of logistics and costs; there are ramifications for marketing and communication too.

Socioeconomic Factors

Socioeconomic factors are likely to impact many aspects of the brand offer, from product design to pricing and communication. As we have seen, differences in disposable income will have an enormous impact on the nature of the brand offer. Products may need to be made more economical to use or sold in smaller unit sizes to make them affordable. Alternatively, a brand might decide not to adapt to the market and reap the rewards of higher margins but lower volume sales.

Physical Needs

Some physical needs are the same the world over. In explaining how Gillette's Fusion came to be a truly consistent global brand, an ex-employee of the company pointed out the common need: "Men's need to shave whiskers is virtually the same around the world." The nature of the product means that it is easy to globalize. "It is made at one factory and so is absolutely identical across the world. Its size and low weight mean you can ship it where needed."

Not all physical needs are so consistent. Speaking of shampoo in Asia, Karen Hamilton of Unilever says, "Asian hair is very different from Caucasian or Black hair. You need to physically tailor the product to suit the individual hair type."[4] By contrast, Hamilton suggests that there is no compelling evidence to suggest that antiperspirants work differently on different skin types.

Local Tastes, Preferences, and Customs

The existence of a common need does not always allow a brand to pursue a common strategy or even offer a common product. For example, an elevated level of cholesterol is recognized as a risk factor in developing cardiovascular disease. Many doctors, therefore, encourage people to lower their cholesterol level through a variety of means, including diet. The potential benefit is universal. However, in offering people solutions to their cholesterol problems, Unilever needed to create different products for different markets in Europe.

Unilever recognized the opportunity to address concerns about cholesterol through products that provide the balance of polyunsaturated fats that can help reduce levels of HDL (bad) cholesterol while boosting the LDL (good) variety. In northern Europe, where butter is commonly used, Unilever marketed a new margarine brand under the names of Flora/Becel/Promise with the claim that the product can lower cholesterol provided the daily intake is at a certain level. But in Spain and Italy, butter consumption is far lower—typically below the level required for the polyunsaturated fats to have a positive influence. For these countries, different products were needed. In Spain, the marketing team chose milk as the carrier, launching the product under the Flora pro.activ name, and in Italy, the company launched Maya pro.activ, small containers of a yogurt-like shot, to provide the same cholesterol-lowering end benefit but using a different delivery system.

Expectations can play a major role in the acceptance of brands. In the United Kingdom, there used to be an expectation that darker beers were higher in alcohol. Many years ago, when I worked for Millward Brown in the United Kingdom, I was responsible for conducting a great many product tests for beers. On two separate occasions, I tested Budweiser from the United States and Castlemaine XXXX from Australia among local beer drinkers. In both cases, people thought that the beers looked weak. Because both beers had a significant alcohol content, I recommended that the colors be changed to match local expectations.

Castlemaine XXXX changed its color; the King of Beers refused to do so. Although Castelmaine XXXX also benefited from an effective launch campaign, the beer's darker color was an important factor in making its launch more successful than that of Budweiser.

Local customs may also dictate a different perception of the category itself. Here in the United States, people think nothing of chugging down a Coke or Pepsi to give them their first caffeine hit of the day. That places colas in direct competition with coffee.

Competitive Context

This is where things get really complex! Unless you are in the fortunate position of creating the category in a country based on success elsewhere, much as Red Bull has done, then it is highly likely that a strong incumbent is going to be the biggest barrier to success. As I noted in Chapter 9, this is particularly problematic if the incumbent already owns the positioning that you have established elsewhere in the world. Retail structure, relationships with the trade, and the media environment will all have important implications for how easy it will be to create a strong brand presence in the new country.

In some cases, establishing awareness of a brand can simply be more difficult in one country than another. Looking at Millward Brown's brand communication database, we observe that in countries where there is a lot of advertising clutter on TV, such as Italy, Spain, Hong Kong, the United States, and Japan, ad efficiency scores are lower than in countries where clutter is low, such as Denmark and Belgium. In other words, advertising has less impact per GRP (gross rating point) because it has to fight for attention. Thus a greater level of media investment is required to have an effect and reach the desired levels of brand awareness.

Local Understanding of Marketing and Advertising

The kinds of advertising consumers see everyday varies enormously across countries, for both cultural and economic reasons. This is an important fact, because it is people's experience with advertising that will shape their expectations of it. It will also, of course, influence their interpretation of advertised messages. On average, 12 percent of the ads in Millward Brown's Link advertising pretest database are intended to be funny. But across countries, the percentage of ads relying on humor varies widely. In Spain and Netherlands, the figure is over 20 percent whereas in many Asian countries, it is under 5 percent.

Ads with implicit messaging depend on a degree of advertising "literacy" among their audience to get their intended messages across. Such ads tend to work better in countries where esoteric advertising with implicit messages is commonplace. These ads will be less effective in countries where explicit messaging is more common and people expect ads to deliver rational claims and benefits.

Brand Status

Another factor that will influence the effectiveness of a brand's communication is the brand's status in its category. If, for an established brand, you intend to recycle copy from elsewhere in the world, you need to bear this fact in mind. For example, ads with implicit messages tend to work best in countries where the brand is very highly regarded and familiar; in these circumstances, the brand has "permission" to invite the consumer to connect the dots. Where the brand is less well known and has lower status, though, consumers are less inclined to make the effort to fill in the gaps. Thus implicit messages are less effective.

In one example, the same ad for an "indulgent" food brand worked well in France but not in Spain, where the basic brand positioning was not understood as well. In another case, a pan-European campaign failed to work well in some countries because the basic brand proposition was not established. In Germany, the problem was exacerbated because people there associated the positioning with another, bigger brand. As a result, almost twice as many people attributed the ad to the competitive brand.

Brand equity research can play an important role in establishing which countries can sensibly be grouped together in terms of brand status. In one project conducted for a multinational corporation's brand, we identified three country clusters, as shown in Table 11.1.

Table 11.1 Clustering Countries for a Global Brand

Cluster	Countries	Status	Action
1	U.S., Mexico, Brazil, Poland, South Africa	Well known but no advantage established beyond cost of entry efficacy	Find ways to add differentiating benefits and/or establish advantage more convincingly
2	U.K., Germany, Turkey, Argentina, Australia	Well known but lacks emotional appeal	Seek ways to establish a stronger emotional connection with target audience
3	France, Italy, Chile, Thailand, Japan	Little known	Create presence and establish what brand stands for

The communication task is clearly different for each cluster, although the same advertising idea could work well for more than one cluster. For example, advertising that differentiates the brand in an emotionally appealing way could work well for both clusters 1 and 2.

Balance Global Scale with Local Effectiveness

Faced with a matrix of all the differences that might exist across countries and cultures, an aspiring global marketer might conclude that no consistent approach can be effective everywhere. For some brands, that may be true, but often it is simply a matter of finding the right balance between global scale and local effectiveness. As noted in previous chapters, the philosophy of most large multinationals is that global should take precedence over local in order to realize economies of scale. There are definitely risks and costs associated with going too local.

Ralph Blessing, formerly with Unilever and Helene Curtis in the United States, and now with the Arbor Strategy Group in Chicago, warns that focusing too intently on a local environment may cause you to lose sight of what made your brand successful in the first place: "Don't walk away from the core proposition just because it is a different country."[5]

He cites the example of the shampoo brand Suave. The U.S. division of Helene Curtis (which owned Suave before Unilever purchased the brand) had successfully established the brand with the proposition "Works as well as the expensive brands for less." But the international division of Helene Curtis was separate from the U.S. company. As a result, in Canada, the brand was launched with a different positioning (not as value oriented) as well as different packaging and a different price point. In Mexico, the brand was placed adjacent to more expensive brands (using a strategy similar to many store brands, trying to draw attention to the price differential). The lack of a consolidated facing diluted the brand's in-store presence and undermined the trial-building effects of mass-media support. In neither case did the brand achieve success as it did in the United States.

Finally, you cannot ignore the cost side of the equation. Can you really afford to optimize every aspect of the brand for each market? Del Levin at Colgate uses the word "bundle" to describe the combination of brand idea, product, and packaging. He suggests that in order to leverage economies of scale, the global bundle should be tried before other options. "The maxim should be globalize to the extent we can," he says. In response to the inevitable local push back, he recommends testing the global idea. "If it works, great. If not, adapt it."[6]

Key Points to Take Away

- The driving force behind taking a brand global differs across product and service categories.
- As Peter Brabeck explains, "The real challenge [to winning locally while realizing the advantages offered by global scale] is to combine an understanding of the complexity of the situation with operational efficiency."
- The objective should be to identify commonalities and differences across the eight key dimensions, focusing on the commonalities:

  1. Political and legal issues
  2. Practical and logistical constraints
  3. Socioeconomic factors
  4. Physical needs
  5. Local tastes, preferences, and customs
  6. Competitive context
  7. Local understanding of marketing and advertising
  8. Brand status

Questions to Consider

1. What is the driving force behind your brand's global imperative? What are the implications for profit expectations?
2. What does the matrix of geographies and brand assets look like for your brand? What are the commonalities? What are the differences you must take into account?
3. What do your answers tell you about the right balance between global scale and local effectiveness for your brand?

For more information related to these questions, visit theglobalbrandonline.com.

Chapter 12

Identify a Global Brand Promise

A consistent global brand promise is a very desirable asset. Identifying something that works across countries and cultures in a way that differentiates your brand and motivates people to buy it is a big step toward unlocking the economies of scale. When you have a consistent brand promise, it becomes more likely that you can share brand assets across markets, perhaps by using the same base product formulation, service offer, or advertising. If something works well in one country or region, a common promise will make it more likely to work well elsewhere. But although the search for a common brand promise is desirable, it must not lead to a bland platitude that motivates no one.

Creating Mass Appeal Is a Big Challenge

The biggest challenge in marketing is not creating a brand. There will always be a market for niche, upscale brands—Innocent, Camper, Gevalia, Patagonia, Williams-Sonoma—that appeal to specific consumer segments. The Internet is making it far easier to reach the long tail of consumers whose tastes diverge from the mainstream. The real challenge is to take a brand and give it mass appeal that transcends its origins. If your analysis of similarities and differences across markets suggests that there are strong commonalities, you may be able to identify a globally appealing promise. Some brands have established a strong, consistent emotional connection across cultures by tapping into fundamental human truths: the commonalities that unite rather than divide people around the globe, such as the desire for love, health, and happiness. Such a platform opens up real opportunities to make your marketing budget work more efficiently, but finding the right idea can be a tough challenge.

Who Is Your Target Audience?

It is easier for any brand to generate loyalty from a well-defined and delineated target group, whether it is smokers, information technology decision makers, or teenage boys. If a brand can identify a target audience with the same needs around the world, the opportunity for a one-size-fits-all positioning is obviously far greater than if it is dealing with a fragmented audience.

Many high-tech business-to-business brands have been able to globalize successfully because their target audience is very consistent. Not only is the target group typically well off and well educated, many of them need to speak English in order to do their jobs properly. Cisco, for example, is global in scope and serves a wide array of needs but in a very consistent fashion. Technical innovation drives its marketing agenda.

Commenting on whether there really is such a thing as a global consumer, Karen Hamilton of Unilever suggests that some groups are more homogenous than others. "The preoccupations of youth are universal," she says, going on to list lifestyle, leisure time, school, music, and "the Mating Game" as being concerns shared by young people irrespective of gender or culture.

"The Mating Game" is, of course, a reference to the promise made by Unilever's successful Axe brand (or Lynx, as it is known in the United Kingdom). Since its launch in France, the brand has gone from strength to strength and country to country with the promise that it will help young guys get girls—according to one TV ad, billions of them. Hamilton recounts the recent launch of Axe in Japan to show how a global platform can produce cost savings. She explains that the local team was at first intent on completely customizing the offering to the Japanese market, but ultimately they adopted the core proposition, product, benefit, name and design, only adapting the fragrance level. The launch ran across multiple communication channels using a mix of global and local creative talent.

It is easier to identify common motivations that can ladder up to a compelling and differentiating brand promise for a homogenous target audience than for a widely disparate one. If your brand promise is to meet this challenge, without running afoul of or getting boxed in by local culture, it must be rooted in essential aspects of human nature—those that are common to people around the world.

Human Nature Is Consistent around the World

Chapter 8 provided some fascinating insights into the factors that make brands successful in Africa. While these success factors are deeply rooted in the local culture and context of the different African countries, the authors of that chapter have managed to highlight broad themes that run across all of them. Many of the factors they identify relate back to human nature. They are traits common to human beings around the world, regardless of race, color, or creed; the traits are simply mediated by differing economic, structural, and social circumstances.

As suggested in that chapter, people who live in the West live a much more individualistic and isolated life, separated from the broad crush of humanity by iPods, cars, and concrete walls. Much of our communication is filtered by technology, and we are denied the opportunity to sense the nonverbal responses of the people we are talking to. Underneath the trappings of the developed world, however, we still have the same basic responses to the environment around us as people in Africa and elsewhere. When I talk about human nature, I am referring to the motivations—the drives and emotions—that underpin our behavior. Safety is one of the strongest drives. One of the main reasons that western brands are trusted in developing countries is because they promise a safe choice versus local, and possibly less responsible, manufacturers. Many people need to demonstrate their success and use brands to publicize their status, whether it is by being seen using Surf detergent or driving a luxury Mercedes.

Culture varies, but human nature is the same everywhere. While it does not dictate the behavior of individuals, human nature does make them more inclined to act in one way than another. By contrast, the cultural differences we observe, based on habits and values, are not inherent but acquired. Rooting the brand promise in some aspect of human nature is likely to maximize the chance that it will work across countries, provided you can do so in a way that differentiates the brand from its competitors.

Motivations Transcend Culture

As marketers, we want to influence people's buying behavior. Drs. Valerie Curtis, senior lecturer in hygiene promotion, and Robert Aunger, senior lecturer in evolutionary public health, of the London School of Hygiene & Tropical Medicine, propose three different types of behavior: reactive, motivated, and executive.

Reactive behavior is instinctive. We react automatically, without thought, to environmental cues. The response is short-lived. An example would be jerking a hand away from a hot object.

Motivated behavior is goal oriented and intended to solve a need and achieve a desirable end state. For example, hunger will cause someone to look for food in order to satisfy that hunger.

Executive behavior relies on the ability to visualize and plan to achieve strategic objectives. This ability allows an individual to override a motivated response in order to achieve a higher-order goal and so achieve a long-term objective. An example would be working through lunch to complete an assignment on time. This makes the worker, who hopes for a promotion some day, look good to the boss.

A chemical/neurological guidance system keeps behavior on track toward specific goals; dopamine and other neurotransmitters are released when progress is being made. Chemicals are also released when the goal state is reached, which reinforces the behavior. The combination of motivations will help the individual weigh and select the best course of action at any one time, given what has worked best in the animal's evolutionary history and in its own lifetime. Intriguingly, we can see how this reinforcement mechanism might lead to the sort of heuristics and habitual behaviors described in chapter 1.

Tapping into a Basic Motivation Is the First Step to a Global Brand Promise

Reactive behavior can lead to us learning specific responses. For instance, children have to learn the hard way that touching hot things leads to pain, even if the basic physical response is part of our evolutionary programming. Some habitual responses to brands involve reactive behavior. For example, if people are bonded to a brand, they may recognize the package by its color and reach for it. However, this will happen only if the connection between brand and color has been established, and the behavior—purchasing that brand—has become habitual. At the other end of the scale, executive behavior involves a significant amount of cognition. Cognitive thought is heavily influenced by local culture and customs, making it more difficult to find a common platform for many product and service categories.

Motivated behavior, however, is consistent and operates more at the level of the gut than the head. Motivations do not need to be consciously felt to operate; nor do their purposes have to be comprehended. Motivations help animals adapt to their circumstances, survive, and prosper. Table 12.1 gives examples of motivations and related adaptive needs.

Note that, unlike marketers, Curtis and Aunger make a distinction between "emotions" and "feelings." They use the term "emotion" to represent a particular type of motivation for behavior, specifically those which relate to improving our social state. What marketers might typically call "emotions" are defined by Curtis and Aunger as "feelings," which, they say, evolved later than emotions. Feelings do not motivate behavior; rather, they are sources of reflection on behavior, which also allow us to imagine what the result of our actions will be, and help us make better decisions in the future. To show how motivations might lead to feelings I have suggested some that might relate to each motivation in the right-hand column of Table 12.1.

Combinations of these basic motivations produce myriad different human needs, which manifest themselves across cultures; identity, achievement, self-worth, stability, fitness, safety, beauty, and justice are just a few. Satisfaction of these needs can lead to positive feelings.

Table 12.1 Human Motivations

Motivation	Adaptive Need	Related Feeling
Hunger, thirst	Provide body with resources	Satisfaction, enjoyment
Comfort	Put self in optimal environment (temperature, humidity, noise, physical obstruction, etc.)	Relaxation, tranquility
Fear	Avoid physical damage (predation, accidents)	Rejection
Disgust	Avoid disease (parasites, pathogens)	Revulsion
Parental love	Put offspring in optimal conditions (nurture)	Caring, affection
Pair-bond love	Get investment in offspring care to assist gene copies to replicate	Love, affection
Attraction	Maximize mate value; humans are attracted to mates who will be good parents	Desire
Status	Maximize social position to get benefits	Victorious, successful
Affiliation	Do what others are doing to be acceptable to the group	Connection, appreciation
Morality	Maximize reciprocal social benefits through cooperation	Righteous, honest
Play	Learn skills	Enjoyment, curiosity

Motivations, therefore, provide a foundation on which to build your global brand promise. The challenge is to identify which one works best with what your brand can offer.

Motivating People to Wash Their Hands

Today many brands are seeking to cross cultural boundaries by appealing to common motivations. Marketers might learn something relevant from a surprising source—work done in Africa promoting good hygiene, specifically hand washing. It turns out that one of the basic human motivations—disgust—is being used to save thousands of lives.

In Africa, 65 percent of all deaths are caused by infection. By contrast, the proportion in the United Kingdom is only 5 percent. The Global Public Private Partnership for Hand Washing (www.globalhandwashing.org/index.html) was created in order to help change behavior and reduce the number of people who die from infections caused by dirty hands. Speaking at a Millward Brown seminar, Dr. Curtis joked, "The only place that Colgate-Palmolive, Procter & Gamble, and Unilever talk to each other is at the meetings of the Global Public-Private Partnership for Hand Washing." Of course, their interest in the initiative is not purely altruistic. Getting more people to wash their hands with soap could reduce the incidence of diarrhea by 47 percent and save at least a million lives;[1] it will also help sell an awful lot more soap. The key question, however, is what motivation will best encourage people to start washing their hands?

The cultural acceptance of hand washing differs from country to country. Where it is practiced, it is largely habitual. Dr. Curtis contrasted mothers in Ghana, who learned to wash their hands as children and accept it as something they have always done, with mothers in Kurdistan, who said "Nobody ever washes their hands with soap round here," "Nobody taught me to do this," "It's not important." What the partnership needs to do is find the right motivation to get people to start washing their hands and help it become a habit.

Just telling people that hand washing is good for their health is not enough to change behavior. Mothers in developing countries do not see diarrhea as a serious illness, and when it becomes so they do not connect it with its true cause; they assume it must have been caused by something else: the evil eye, stepping on an egg, or a change in the weather. The logic chain from dirty hands to germs to illness does not work for them. Add to that the fact that the future health of a child is not an immediate, urgent concern compared to getting water and buying food, and teaching is just not going to have the desired effect.

Many brands face exactly the same problem. Repeatedly extolling a brand's virtues is not going to get people to buy when there are many other things competing for their attention. What you have to do is engage their attention and establish the relevance of the brand to them.

With this in mind, the partnership has explored what motivations might help them achieve their goal. They found a universally powerful motivator: the basic human motivation of disgust. As Curtis put it, "The voices of our ancestors say stay away from disgusting stuff because it might make you sick. It is not planned, logical, or rational."[2] She added that disgust keeps us away from the things that might harm us from the inside, just as fear kept our ancestors away from the snakes and saber-tooth tigers that could have inflicted harm from the outside.

How Can You Use a Relevant Motivation to Differentiate Your Brand?

The real issue for a brand is not identifying a relevant motivation but building a differentiating promise around a relevant motivation. Doing this requires finding a point of connection between what the brand can uniquely offer and people's needs, desires, and aspirations—which is by no means easy. Many brands struggle to find a differentiating promise based on a motivation.

Mothers are motivated to care for their children, but how do you turn that motivation into something a brand can own? Identifying that "insight" is crucial to unlocking the power of your brand and creating a promise that will transcend culture. Research has an important role to play in the process of identifying insights like these, and I return to how it can help do so in Chapter 14.

Even though most people have a tough time vocalizing what motivations underlie their behavior, they find it easy to describe their needs. Typically these needs, once you dig into what people really mean, fall into three basic groups: functional, emotional, and identity.

Shared Functional Needs

People buy products because they need to achieve some functional end. They may buy a particular brand as a means to demonstrate their status or signal which tribe they belong to, but if that brand does not deliver a functional benefit, their allegiance will be short-lived. As we saw from the BrandDynamics Pyramid in Chapter 3, product performance is a key stage in the development of a strong bond between consumer and brand. That is why innovation is so critical to long-term brand success. A brand must deliver a consistently good experience in order to stave off the competition. Many brands today seek to create an emotional connection with consumers while seeming to forget the functional benefits that people are also looking for. This lack of attention to product-based benefits seems strange, considering that one of today's best-known brands owes its success to very strong functional credentials and almost no use of the traditional mechanisms of brand building, such as broadcast advertising.

Google: Meeting Modern-Day Needs

Few people today come into contact with snakes or saber-tooth tigers, but many of us around the world feel overwhelmed by information. We seek out information that may help us, and we feel fearful that we will miss out on something important. Google offers a promise of empowerment: "to organize the world's information and make it universally accessible and useful." And Google delivers on that promise. The brand's initial growth in the United States was fueled by word of mouth, because people were eager to tell friends and family about the search engine that really did seem to work better than others. Yahoo!, Lycos, and HotBot were forced to adapt to the changing standard represented by Google. A whopping 44 percent of U.S. Internet users are bonded to Google, and 73 percent agree that it returns the most relevant links to your search criteria. While only 21 percent of people say they have recommended Yahoo! to others, 43 percent of respondents claim to have recommended Google.

Google continues to provide accurate search results, and it has expanded its domain to include e-mail, photo-sharing, online documents, and other useful tools. These applications work well and are free, creating even stronger allegiance to the brand, while also drawing more eyeballs to fuel the company's business model. Adding to the brand's strong functional benefits is the authenticity of the garage-to-riches story of the company's founding by Larry Page and Sergey Brin. Today the company's innovative, egalitarian, and playful image is in tune with the times but at odds with that of many big corporations.

Shared Emotional Needs

Most people, irrespective of country and culture, enjoy spending time with their families. Combine that with a promise of fun, and you have the winning combination that helps make Disney theme parks so successful. Many brands have succeeded by appealing to these basic human motivations. Apple, for example, embodies the belief that everybody has the right to express their individual creativity. Nike taps into the desire to make the most of our abilities. Coca-Cola has also tried to tap into the basic motivations of fun and friendship. None of these brands, however, can afford to forget the functional need that they serve. Disney must deliver on its promise of entertainment. Nike products need to help people perform better. Coke needs to be refreshing and taste good. As we shall see in the next chapter, brands like these have permission to use higher-order emotional needs as the basis for their communications because their functional credentials are so well known that they are accepted as a given by most people.

Shared Identity Needs

The most famous luxury goods brands are not global by chance; these brands depend more than others on values that are largely symbolic and intangible. Louis Vuitton attracts thousands of people from around the world to shop at its flagship stores because of the aspirational nature of the brand. For some, possession of one of Vuitton's iconic, monogrammed bags is a signal of achievement and status. But brands can signal many other more specific aspects of a person's identity and "tribal" affiliations. A person who wears Patagonia clothes is making a statement about an outdoor, ecofriendly lifestyle (even if she never makes it out of the city). Someone who rides a Harley is espousing the identity of a rebel (even if he really works in insurance), and there is a good probability that he has a bottle of Jack Daniel's in his liquor cabinet. The statement often is not as overt as these, but our choice of brands says something about us as people, and we are drawn to brands that fit with the identity we seek to project.

Table 12.2 Positive and Negative Archetypes

Positive Character	Negative Character
Joker	Fool
Seductress	Vampire
Rebel	Anarchist
Hero	Villain
Wise	Charlatan
King	Tyrant
Mother	Stepmother
Friend	Traitor
Maiden	Witch
Dreamer	Fantasist

Archetypes offer one way to project a consistent brand persona that will be understood around the world. Archetypes are commonly understood characters—stereotypes if you like—that are found in stories and fables around the world: the wise king, the seductress, the joker or trickster. Qualitative research conducted by Millward Brown (in 14 countries during 2003) identified 10 easily recognizable archetypes found in storytelling across all cultures. These "characters" could be expressed in either a positive or a negative way. Table 12.2 lists the 10 positive and 10 negative characters.

Subsequent research and development, including pilot testing in the United Kingdom and Japan, resulted in a survey tool that assigns brands to different archetypes based on how people perceive the brands' personalities. If a brand is perceived as "playful" and "fun," it would be characterized as the joker, for example, but if it is associated more strongly with being "hasty" and "dishonest," then it would be designated a fool.

Some brands maintain remarkably consistent identities across countries and cultures. Nike is a hero, Gap a joker, Diesel a rebel, Chanel a seductress, Apple a dreamer, and Toyota the wise. For brands like these, it is relatively easy to transfer marketing communication from one country to another because the tone is likely to be consistent and appeal to similar target audiences. Honda by contrast has a fragmented identity, being seen as a joker in Canada, a seductress in Brazil, and a mother in South Africa. Because consumer perceptions of what the brand stands for are so different, it might be difficult for Honda to transfer advertising successfully between Brazil and South Africa.

Building on the Brand Promise

Earlier in the book, I highlighted the fact that while many Unilever brands share a common positioning and product across countries, the brand name may vary.

This reflects a hierarchy of importance reputedly created by Simon Clift, the company's chief marketing officer. According to this hierarchy, it is critical to identify a global brand promise—this maximizes the likelihood that brand assets can be created on a one-size-fits-all basis—but it is far less important to have a common name, because few people will seek out the same brand across countries.

Table 12.3 presents a hierarchy like the one identified by Clift. It allows us to architect an approach that makes sense for a brand across countries and cultures while retaining the ability to customize the offering as necessary to meet local needs. The table works well for food or personal care, but different product and service categories will dictate a different hierarchy. Obviously, if your target audience is international travelers, then it is far more desirable that the brand has the same name everywhere.

If you can identify a promise that works across cultures, it will be a lot easier to make the remaining components work on a unified basis. If the basic positioning can be unified, then it is likely that many of the elements farther up the hierarchy can too. Strategy combines the positioning with what the brand needs to achieve to be successful. Again, a common strategy

Table 12.3 Hierarchy of Brand Properties

Importance	Brand Asset	Rationale
Least	Name	Can differ in order to retain local familiarity
	Formulation	May need to be adapted to meet local needs
	Graphic look	May need to be adapted to meet local aesthetic or legal requirements
	Communication	Common positioning and strategy makes it easier to share communication assets
	Packaging	Common packaging format can create significant cost savings
	Strategy	What the brand needs to achieve
Most	Global promise	The idea on which the brand is built

makes it far easier to create the remaining brand assets to achieve that common purpose. From there it becomes a matter of weighing the need for a customized approach to ensure local brand success against the cost of doing so.

Obviously this hierarchy works for product categories where there is leeway to adapt to local circumstances. Some brands may not have that luxury. In every case, however, if you can identify a global promise, it makes sense to work up from there to the other aspects of the brand.

Before I close this chapter, however, let me issue a word of warning. Finding a common brand promise that is both motivating and differentiating is not for the faint of heart. Economies of scale are realized once you have found a promise that works. Unfortunately, the iterative process necessary to find such a promise takes significant time and resource and may simply confirm that it is not possible to find something that works well everywhere. If that is the case, whether it is better to be as consistent as possible or as effective as possible will become a judgment call.

Communicating Your Global Brand Promise

The Axe brand has succeeded in creating a strong brand in most of the countries in which it has been launched because it has successfully tapped into an underlying motivation in a way that engages its audience. The fact that teenage males have very similar preoccupations across cultures makes creating and redeploying content across markets relatively easy. While a brand is clearly more than how it presents itself to the world, the development of successful global advertising is one of the biggest challenges our clients face. Communication is intimately bound up with culture and makes creating effective global campaigns a big challenge. In the next chapter, we turn to the thorny issue of developing great global communication.

Key Points to Take Away

- A global brand promise helps unlock the advantages of scale but may not be easy to find.
- A promise founded in basic human motivations is likely to work across countries and culture, but it needs to be interpreted in a way that can be owned by the brand.
- Once you have created a compelling and differentiating promise, you can decide which brand assets should be kept the same and which should be adapted to meet local needs.

Questions to Consider

1. How homogeneous is your target audience? Which of their motivations are relevant to your brand?
2. How does what your brand can offer in functional, emotional, or identity terms intersect with those motivations?
3. What is your brand's hierarchy of assets?

For more information related to these questions, visit theglobalbrandonline.com.

Chapter 13

Identify How to Communicate
Your Promise

Communication: The Toughest Nut to Crack

One of the most difficult aspects of developing a global brand is creating effective, controlled communications that will highlight the brand promise across touch points, countries, and cultures. As demonstrated by Disney, Apple, and Nike, it is possible to create a brand promise that can travel. But even when a brand promise can be embodied in a global campaign, the choice of media and the individual creative executions may need to vary by country.

In this chapter, I outline an approach for working through the issues involved with creating a global campaign: finding the right communication channels with which to engage consumers along each step of their path to purchase and identifying a creative approach that will work well across those multiple touch points.

How Consistent Does Your Communication Need to Be?

Brian Fetherstonhaugh, chairman and chief executive of OgilvyOne Worldwide, says, "When someone glibly announces that they're fulfilling a longtime dream and 'going global' with their next campaign, I feel a deep chill."[1] He believes that ambition as much as business needs drives the desire for many wishing to advertise globally. After all, he suggests, there are many other ways to derive value from a strong brand without "doing another IBM" (referring to the occasion in 1994 when IBM consolidated its global advertising with Ogilvy & Mather).

Axe has been able to realize economies of scale because its basic promise easily translates into campaigns that work across cultures. The Japanese launch mentioned in Chapter 12 was able to use TV and online advertising created for other markets once the brand concept—"Helps get the girl"—had been established using locally produced executions. Although a truly global campaign is desirable for this reason, it is *necessary* only if the same consumers are going to be exposed to the same campaign across multiple countries. Such a condition applies to brands that are actively targeting the small minority of truly global customers: British Airways, Accenture, and Cisco, for example. In reviewing whether a global campaign makes sense or not, Fetherstonhaugh considers many of the factors reviewed in Chapter 10, focusing on whether the customer base is global, the brand status is consistent, the nature of the competitive context, and legal constraints. When a global campaign makes sense on these criteria, Fetherstonhaugh agrees that you need to look for an advertising idea that will work across cultural differences.

Beyond Television

It is tough not to think of communication in terms of TV advertising. After all, it is said that over 2 billion people around the world watch TV for more than three hours a day. Even in the United States, television now accounts for more than half of the time people spend with media, up from one-third in 1955. Far from watching less TV, U.S. consumers are watching more today than ever. In fact, they are spending more time with all media. The time spent with TV, radio, magazines, newspapers, and lately the Internet has doubled over the last 50 years, and that does not even take account of one of the most ubiquitous means of communication: the mobile phone. All young, well-educated people in the world are likely to have three things in common: They watch television, they access the Internet, and they carry a mobile phone.

Resequencing the Marketing Process

Tony Palmer, chief marketing officer at Kimberly-Clark, agrees that in the past, the 30-second spot developed by the marketing team tended to come first, before the idea was "thrown over the wall" to the sales team. Engaging consumers in new ways, particularly by creating a dialogue using alternative consumer touch points, is a key aspect of Palmer's marketing philosophy. Citing the example of Depend, Kimberly-Clark's adult incontinence brand, which is built around the promise of "preserving relationships through greater discretion," he explains why TV, in spite of its superior reach, is not always the right approach. "We know it is embarrassing to be seen buying them, to use them, and for others to know you use them," he said. "We have to preserve people's dignity, and we can't do a 30-second spot. Instead we need to examine alternative ways to communicate and live up to the brand promise."[2]

Palmer says, "We have to completely resequence the way we go to market," and he outlines four steps in that process:

1. Identify a compelling and differentiating brand promise.
2. Identify how to overcome barriers to engagement.
3. Identify the consumer touch points that add value.
4. Figure out which creative approach will work best.

In Chapter 12, I discussed the issues involved in finding a relevant and differentiating brand promise. In the remainder of this chapter, I consider how brands can translate that promise into effective communication.

Identify How to to Overcome Barriers to Engagement

As Palmer implies, communication planning is about problem solving. How can you best remove the barriers that prevent people from engaging with your brand? But what do we mean by "engagement"? The advertising industry has talked itself into a frenzy, asserting that "we must engage people, not interrupt them," as if this were something new and profound. The truth is that advertising has always needed to engage people, but the most important form of engagement comes when people buy and use your brand. Engagement should refer to every touch point, from initial perceptions created by TV advertising or word of mouth, to point of purchase and experience of the brand itself. And because the barriers to engagement will differ across brands, countries, and stages of the path to purchase, the solutions will be different too.

Mapping Out the Barriers to Engagement

Research conducted to map out the path to purchase in the beer category finds big differences between the United States and China in terms of the barriers to building preference and promoting purchase.

In both countries, broadcast advertising plays an important role in creating preference, but the barriers to purchase differ in one important respect. In the United States, the biggest barrier is simply finding one particular brand among all the brands on the shelves. Therefore in-store displays need to work in tandem with broadcast advertising. Broadcast advertising seeds people's interest in a brand and keeps it top of mind, and display is used to make it as easy as possible for consumers to find the brand they want. The location, scale, and visibility of the fixture, the location and prominence of the brand within the fixture, and the ability of consumers to instantly identify the brand through its packaging all contribute to making a brand easy or difficult to find.

In China, however, price is a bigger barrier to making a sale. Lowering a brand's price through price promotions has become an accepted means of overcoming that barrier and, as a result, has far more influence on purchase.

Essentially brands are bribing consumers using a variety of financial incentives. This strategy can prove to be very dangerous, lowering margins in the short term and teaching consumers to buy on price in the long term. The challenge is to find other ways to overcome the price barrier. One solution would be to engage people before they get to the store. Loyalty schemes, cross-promotion, and added-value consumer promotions are alternative ways to distract consumer attention from price and reinforce brand preference.

If you want to create a strong brand, you need to understand all the potential barriers along each step of consumers' paths to purchase. Knowing how people start their active engagement with a category is critical. For instance, while broadcast advertising creates familiarity for digital camera brands, once people start actively seeking information to help make their purchase decision, they turn to search engines, friends and family, and print advertising. As they move closer to the point of purchase, store advertising, Web sites, and displays have more influence. A marketer of a digital camera brand needs to understand the potential barriers to consumers proceeding along the path to purchase its brand. A big brand may take it for granted that it will come up in the organic search listings; a small one may need to buy sponsored links to ensure visibility at that crucial first step.

Identify the Consumer Touch Points that Add Value

The best form of advertising is the unsolicited testimonial. Advocacy is the single most important form of communication for many brands, and it is rooted in one thing: an exceptional brand experience. A brand experience, however, is not just the outcome of experiencing the product. It is the outcome of the combined effect of experiencing the brand through all of its touch points: product design, customer service, packaging, direct mail, brochures and videos, online and in-store communications, sales representatives and celebrity spokespeople. The brand promise needs to run through all the ways in which people come into contact with the brand. Think MINI, Nike, and, of course, that recent technology brand phenomenon, Apple's iPod.

iPod: The Embodiment of Simplicity
In an age when high-tech gadgets come with a dizzying array of buttons and features, the iPod offers simplicity—of design, of use, and of packaging. The advertising exploits these properties. The simple silhouettes of people enjoying music through their sleek white iPods work well across countries and cultures. The brand promise is implicit across all its touch points.

The Apple design aesthetic is easy to recognize but not easily imitated. And that is just the sort of competitive advantage that manufacturers are looking for these days: easy for customers to recognize, tough for the competition to replicate. Cadillac, Nissan, and Alfa Romeo have all focused on creating a differentiated look for their vehicles. Mobile phone companies such as Motorola, Samsung, and Philips are also boosting design spending in an attempt to outdesign Nokia. But as Apple has demonstrated, good design implies more than just good looks. It's also about ease of use—a feature that appeals to everyone—and easy access to a vast library of music through the iTunes Web site. The iPod's physical distinctiveness—the white earbuds, cord, and player—also reinforces the link between brand and advertising.

Media, More Local than Global

Today there are more international media options than in the past, but it would be very difficult to pull together a completely global campaign, and probably far less cost effective than negotiating the separate parts of the deal locally. Global channels like CNN, BBC World, Discovery, the Cartoon Network, and MTV offer the prospect of reaching a global (albeit upscale) audience on TV and online, but their reach does vary by country. To reach a reasonable proportion of the target audience, local media must be purchased to fill in the gaps. Similarly, global magazines like *Cosmopolitan, Elle*, and *Maxim* vary not only in penetration but in the characteristics of their readers. Like brands, media channels must adapt their offers to appeal to their audiences. The lack of truly global channels (online or off) is testimony to the power of local culture.

Most campaigns, in whatever medium, are going to be constructed locally, based on the availability of the various communication channels and their ability to overcome a specific barrier to purchase. Next you need to find creative content that will achieve the task required of each communication channel. Here too a global campaign may need to bow to local necessity.

Figure Out Which Creative Approach Will Work Best

Dr. Valerie Curtis of the London School of Hygiene & Tropical Medicine made one other important observation. "All of those [motivations] are tuned by the local circumstances, and obviously if you are going to produce effective communications and change behavior, then you have to ground your universal human truths in people's own life experience of the local culture." A strong global brand, while leveraging a fundamental human motivation, still needs to find distinctive and compelling ways to deliver its message. And therein lays the challenge. As Curtis notes, just because you have identified a universal motivation that is relevant to your brand does not mean that you can communicate it the same way across cultures.

The process of communication is inextricably linked with language, society, and environment. Of course language varies by country, but so do idioms and cultural references. As a result, it is difficult to make creative executions work equally well everywhere. Slapstick humor may be appreciated worldwide, but many other forms of humor have distinct cultural biases. In the Netherlands, the use of humor is a very powerful way to engage people in TV advertising, but very few of the international ads that intend to be funny succeed there. Apparently international advertisers have not been able to tune in to the Dutch sense of humor as well as the locals.

We have also observed differing responses across countries as to what is considered socially acceptable—for example, nudity, references to religious subjects, and attitudes toward women. Consumer identification—in relation to ethnic type—continues to be an issue in some countries, where ads featuring indigenous actors are more acceptable to consumers. Additionally, brands that market themselves as American may not be well received in some parts of the world; similarly, colas from Muslim countries may not be universally appreciated. Advertising environments also differ. In Brazil, the quality of local advertising is particularly good; this makes it harder for international ads to shine. What all of this means is that it is very rare for a global campaign to work well everywhere.

Creating Communication that Differentiates

A brand that has developed an appealing brand promise is off to a good start. It has a platform on which it can build. Then the question becomes one of how to take the idea and link it to the brand in a distinctive manner. Many of the ads that we have seen used successfully across the globe have done this by creating their own unique "brand space." This brand space isn't tied to any particular place or time; rather, it is owned by the brand. Richard Swaab of AMV BBDO believes that this approach of carving out an emotionally based territory for brand communication is becoming more common.

Swaab explains: "The world is moving to a place where brands can voice real convictions about what they stand for and believe in. So Apple believes that everybody has the right to express their creativity. Dove believes that every woman has a right to feel beautiful. Those are the territories we operate in [today], and if you can make those convictions come alive, it's brilliant, it's exciting, and it does work across borders."[3]

Developing cultures, however, tend to place more emphasis on functional benefits than emotional ones. But even in developed markets, we have to remind ourselves that brands cannot lose sight of their functional purpose. Remember, the strongest brands are those that can establish strong perceptions across the three areas of knowledge, action, and emotion. A brand that is weak on any one of these will be weaker than one that has a balanced profile.

Speaking at the Millward Brown Global Advertising Conference in London in 2007, Swaab reiterated that functional benefits are the key to opening up emotional territories and big multimarket ideas.

> Coke has the right to play in a world of optimism and positivity because that is what Coke has done for a very long time. You earn the rights to those kinds of things. Persil (or Omo as it is in some markets) can do something like "Dirt is Good," because it has had years and years of establishing that "Persil Washes Whiter." That's what gives it the right to make such an enormously brave flip. If another washing powder had said "Dirt is Good" or another brand of soft drink had claimed "we own optimism," it wouldn't ring true.

The Unilever campaign "Dirt is Good" does not explicitly demonstrate that Persil/Omo will get your clothes clean no matter what your kid does. Nor does it show the brand's superior cleaning power in a side-by-side demonstration. But there is a strong implicit communication that the brand will do its job—that you can let your kids get dirty because you can trust the brand. Even so, the brand promise may need to be interpreted differently according to culture and context. Omo in Asia delivers its "Dirt is Good" message in a different way than Persil in the U.K., because attitudes to dirt differ. In Asia, dirt is dangerous and threatening, something to be avoided. In the U.K. it is more an unsightly nuisance.

Exceptional Advertising Can Travel
Millward Brown has validated two key measures in terms of their ability to predict a short-term sales response: the Awareness Index and persuasion. The Awareness Index captures an ad's ability to engage the audience and establish long-term memories that are linked to the advertised brand. The persuasion measure captures the immediate motivational power of the ad. Combined, the two allow us to predict the likelihood that an ad will produce a measurable short-term sales response. Figure 13.1 shows how ads that performed

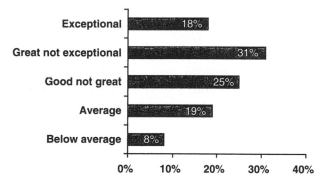

Figure 13.1 Degree to Which Exceptional Ads Perform Well Elsewhere

Source: Millward Brown Link pre-test database.

exceptionally well on these two measures in one country (ranking in the top 5 percent of the Link pretest database in that country) worked when aired someplace else.[4]

It is clear that, on average, these exceptional ads perform well in other countries, with a total of 74 percent of them performing above average (that is, exceptional, great, or good). Eighteen percent achieved exceptional performance in more than one place. These data suggest that a great ad will have the potential to travel but also confirm that there no guarantee of it doing so. Of our exceptional ads, 27 percent performed below what is generally deemed to be an acceptable standard, suggesting that they are too intrinsically linked to their country of origin to be effective across borders.

In six countries, the proportion of international ads among those classified as great or exceptional (top 15 percent of the database) is significantly lower than expected: Germany, France, the Netherlands, Poland, Brazil, and Japan. Japan stands out in particular—none of the ads in the top 15 percent of the Japanese Millward Brown database have international origins. It is important to note, however, that apart from Japan, many international ads have worked well in all these countries. This fact suggests that global advertisers need to place a premium on finding exceptional advertising that can transcend local culture. Further, it confirms the need to test advertising before running it in a new location. You cannot assume it is going to work the same way it did in its country of origin.

Success in New Media also Requires Local Engagement

The Internet has been heralded as the first truly global medium, and it is increasingly true that the people marketers most want to reach are online. All global marketers must consider how to use this medium to benefit their brand, but its potential goes way beyond search and display advertising. The most innovative brands are seeking to engage their consumers in ways that go far beyond traditional advertising.

The latest evolution of the Internet has empowered people on an unprecedented scale, both to express themselves and to connect with others. At the nexus of connectivity and creativity are such sites as YouTube, MySpace, and Facebook, which allow users to share videos, pictures, and ideas. The visibility of consumer communication and creativity, and the speed with which it can spread (albeit usually with the assistance of traditional media), has increased dramatically in the last 10 years. However, as Jeben Berg, product marketing manager at YouTube, explains, this does not automatically make the Web a great showcase for brands, global or otherwise. You still need to find compelling and relevant ways to communicate your brand promise.

Project Direct, conducted for Hewlett-Packard's printer division in cooperation with Fox Searchlight Pictures, is a project that, according to Berg, was a big success in terms of taking an idea and effectively localizing it. The project involved a competition, hosted by director Jason Reitman, to discover new film directors. Entrants simply needed to submit a video that showcased their talent. Berg says that one of the factors contributing to the success of Project Direct was the fact that HP took his advice not to force people to say the brand name in their films. "You need to be very casual about your branding, but the HP tagline, 'What do you have to say?' did work to their advantage. Everyone gets it."[5]

Once the details of countries, contest, and timing were agreed, YouTube took the introductory videos, added subtitles, and prepared a local public relations action plan in conjunction with HP's local teams. YouTube's country managers personally handled queries from the contest. Of the more than 650 submissions, nearly 50 percent were from outside the United States. The top 20 films alone generated almost 3.5 million views. Flávia Lacerda from Brazil submitted the winning entry, a film titled *Laços* (Ties).[6] Her prize is a trip to the Sundance Film Festival to meet with Fox Searchlight and screen her video.

In contrast to the success of Project Direct, Berg described a holiday-based promotion he put together for another big global company. Although he believed the idea would have worldwide appeal, the promotion failed to accomplish its goals. Two things held it back. First, according to Berg, the holiday in question was an occasion where people really just wanted to be "in the moment." It wasn't a time they necessarily wanted to capture for posterity. Second, the client insisted on adapting the contest questions to be specific to their products. "It boxed people in," said Berg. "The content became relevant only to the person uploading it and unappealing to everyone else."

Embedding Brand Directly in Popular Culture
Increasingly brands are reaching out to embed themselves in popular culture with events, sponsorship, and—the ultimate engagement opportunity— alternative reality games, in which fans interact with the brand in a blend of real and fictional events. The United Kingdom's *Contagious* magazine highlights *La Leyenda del Domino Dorado (The Legend of the Golden Domino)*, the latest online viral marketing campaign created by Guinness and its agencies AMV BBDO and iChameleon. This treasure hunt involved following a series of clues from the initial, enigmatic video by the mayor of El Dorado, Juan Ramon, to the location of the brand's latest video commercial. The first clue, "119500," just may be connected to the fact that it takes 119.5 second to pour the perfect pint of Guinness. Throughout the game, a recurring theme is that good things come to those who wait.

When people engage with a brand on a large scale, that brand becomes a part of popular culture. This is the ultimate benefit of consumer-generated content fueled by social networking. But, of course, leveraging the power of community is not limited to the online arena. In the United Kingdom, Coke sponsors the Football League. James Eadie, integrated marketing communications director for Coca-Cola Great Britain, points to the delicate balance between engagement and intrusion. "In that environment, you have very local clubs and it is a local passion point. It is important there that a brand like Coke is not seen to be coming into the community and crashing the party. And that was actually one of the thoughts behind our club colors route, where we actually took the 72 different clubs and changed the color of the Coca-Cola logo into that of the individual clubs. It was a case of being humble and saying we recognize the importance of your club in your life and that even a big brand like Coca-Cola needs to adapt to that particular situation."

There is No Guarantee of Success

Many of the global advertisers Millward Brown works with struggle to find a campaign idea that will work everywhere. They find that they need to adapt their message to work in the local context, interpreting the global promise in a way that is acceptable to the local culture. The challenge with all communication— whether it is a TV commercial, branded content, or an online campaign—is to ensure that there really is a connection between the brand and what people find engaging. A great idea does not necessarily translate into great communication. Given the strong influence of culture, we cannot assume that the same executions will work effectively everywhere. Whether agencies like it or not, if you want to avoid the spaghetti approach to advertising—throw it at the wall and see what sticks—then a strong focus on communication development and testing is a must. Trial and error is not only wasteful; it could potentially undermine a brand's standing. In the next chapter, I consider two basic ways in which research can help global brand marketers: by helping to uncover insights and by providing a common currency to help marketers manage their brands across borders.

Key Points to Take Away

- Communicating your brand promise through a global campaign is desirable to realize economies of scale, but it is truly necessary only if the same customers are going to be exposed to it in multiple countries.
- Growing a strong brand requires understanding the potential barriers to engagement along the path to purchase. These barriers will differ across brands, categories, and countries.
- Communication is inherently linked to culture. Great advertising *can* travel but may not always be able to do so.

Questions to Consider

1. How consistent does your communication need to be?
2. What are the barriers to engagement for your brand?
3. Which consumer touch points would help overcome those barriers?
4. Whatever form it takes, can your advertising travel?

For more information related to these questions, visit theglobalbrandonline.com.

Chapter 14

Harness the Power of Research

Research plays a critical role in helping global marketers identify the means to position their brands to best effect. While our intuition may serve us well at home, we are on unfamiliar ground when working in foreign countries, and it's tough to rely on gut instinct if you don't like the food. It's unwise to make judgments about what will or won't work without really understanding the local culture and the implications of that context.

Insight is the lifeblood of all successful marketing programs, whether we are talking about new product innovation, brand positioning, brand planning, or communications. All the marketers I've talked to are in agreement that real insights are scarce. Research has an important role to play in facilitating the process of identifying insights, but it will not produce them without active involvement from people who work on the brand. Unlocking insights requires individual understanding and intuition. The challenge, then, is to facilitate that intuition rather than relying on random flashes of inspiration. In this chapter, I suggest how research can fuel the insight process, helping to cross-reference personal understanding with hard facts.

But the challenge does not stop there. Once you have found an insight, you need to develop processes to keep it on track from ideation to implementation. During the development process, it is all too easy for a real insight to get lost, so that what makes it to market bears little resemblance to the original idea. Once the insight has been developed and implemented, you need a common research "currency" to understand its impact across different countries.

What Do We Really Mean by "Insight," Anyway?

At Diageo, the world's largest beer, wine, and spirits company, an insight is defined as "a penetrating discovery about a consumer motivation applied to unlock growth." The fact that marketing management at Diageo took the time to craft a definition is telling. Although a million and one observations might be made from personal experience and research data, smart marketers know that precious few of them really qualify as "insights."

A real consumer insight changes our understanding of a situation, an idea, or a product. It reframes our perceptions. It helps us make new connections, by bringing new, previously overlooked details to light. If we can act on that new understanding, we may be able to disrupt the status quo in a product or service category by reframing consumer expectations and perceptions. The case study that follows shows how an insight was used to unlock substantial growth for a U.K. brand.

Using an Insight to Drive Growth

It cannot be taken for granted that people will recognize the superiority of most brands through use, even if their primary appeal is a functional benefit. The Nicorette 2006 case study by Toby Horry and James Miller, awarded Best Idea and a Silver IPA Effectiveness Award from the Institute of Practitioners in Advertising, is an interesting one because it demonstrates how a strong brand with a common functional appeal can unlock cross-country growth.

AMV BBDO was appointed late in 2000 by Pharmacia (later Pfizer) with a brief to establish Nicorette as the dominant player in nicotine replacement therapy (NRT) across Europe in the face of increasing competition and category stagnation. There were several business challenges to be overcome, not least the fact that the competitive brands were largely undifferentiated, with similar names and products. Attitudes toward smoking differed across countries, as did legislation. Advertising tobacco was banned in some countries and not in others, bans on smoking in public varied, and a claim that could be made in one country might not be approved in another.

The IPA Award paper states: "The key to unlocking international growth came from one core insight: Pharmaceutical brands don't cross borders, consumer brands built on fundamental human truths and insights do." Qualitative consumer research identified that for smokers, smoking is a lifestyle choice. It is part of who they are, and even if they want to quit, the challenge seems insurmountable. They can, however, envisage giving up one or two cigarettes at a time. As the paper explains:

> They can imagine winning a battle but not the war. Brands that focused on the end point of being smoke free put smokers off because they presented an "unattainable" goal. We could make smokers feel better about Nicorette and their quit

attempt by presenting a more honest and accessible goal. Nicorette will help you fight the battles with individual cigarettes. By focusing on the individual battles we could move smokers from a losing psychology to a winning one—every cigarette craving you beat is a victory."[1]

The core idea of "Beat Cigarettes One at a Time with Nicorette" was found to appeal successfully across borders. Advertising across a wide range of media featured the "Cravings Man," a 2.5-meter cigarette with arms, legs, and a face, and surrounded consumers with the message "Beat cigarettes one at a time. You're twice as likely to succeed with Nicorette." The paper states: "'Cravings Man' has been absolutely essential to Nicorette success in Europe. From 2000 to 2004, based largely on the success of the Cravings Man campaign, Nicorette grew from 7 advertised countries to 16, from $194 million to $295 million in sales and established itself as the clear market leader."

Adhering to the IPA requirement to prove that advertising was the growth driver, Horry and Miller report on the success of the campaign from Millward Brown's pretesting and tracking research as well as a sales decomposition model conducted by OMDMetrics. They conclude: "Across Europe we have seen 30% growth in value sales over the course of the campaign (2001 to 2004) and we have a clearly established market leadership. The category grew by 24% over the same period, so we are keeping ahead of a very dynamic market. Our share of market grew from 33.2% in Q1 [quarter 1] '01 to 41% in Q4 '04 across Europe."

Commenting on the example of Nicorette, Richard Swaab of AMV BBDO suggests, "It's very easy to generate advertising for functional truths like that."[2] However, it is important to note that while rooted in a functional benefit—the means to quit smoking—the Nicorette campaign succeeded by recognizing the inherent emotional issues and benefits to quitting as well. Smokers do not want to be hectored into giving up. They need to feel that they can succeed and that someone—in this case Nicorette—is on their side. Critical to the success of the Nicorette case is that the agency not only found a motivating way to position the brand, but they also created a unique communication vehicle, in the Cravings Man, which helped the ad engage people and differentiate Nicorette from other brands.

If insights can be this valuable, why are they so hard to find?

Barriers to Insights

One of the biggest problems we face in uncovering insight is our habitual way of looking at the world. To make a new observation, we need to look at things in a different way; we need to look through something other than our existing lens.

Unfortunately, market research often creates a lens all by itself. We tend to get sales data for a certain group of companies. We tend to track among a certain target market. We even create new lenses through which to view the world. Many years ago, I remember a U.K. brand manager at Cadbury redefining the market for his brand. By proclaiming that Cadbury's Drinking Chocolate competed in the category of "real" chocolate versus "instant" chocolate (which combined chocolate and milk powders), he could claim that his brand was maintaining share over time, even though the brand's sales were plummeting as consumers opted for the convenience of the instant brands. There are plenty of other examples of major marketers overlooking looming threats because they failed to look at their brands in the right context. For example, Levi's congratulated itself for growing share in a declining denim category. In the toothbrush category, Johnson & Johnson didn't consider the impact that handheld electric brushes would have on their own Reach brand because electric brushes were outside the company's frame of reference. Marketers and market researchers should be careful not to look at a brand or a category in isolation; they need to keep an eye out for emerging trends that might disrupt the status quo.

The People Problem: Consumers

People don't make it easy to find crucial insights. When questioned, consumers tend to stick stubbornly to the world of the rational. They have trouble articulating their real motivations. Researchers have three main problems to overcome, if they want research findings to lead to relevant insights:

1. Lack of introspection
2. Self-interest
3. Lack of imagination

Lack of Introspection
People can't always tell you why they do what they do. Various qualitative research techniques exist to help overcome this problem. The techniques all have one thing in common: They enable the researcher—the person seeking to understand why people do what they do—to see the world from the consumer's point of view.

Self-Interest
It is commonly accepted in marketing that you should meet people's stated needs before addressing their unstated ones. But before you ask people to describe their needs, you should have a clear idea of what's in the best interest of your brand, because what people are most likely to tell you is what will add

value for *them*. They will say "make it cheaper," "make it faster," or "give me more." It's up to you to ask questions that will lead to a value proposition for both the consumer *and* the brand.

Lack of Imagination

When questioned, people tend to give answers that reflect their experience with the world as it is. They can't imagine products or processes that don't exist. It is often said that if Henry Ford had listened to consumers, he would have created a faster horse. If you want people to visualize something new, you have to help them. Doing that might involve using a concept board, a video, a complete scenario, or some other technique.

The People Problem: Marketers

Marketers are people too. We share the shortcomings of consumers and bring along our own problems as well:

- We suffer from data overload. We have too much data to digest and too little time to do it.
- We have our own preconceptions. We use research to reinforce our existing beliefs and experience rather than to challenge them.
- We are risk averse. We use market research as a CYA (cover-your-ass) tool because we are afraid to go out on a limb.

How can research surmount the limitations of lenses, marketers, and consumers?

Immersion Offers One Way to Unlock Insight

In 2007, senior management at Procter & Gamble were busy proselytizing "immersion"—direct interaction with the people who buy their brands—as the best means to get in touch with the needs, wants and desires of consumers.

An article in *Strategy Magazine* on the turnaround led by P&G chief executive A. G. Lafley reports that as part of the "internal revolution" there, research methodologies were reexamined along with operational structure and processes.[3] Much of P&G's traditional research, in which the marketer plays the role of objective witness, has been replaced with programs that bring marketers directly in touch with consumers and their everyday lives. Jim Stengel, global marketing officer at P&G, calls these programs "consumer immersion experiences." In the name of consumer immersion, P&G marketers are spending time working in shops in Mexico and conducting in-home observations of U.S. pet owners.

For Stengel, immersion is one of the keys to consumer-centric marketing. In an interview reported on the blog Magnosticism, he said "Consumer-centric marketing makes no assumptions. It begins with 'who is your consumer, and what's different about her?'" He explained P&G's new emphasis this way: "What we're now trying to do is let people, without a filter, really be with our consumer and be in her life."[4]

I would agree with Stengel that there is much to gain by combining the somewhat shallow view provided by traditional research with the more in-depth view gained by immersion. It's hard to infer consumers' thoughts and feelings from a written report or a summary of data. Businesspeople who rely on secondhand accounts and interpreting them based on their own experience and concerns are out of touch with the reality of people's lives; thus they may fail to understand how their company's products and services might be improved. This is even more likely when your consumer is a world away. The immersion process, which allows marketers to see someone wrestle with packaging, deliberate between spending the remains of the week's budget on snacks or cereals, or select clothing based on comfort rather than appearance, can bring home the results from research in a much more meaningful way.

However, immersion is not a substitute for traditional research. Without the context provided by professionally conducted qualitative and quantitative research, the risk of an insight from immersion turning out to be trivial, biased, or just plain wrong is high. Personal observation alone is not enough to obtain a truly holistic view of consumer relationships with brands. Identifying a true insight requires a blend of facts, observation, and intuition. You need hard data on sales trends, brand equity, and competitive spending to understand the dynamics of the current situation. Then you need to get behind the numbers to understand why things are that way and how they might be changed to the brand's advantage.

Developing a Customer-centric Viewpoint Is Critical

Stengel sees immersion as a means for marketers to adopt a customer-centric point of view. I would agree that this is a critical goal. Too many marketers look at the world through the eyes of their brand, not those of their customers. A good discipline for developing a customer-centric view is to lay out the different contact points that consumers have with your brand, starting from their first contacts, when they may not even be considering a purchase in the category, through the purchase process and the experience of

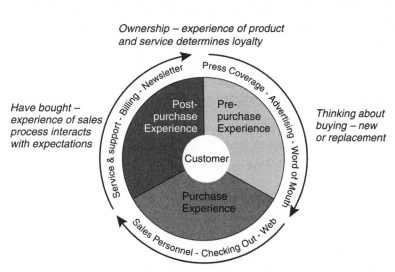

Figure 14.1 Customer-centric View of Mobile Phone Touch Points

Source: Adapted from Davis and Dunn, "Building the Brand Driven Business."[5]

the brand in use. Figure 14.1 shows this product experience life cycle for a mobile phone brand.

In adopting a customer-centric view, you should be looking for the point where the needs, desires, and aspirations of consumers might connect with what your brand can deliver. What is the context in which your brand operates? How might that context change? Are consumers using your brand or others in ways you had not expected? What needs are going unmet? What can your company or brand bring to the party that others can't? And how does the viewpoint differ across countries?

This is just one approach. Many companies expand the line of questioning to ask "Who, when, where, why?" By seeking answers to these questions, they build up a detailed understanding of what the brand is about. Many different tools can be used to flesh out this picture: immersion, ethnography, one-on-one interviews, customer diaries and videos, and deprivation research. But an insight may also come from personal observation, friends, family, the sales force, or data from a variety of sources. One valuable insight resulted from inspection of tracking data. The findings suggested that customers did not pay attention to the newsletters sent to them on a regular basis. Seeking an alternative approach, someone realized that there was one communication that everyone looked at: their monthly bill. By including information sheets in with the bills, the brand improved communications and saved $10 million in unread newsletters.

At a Millward Brown seminar on global advertising, Jaroslav Cír, Unilever's global consumer and market insight director for the Rexona brand, revealed one way his team is keeping in touch with consumers. "We have moved away from using respondents as laboratory rats and co-create with them more. On Rexona we have our own Internet panel called Window on Women. And it is kind of an elitist panel of 40 women from Shanghai to São Paulo, London to Moscow. Idea writers, journalists, fashion designers, and they know what they are there for. Paid by us, they know about the brand, but also get the pleasure of talking to each other and sharing ideas."[6]

Levi's uses an annual "Youth Panel" to perform a similar function. Composed of 50 to 100 people, it brings fashion-forward people from art, media, and photography schools together with typical young people from significant European cities. During the panel, which meets once a year, a variety of techniques are used to gain an understanding of respondents' lives (scrap-books, ethnography, accompanied shopping trips, and creative workshops). Feedback on people's values and passions, sources of fashion influence, brand relationships, and the impact of recent product, retail, and marketing initiatives help guide future action. The forum is attended by a cross-functional Levi's team from research, marketing, retail, merchandising, and design who use the resulting feedback for innovation, such as the launch of Levi's Engineered Jeans in 2002, as well as trend spotting, sponsorship evaluation, and troubleshooting.

Insight Generation Is a Collective Responsibility

Many companies have renamed their market research departments consumer insight or strategic planning departments. The implication seems to be that it is the job of the people in those departments, and those people alone, to discover insights. While researchers are well positioned to lead in this process, the critical job of identifying strategic insights cannot be the sole responsibility of just one group or department. As I explained earlier, even the most diligent marketers and researchers sometimes may have difficulty seeing past their own biases and preconceptions.

To counter this problem, many companies use ideation sessions involving multidisciplinary teams to uncover new insight. People from sales, production, and outside agencies all see the brand from different perspectives; this helps to overcome the single-lens effect. These sessions create an environment in which people are better able to identify insights because they get to see the brand and its context from different points of view. A professional facilitator who can manage the debate without taking sides usually moderates the sessions. A wide variety of techniques are used to encourage creative thinking. One popular approach is to list all consumer touch points and, for each, describe two things: the desired response that each one should elicit from a customer and the actual response that session participants think is elicited. This activity is particularly helpful in highlighting inconsistencies in messaging and barriers to initial purchase or repeat purchase.

Keeping the Insight on Track to Implementation

How do you know you have found a real insight? Ask yourself how the world will be different if the insight is turned into action. What would it mean to your customers, and to your brand? A real insight should have the potential to transform the competitive standing of the brand, to give it a new advantage.

Of course, most of us are not in the position to take an insight and implement it on the basis of our intuition alone. First we need to justify the business case for our idea, and then we must ensure that subsequent stages of development hold true to it.

Every significant brand innovation will go through stages of development, research, and testing. Qualitative research typically is used to develop ideas into fully fledged brands or communication. Quantitative research, in the form of concept, product, ad, and store tests, is used throughout the development process to ensure that the incarnation holds true to the original insight and that consumers do in fact respond to the idea as intended. The challenge here is to keep track of what the real insight was in the first place.

Bringing an idea to life is not an easy task. Take the example of creative development. By the time an individual ad is developed and aired, so many people have had a hand in its development—the creative team, the account team, the client, the client's spouse—that the finished product may resemble the original idea as much as a camel resembles a racehorse. Thus the original great idea may never reach the people it was intended to influence.

Keeping the Insight in Sight

A couple of years ago, Millward Brown worked with BASES, the new-product forecasting unit of The Nielsen Company, to understand why our ad pretesting results did not match its product concept results. We found that often the ads tested did not reflect the original ideas that had made the original product concept successful. Interviews with clients and planners in some of the major New York ad agencies suggested that:

- Agencies did not get involved at the concept test stage (and clients did not ask them or pay for them to do so), and their briefing did not focus on what it was that made a product concept successful.

- Agencies did not see the role of advertising to be the communication of functional benefits. They saw their job as "to create a resonance with the consumer."

However, particularly when it comes to new products, people need to know why one brand is better than the competition. Advertising needs to take this fact into account. Although agencies may discount the importance of communicating functional benefits, emotion alone is unlikely to create a compelling reason to buy.

Creating a Common Currency

One of the challenges of managing a brand, or a portfolio of brands around the world, is being able to make apple-to-apples comparisons. You cannot judge whether a brand is performing well in one market versus another or identify which TV commercials are most effective if different research techniques are used to assess them. This applies to all types of quantitative research, whether it is pretesting advertising, measuring brand equity, or tracking in-market performance. A common set of metrics will facilitate decision making. A lack of such a common set of metrics undermines the potential to reap the benefits of scale.

In speaking of the need for a common marketing currency, Brian Fetherstonhaugh of OgilvyOne Worldwide recommends that research always be conducted in the country where the company is headquartered, to provide a benchmark against which senior management can observe similarities and differences.[7] Many of the people I talked to shared Fetherstonhaugh's views—hard data helps to put personal opinion in context and speed up the process of reconciling differences of opinion. David Wheldon, global director of brand for Vodafone, says, "The brand pyramid is a phenomenally useful tool to a company like ours. Having these brand metrics allows you to demonstrate the power of a strong brand across different businesses and countries and encourage people to learn from what others do right."[8]

The adoption of a common approach to testing products, packaging, and advertising also benefits companies pursuing a search-and-redeploy strategy, by allowing people to anticipate what will work in their markets based on what has worked in others. An analysis of Link pretesting results in Asia, for instance, identified that ads created in Thailand typically were likely to do well in the Philippines and Indonesia. By contrast, ads created in Japan were unlikely to perform well in Korea or Taiwan.

It can be challenging to ensure that the common currency approach also provides flexibility and value at the local level. The way in which international research is organized and managed varies greatly among companies, often in line with their approach to brand management, but it always presents global/local issues. Where budgets are held locally, it can be very difficult to persuade individual markets to adopt a common approach. The opportunity to obtain a global overview is lost if there is too much variation between local research programs. If budgets are held centrally, the local market can feel it has lost control. We return to these issues in a more general sense in the next chapter, but the ideal solution is to give the local client ownership over research that is integral to both local and global strategy, but require that the research be executed within a common set of agreed guidelines.

One Size Fits All Does Not Work for Research Either

In order to give marketing a global view, research must overcome a number of challenges inherent to the practice of research itself. By far the biggest problem is that absolute figures are not comparable across countries due a wide variety of factors:

- Rarely is it possible to use exactly the same research methodologies across countries. In the United States and the United Kingdom, online research has become the norm, but elsewhere, the standard approach for reaching a representative cross-section of people is telephone or face-to-face interviewing. Results vary widely between methodologies even within a single country. Looking at them across countries adds further confusion.
- Wording and translations can have a great impact on results and must be carefully considered. In the United Kingdom, for instance, the term "food miles" is widely used and understood to describe how far goods and groceries have traveled to get to the store shelf. In the United States, the term is neither used nor commonly understood.
- Response to questionnaires is intimately bound up with culture. Results can vary across countries because people respond to questions differently. For example, scales may be interpreted differently; in some countries, respondents are prone to top-boxing, while respondents in other parts of the world avoid the extreme ends of the scale. The average response to the enjoyment scale asked in Millward Brown's Link pretest shows a wide variation in response from developing countries of Indonesia, China, and India to western European markets such as Sweden, Germany, and the United Kingdom. (Notably, the United States sits in the middle of the pack.)

There are no easy ways around these differences. Beware any research company that presents data without acknowledging the possible biases involved. The best solution is to database the results across different countries and then find ways to make the data more comparable. You can create a normalized index by mathematically transforming the distribution on each scale, so that for any given measure, an indexed score represents the same relative standing in every country. Similarly, brand health metrics like Voltage (described in Chapter 3) take into account a brand's relative standing within a category and country, facilitating an apples-to-apples comparison. Using approaches like these, senior managers can compare performance across countries without worrying about the underlying complexities involved.

Measure What Matters

The risk today is that managers, senior or junior, will be so inundated with information that they will not be able to absorb or act on it. Research data should be separated into two groups:

1. Forward-looking metrics, such as Voltage, which relate to future business outcomes. These metrics should be readily available and presented in an easily digestible format—on a dashboard, to use the industry jargon. A dashboard is the visual representation of a brand's health and provides a snapshot between actual performance and key benchmarks, such as targets and key competitor performance. A good dashboard facilitates action. It not only reports on the metrics being monitored but also serves as a means to identify and prioritize next steps.
2. Information related to why that situation exists and what might be done about it. No dashboard, however complete, can provide all the answers. You must have the diagnostic information to dig deeper and help understand what specific actions need to be taken. Again, any company experienced in the field of global measurement should be able to provide diagnostic information from its research to tell you not only what is happening but why it is happening, and to suggest potential actions.

Good research that combines both forward-looking evaluative measures and diagnostic questions can play a valuable role in helping to manage a global brand. It can provide not only a currency but also a potential source of insight. Almost every global company that Millward Brown works for recognizes the value of research to identify best practices and ensure a proper balance between global and local. In the next chapter, I widen my scope to consider how companies need to align not just their research programs but also their marketing practices.

Key Points to Take Away

- Insight generation is a collective responsibility.
- Finding insights that create real value is a combination of art and science. You cannot rely on personal observation alone; rather you must combine that with research to ensure that an insight is real, not imagined.
- Use different techniques in order to create a customer-centric view of your brand, your category, and the cultures in which they exist.
- A common research currency in terms of methodologies, metrics, and terminology facilitates the process of managing brands and assets across countries.

Questions to Consider

1. How does your company go about discovering insights? Is it a collective responsibility, or someone else's problem?
2. What processes do you use to ensure that a valuable insight does not get lost in translation from idea to implementation?
3. Do you measure what matters on a consistent basis around the world?

For more information related to these questions, visit theglobalbrandonline.com.

Chapter 15

Align Your Organization

One theme runs throughout all the interviews that I have conducted for this book: It is impossible to create a strong, profitable global brand unless the organization is aligned to that purpose. As noted elsewhere in the book, this is mission critical for service organizations, where there is a direct human or technology interface with customers. However, alignment is also fundamental to the success of such brands as Apple, Dove, and Jack Daniel's. The people who run those brands believe in them and are working efficiently across functions and geographies to deliver on their brand promise. Unfortunately, these companies are exceptions, not the rule. Many businesses appear to operate in silos that are not coordinated to deliver a great brand experience.

The essential problem of the global brand is that without a common internal mind-set, and without systems to facilitate that mind-set, the confederation formed by the local brand teams will fragment as each one seeks to do what it believes is in its own best interests. Not only will potential economies be lost, but the energy so crucial to success in today's marketplace will become diluted.

Like many of the problems facing global brands, lack of alignment is not unique to operating on the world stage, but the issues involved become far greater. Nor are the issues unique to any specific industry. The problems I observe in major client companies are exactly the same ones that I have wrestled with over the years at Millward Brown. The biggest of these is that distance undermines communication and breeds distrust. Unless this problem is recognized and addressed, it can completely undermine the advantages of scale.

In this chapter, I focus on the global/local tension within the marketing function and consider what practices can help alleviate inefficiencies and frustrations. The biggest challenge is to unite the team around a common understanding of what the brand stands for and what it is trying to achieve. Then you can align the structure of the team to facilitate the process of global brand building. Doing that means minimizing the degree to which people work at cross-purposes and encouraging them to share best practices.

It Is All about People

Commenting on what makes a global brand successful, Brian Fetherstonhaugh of OgilvyOne says: "The biggest lesson perhaps is the obvious one: it's all about the people." Left to their own devices, however, people may have trouble working toward a common purpose. Lack of success for global brands is also most often attributed to people; these comments, from various people I interviewed, attest to that.

> "A huge barrier to success is in the mind of the managers and a need for control."
> "There is not a consistent policy of search and redeploy so you end up with a lot of 'not invented here.'"
> "If the local team does not feel it is right, it will not happen."

Some people do recognize that the tension between global and local is not insurmountable. Ben Haxworth, who has worked in both global marketing and as a local marketing director at Colgate-Palmolive, has this to say: "Effective global brand management is a continuous process of integration and alignment. Multiple views of what makes sense at a local level are synthesized into a single plan that delivers global strategic objectives. There are two ways of viewing this: endless conflict or enhancing global best practice."[1]

So the question is, how do you get people to work with both local and global goals in mind?

Inconsistency Undermines Purpose

The biggest internal threat to a strong brand is inconsistency of understanding in terms of where the power lies, what the brand stands for, and what the priorities are.

One of the biggest contributing factors to this inconsistency is the relentless turnover of chief marketing officers and brand managers. Every new person on the job wants to make a mark. A new CMO may choose to change the organizational structure or overhaul the brand management process. A new player on the global brand team may seek to reinvent what the brand stands for. Change is never easy, but change that is perceived to be based on personal whim breeds cynicism and discontent. If the brand teams in different countries don't believe in the changes they are asked to make or don't understand how they are meant to modify their approach, chaos will ensue.

Create a Common Language

Kimberly-Clark markets its brands of health and hygiene products in more than 150 countries. Tony Palmer is the first CMO in the company's 136-year history.

Because of his general management background at large global companies like Coca-Cola, Mars, and Kellogg's, Palmer understands the importance of getting everyone on the same page. On a global team, not only do people's backgrounds and experiences differ but the nuances of language and culture introduce a further barrier to communication. As Palmer states, "The very first challenge is to get everyone talking about brands the same way."

Ensure a Common Understanding of Purpose

A McKinsey consultant would suggest that the only goal worth pursuing is revenue growth. Palmer expands on the growth mandate: "At Kimberly-Clark, we have a very simple perspective on the role of marketing. It is to sell more stuff to more people, for more money, more often."

But behind the simplicity of that statement is the vast complexity of making that objective a reality. Are people aligned to achieve the right goals? Should managers focus on launching new brands or strengthening existing ones? Are the growth drivers the same everywhere, or does the marketing mix need to differ by region or market? A CMO needs to ensure that the rules of the road are clearly understood. It is impossible to mandate what happens under every set of circumstances, but a set of general principles can help smooth the way.

Ensure a Common Understanding and Passion

A brand has a soul, an intangible quality that is easy to undermine if people are not familiar with it. Peter Brabeck of Nestlé says, "You need people who understand and live their brands, who keep their spirit alive." People sometimes shy away from words like "passion," preferring less emotional phrases like "shared understanding," but whatever you call it, as we saw in Chapter 4, strong, shared understanding and values are important. It is often said that in a professional services company, the people are the brand. But does the lack of a direct interface with customers make it any less important for people who work on a brand to share a common passion for it? In any company, it is critical to create an environment where people can be passionate about their work. Strong, inspiring leadership created such an environment in many of the case studies in this book. Once established, that passion needs to be stoked and centered on what the brands stands for.

Mike Keyes, the global brand director of Jack Daniel's at Brown-Forman, commented on the difficulty of communicating the spirit of that brand (no pun intended) as new people joined the increasingly widespread brand team. Brown-Forman is unusual because people tend to stay with the company a long time—particularly on the Jack Daniel's brand—so in the past, team members had an intimate knowledge of what the brand stood for. But as the brand has grown, Keyes said it has become a challenge to instill the same understanding of the brand's essence and heritage in new team members. And without that understanding, it is too easy for someone to implement something at odds with the brand's character simply to get sales. You cannot rely on osmosis to convey what the brand stands for. You have to write it down, share it, and encourage people to walk the talk.

To address this problem, the global Jack Daniel's team has implemented a one-week "Camp Jack" to train new staff members. They have also created a 30-minute DVD documentary to speed up the learning process and codify the brand's values. Other companies summarize the spirit of their brands in a brand "bible," which covers the details of the positioning, the target audience, and how that audience feels about the brand. Levi's developed the *YP* magazine to communicate key brand insights across the company. Vodafone created a mobile day insight book. Hewlett-Packard took it one step further with a mobile life road show.

Senior management also needs to be reminded of what the brand stands for. If top management has a good understanding of what the brand represents, they will be less likely to put cost savings ahead of building brand value. At McDonald's, management has to flip burgers once a year. Executives from Pepsico International have participated in immersive research in Brazil—including meeting consumers at their homes at 5 a.m. and commuting with them for two to three hours—to observe their on-the-go snacking and breakfast behavior.

If people across the whole organization speak the same language, know what the company is trying to achieve, and know what their brand stands for, it will be far easier to get them aligned and reduce the amount of unnecessary politics that take place. What is then needed is the structure to facilitate the brand strategy.

Structure Follows Strategy

Bob Meyers, longtime CEO of Millward Brown, liked to quote the business historian Alfred Chandler: "Unless structure follows strategy, inefficiency results." There are four structural mechanisms by which organizations can efficiently manage their global brands.

Assign Clear Managerial Responsibility

People need to know who has the responsibility to make key decisions regarding the brand. Do decisions rest with the executive board, the global brand team, or the local operating company? As with so many other aspects of marketing a global brand, there is no single recipe for success. What works best will differ according to the brand, category, and company.

The basic question is: Where do authority and budget responsibility lie? Should the local team have the power to adapt the brand to meet local needs, with the global brand team taking responsibility for protecting the trademark and sharing best practice? Or should the global team have the power to control what happens to the brand? The situation is further complicated by the need to manage a portfolio of brands within a product category. Most companies continue to wrestle with what makes the most sense, reflecting a local-first or global-first philosophy and the nature of the brands involved.

At one time, management of brands at Unilever was arranged by country, with the global team offering strategic input and advice but having little control over what happened on the ground. In last few years this has shifted. The category now takes the lead. The global category senior vice president has sole responsibility for decisions concerning product, packaging design, advertising, and promotion development. These decisions are communicated to the geographies (clusters of countries), and it is the job of the local management team to deploy them in the best way possible. The regions are responsible for customer marketing, merchandising, display, and promotional pricing.

By contrast, at Colgate, the matrix is different. Global business development is organized by category, with responsibility for brand consistency (signing off on packaging graphics and advertising strategy) and best practice. Reflecting on his role as director of global business development on toothpaste, Ben Haxworth says his job was to create a "synthesis of the best local strategies so the brand can perform effectively and efficiently on the global stage." Procter & Gamble shifted from this type of structure to one more like Unilever's, with the categories holding the P&L.

Whatever the best solution for a particular brand and company, you need some form of matrix with a global team responsible for trying to identify and share best practices, even if it is not their job to implement it. Some companies have tried clustering markets by stages of development, but with no overarching organization, collaboration usually fails. Geographically and culturally dispersed countries, with little incentive to share, can too easily write something off as not invented here.

Create a Common Global Brand-Planning Process

At Diageo, global brand teams report into Rob Malcolm, the president of global marketing, sales, and innovation. Team members are the custodians of the brand, responsible for trademarks, positioning, and best practice. In-market companies hold the profits and losses and have their own local planning resource when warranted by the size of the market. Diageo recognizes four brands as truly global: Guinness, Johnnie Walker, Smirnoff, and Baileys. Each brand has its own global team and works with global agencies to develop advertising. Each brand pursues a policy of "create and reapply." Create is mostly limited to the lead markets—for example, Ireland and Great Britain for Guinness. The job of a reapply market is to execute the overall strategy.

One of the reasons that Diageo can achieve alignment between global teams and markets is DWBB: the Diageo Way of Brand Building. DWBB is built around the five *I*'s: consumer issue, information, insight, implication and implementation. A "Brand Essence Wheel" helps define not just a brand's core essence—three or four words that reflect the core belief—but also describes how the brand makes its target consumer feel and what it signals to the outside world.

When Malcolm joined Diageo from P&G, he soon came to realize that communication within the company was highly inefficient. Coming as they did from a variety of different companies, each with its own internal culture and practices, everyone was applying their own model to how brands should be managed. This led Malcolm to make a huge investment in creating DWBB and then developing training and documentation to establish the consistent brand-planning framework worldwide. DWBB is strictly enforced—no plans are accepted unless they adhere to the accepted format. Now, however, global and local have a common understanding of what their brands stand for. Business plans, documentation, and process are the same worldwide, which facilitates movement of staff between brands and regions. Warwick Nash, who used to work at Diageo, considers it one of the most successful programs he has ever seen.

Encourage Sharing of Insights and Best Practices

Commenting on his role as a global business development director at Colgate, Ben Haxworth states, "Sixty-five countries competing to execute the same strategy is going to pay off pretty quick in terms of best practice."[2] The best way to resolve global/local issues is by providing value between the regions, and only someone sitting on a global level can look at what everyone is doing and identify global best practices. James Eadie of Coca-Cola Great Britain says, "A center that can recognize good ideas, understand the power of those ideas that are happening in the local market, and quickly take them and reapply them elsewhere is absolutely crucial. And that also demands a sense of humility in the center because sometimes that's about ripping up a strong global campaign and saying 'You know what? That campaign the guy is doing over there is very strong.'" He gives the example of Coke's 2006 World Cup Advertising, developed by Santo in Argentina, which featured claymation characters celebrating the scoring of a goal. This campaign was identified as having more potential than campaigns being developed in other countries, so after it performed well in testing, it was rolled out globally. "Almost every country that activated the World Cup was running an Argentinean ad developed for the Argentinean local market," said Eadie.[3]

To ensure good global/local cooperation, chief marketing officers need to create a culture of teamwork and trust, with a mind-set that searches for and focuses on commonalities, not differences. A policy of rotating managers between global and local roles also helps encourage the understanding of both sides. But at the end of the day, global/local cooperation comes back to personal relationships.

Jaroslav Cír of Unilever says, "I have seen the most successful working relationship between category and region based on successful human relationships . . . and on trust. If they trust you as a professional, even though you are coming from outside their market, and you are open enough to listen to what they know about their own market, it is a win/win."

Creating good relationships requires personal contact. There is no substitute to meeting people face to face to realize how much you have in common. Brian Fetherstonhaugh puts it this way: "Good relationships are wine-enabled, not web-enabled." Getting global and local teams together on a regular basis for workshops, training, and team building is critical to success. Contacts like these help establish stronger relationships between individuals and facilitate the transmission of knowledge.

Whatever you do, there will always be some conflict and tension between global and local, but as Christene McCauley, global consumer planning director at Diageo, says, "An open and honest relationship is half the battle." She also believes that Diageo's strong corporate culture helps to break down barriers. James Eadie points out the risks of having the local team toe the party line: "It is the job of the local market to say no as well. I think there are examples where centrally produced stuff can destroy value rather than create it and understanding that and having a mechanism where in the right circumstances you can say no is also important."

Reward Good Behavior

A fundamental conflict often exists between what defines success for the global brand team and what defines success for the people in a specific market. If success is defined on the basis of global performance, it may become "somebody else's problem" and reduce the incentive to make the brand successful locally. Alternatively, if success is defined as maximizing market share within a country, managers will instinctively, and often correctly, assume that localizing the brand offer is the best path to success.

Few organizations are aligned so that global and local share the same targets. A company's incentive scheme is bound to reflect the way the executive team believes it makes its money. A brand-first company may well end up with a very different scheme from a business-first one. The former might favor a scheme where bonuses are linked to shareholder return and regional performance, while the latter will probably favor local incentives tied to local business performance. There is no single "right" answer. It depends on the company philosophy, the nature of the product and service, and the competitive environment.

Staff objectives can also provide a means to encourage share and redeploy strategies, says Eadie, if people are rewarded not just for creating and executing great ideas but reapplying them internally as well. "If you can reward internal 'borrowing with pride,'" he said, "that also helps considerably."

He extends the idea to suggest that in addition to acknowledging people for using a great ad that's been made elsewhere, companies should consider rewarding the exporting country in the form of shared research, development, and production costs.

No Easy Answers

As the pace of change speeds up, brands cannot afford to rely on command and control structures or include every stakeholder in the decision-making process. As the ever-changing multinational corporate structures testify, there is no single, optimal answer to the question of how best to manage a global brand. The solution is to create a common vision and understanding of what the brand stands for and what it needs to achieve across the organization. Then local operations can take on the responsibility of implementing the brand promise for their market within the context of the global strategy, and global teams can focus on identifying and sharing common best practices. Companies that can crack their specific organizational code, align incentives with strategy, and maximize business efficiency without incurring significant local opportunity cost will be well positioned to grow strong global brands.

Key Points to Take Away

- The greater the distance between managers, the greater the barriers to communication and trust and the greater the work required to align the organization.
- Unite the team around a common vision of what the brand stands for and what needs to be achieved.
- Align the structure of the team to facilitate the process of global brand building:

  1. Assign clear responsibilities: global and local.
  2. Create a common language and brand planning process.
  3. Encourage the sharing of insights and best practices.
  4. Reward good behavior.

Questions to Consider

1. How consistent is the understanding of what your brand stands for and what the priorities are?
2. Does the brand team share a common understanding and passion for the brand?
3. Is there a clear decision-making structure? Is it working for or against building a strong brand? Are incentives aligned with that structure?
4. How much sharing of insights and best practices takes place? How is sharing rewarded when it happens?

For more information related to these questions, visit theglobalbrandonline.com.

Chapter 16

Look to the Future

We are aware . . . that the incredibly rapid development of communications has telescoped time and space. We know that prosperity is interdependent, that currencies are linked, that commerce is international. But only a few (mainly business men whose pockets are affected) take all this for granted.

These words, written in 1936 by Cecil Lewis, pilot, author, and administrator, are just as true today as they were then. Change is not new. Although the global economy continues to strengthen ties between countries and companies, most people remain blissfully local in their daily lives. When I asked Peter Brabeck, chairman and chief executive of Nestlé SA, about the balance between global brand strategy and local execution, his immediate response was: "There is no global consumer. In fact, consumers are becoming less and less global—they are more local than ever before."

This assertion seems to fly in the face of conventional wisdom, but I believe Brabeck is correct. The world is not yet a global village and in all likelihood is not going to become one. In this final chapter, I review a few of the macrotrends apparent today and consider the implications for global brands. Your mission is to figure out which ones present opportunities or threats to your brand.

The Pace of Change Continues to Increase

If you feel overwhelmed by the pace of change, you are not alone. Sixty-three percent of people in our global survey agreed that the world is changing so fast it is difficult to keep up. The results for each country are shown in Table 16.1.

The highest level of agreement came from China, a country that has been no stranger to change over the last two decades. The Europeans appear less concerned, but even there, only one in five disagreed with the statement. Most people seem challenged by the pace of today's world. But it seems unlikely that the pace of change will slow; in fact, it will probably continue to accelerate. The

Table 16.1 Agreement with Statement: The World Is Changing So Fast It Is Difficult to Keep Up

Country	USA	Mexico	Brazil	UK	Germany	Russia	India	China
% agree	60	56	63	52	54	62	67	84

Source: The Millward Brown Global Brand Survey, January 2008.

question for all of us, then, is: What opportunities and challenges might change bring?

Like consumers, marketers are concerned about change. Media fragmentation, changing technology, and the rise of new media all affect their ability to build strong brands. But marketers also add to the pace of change by introducing new products and services. It is often reported that 90 percent of new products fail. Might less haste in the process of launching them make for more success?

It is not speed to market that is so important; it is finding a truly differentiated and compelling offer. It is about creating strong brands. That is one reason multinational corporations are so successful. Where possible, they avoid the risky process of launching completely new brands. If they have a brand that has proved its worth in one market, they consider how it might be adapted to meet local needs elsewhere and then promote it appropriately. As we have seen, that process is certainly not risk free, but the odds of success are probably far better than 1 in 10.

The greater risk for MNCs may be in going too far in trying to realize efficiencies from their global marketing. They may lose sight of the diversity of needs around the world and forget to adapt their offer to the local culture. I believe that the fast-paced world we live in offers more opportunity than ever to build strong brands, but they must be tailored to meet local needs. The trends we observe and the issues we face are global in scope, but they may be just as likely to increase cultural diversity as to decrease it. This fact has important ramifications for global brands and their ability to create strong relationships with their consumers.

Global Warming Has Big Implications for Global Brands

As I said in Chapter 14, marketers need to keep the big picture in mind when planning for the long-term health of their brands. It is important to look beyond what is happening to your own brand or your own category. Today it behooves marketers, and in fact all businesspeople, to consider what is happening to our planet.

Global warming has big implications for brands. A *McKinsey Quarterly* survey conducted in December 2007 finds that 36 percent of executives see global warming as a very important consideration for managing corporate reputation and brands. An additional 32 percent say it is a somewhat important consideration.[1] Some companies are already feeling the impact on their brands while others are turning it into an opportunity for innovation.

Strong Brands Will Weather the Storm Better

Global warming will affect almost everything that consumers and businesses purchase. For example, the increased demand for the biofuel ethanol in the United States has already caused corn prices to soar. In Mexico, which gets much of its corn from its neighbor to the north, the price of corn tortillas doubled from 2006 to 2007, setting off large protest marches in Mexico City.

The rising food costs fueled by ethanol demand are also affecting U.S. consumers. "All things that use corn are going to have higher prices and higher cost, to some extent, that will be passed on to consumers," says Wally Tyner, professor of agriculture economics at Purdue University.[2] So we can expect to see higher prices not just for meat and poultry products, but also for processed foods, such as soft drinks, breakfast cereals, and snacks. Strong brands should be better able to justify the necessary price hikes, while low-cost and private-label brands may benefit from the increased numbers of people forced to budget. Brands in the middle will feel the pressure.

In the United States, major branded goods manufacturers are already responding to the crunch. At Kraft, chief executive Irene Rosenfeld promised to increase marketing spending between 8 and 9 percent in an effort to improve equity and justify higher prices.[3] Kellogg's experienced a net income decline in the fourth quarter of 2007 as a result of higher prices but staunched the loss at 3 percent through increased ad spending. A February 2008 article in *AdAge* noted a significant increase in media spend at Procter & Gamble and reported CEO A.G. Lafley's intention to coordinate the company's price increases with innovation and marketing initiatives because "the value stays right for the consumer when we do that."[4]

Although food and beverage companies are feeling the squeeze now, it seems likely that, before long, the combined effect of global warming and increased demand from developing economies will affect all commodity prices. If prices rise as a result, consumers will respond by making trade-offs across all product categories, from cereals and cheese to cars and computers. In order to pay for the brands they really want, they will scrimp in other areas they feel less strongly about.

Will Global Warming Send Production Home?

A global brand is built on a strong, scalable business model. But what if the advantages of outsourcing production to the other side of the planet disappear?

China's exports to the rest of the world are booming. The *People's Daily Online* reported that exports hit a record $56.2 billion in July 2007, a 28 percent increase from the previous year. The reason behind China's success as an exporter is simple: low prices. Cheap labor and cheap land have fueled China's growth as manufacturer to the world.

But in the long-term, global warming may bring a change in China's status as the world's factory. With more stringent environmental controls, higher taxes, and rising transport costs, the economics of sourcing materials from the other side of the planet will change. Manufacturing products in energy-efficient factories in the West might seem a better bet than transporting goods thousands of miles. But even if they are manufactured closer to home, as the cost of raw materials increases, branded products from toys to MP3 players are likely to sport higher price tags. People may be willing to pay more for an iPod, but the margins of weaker brands will suffer.

Even if the economics of the situation do not militate against production in low-cost markets, consumer concern over climate change may take its toll. A 2006 TIME/ABC News/Stanford University poll in the United States found that 68 percent of Americans think the U.S. government should be doing more to address the issue.[5] In the United Kingdom, it is now common to see food miles displayed on the labels of many products. A carbon-labeling system, introduced there in March 2007 by the Carbon Trust, is used by many well-known brands, such as Walkers Crisps, Innocent Smoothies, and Boots shampoos to highlight their carbon footprints. Even if people are notoriously lax when it comes to following through on their own good intentions, brands that are not seen to be doing their part to offset global warming will be missing a trick. Green credentials will become one more heuristic people will use to make their brand choices easier.

Global Warming: Business Threat or Opportunity?

Global warming may drive up costs for some companies but provide others with unexpected savings. In taking steps toward being more environmentally responsible, retailers such as Wal-Mart, Tesco, and Marks & Spencer are reaping an economic benefit.

In a speech made in October, 2005, Wal-Mart's CEO Lee Scott outlined three large sustainability goals for the company:

1. To be supplied completely by renewable energy
2. To generate "zero waste"
3. To sell products that sustain the environment[6]

One of the specific waste-reduction initiatives cited is a call for the improvement in packaging of all private-label products within two years. Not content with simply improving the packaging of his own company's products, in 2007 Lee Scott told a conference of 250 chief executives that if they want their products to continue to be displayed on the shelves of the world's largest retailer, they needed to reduce their packaging as well.[7]

Of course, Wal-Mart's green initiative is not just altruistic. There is good business sense behind it. In an interview with Amanda Griscom Little of online environmental magazine *Grist*, CEO Scott stated: "It is clearly good for our business. We are taking costs out and finding we are doing things we just do not need to do . . . there are a number of decisions we can make that are great for sustainability and great for bottom-line profit."[8]

No industry or brand will go unaffected by global warming. And while some companies look for ways to reduce their carbon footprint and save money, innovators are looking to create new businesses. For example:

- Goldman Sachs intends to make up to $1 billion available to invest in renewable energy. It aims to become a leading U.S. wind energy developer and is now partnering with Shell Wind Energy and BP Solar.
- GE is looking to boost earnings while making progress on environmental issues through its Ecomagination program. The Ecomagination line of products, which range from locomotives to light bulbs, incorporate technologies that are good for the planet while offering real value to customers.

The impact of global warming will add a further moral, financial, and legal imperative to the existing predisposition to "act local." A reduction in travel and outsourcing of production may slow down the cross-pollination of cultures and business practices that seem to make the world smaller. As we shall see in the next section, there are signs that the world is already becoming more diverse. Global warming may simply exaggerate that trend.

Diverging Trends: Coming Together and Drawing Apart

Underlying the current push to globalize brands is the assumption that the world is becoming more homogeneous. But there are some scholars, such as Professor Pankaj Ghemawat of Harvard Business School, who are far from convinced of this. "The most commonly cited figure concerns international trade, which represents more than 25 percent of most economies. But when I began to research a broader range of measures including investment, phone calls, tourism, and immigration, I found that, surprisingly, the average extent of globalization is only 10 percent."[9] Ghemawat suggests that some indicators of globalization are not increasing (contrary to what many experts have claimed) and points to the decreasing international share of total Internet traffic (presumably brought on by the localization strategies pursued by companies like Google).

In an interesting convergence of numbers, Sir Martin Sorrell, chief executive of WPP, suggests: "Truly global products only account for around 10 to 15 percent of our worldwide revenues. Consumers are probably more interesting for their differences than their similarities."[10]

In fact, a lot of evidence supports a case that while the world is becoming more similar in some respects, it is becoming more diverse in others, as illustrated by the examples in Table 16.2. Of course, these examples may not represent a growing trend so much as a steady state. We share much in common, yet we differ in many ways. Although popular culture can be global in reach, the same people who applaud 50 Cent may also enjoy local folk music. BBC's *The World* reported on a revival in traditional melodies in Borneo that typifies the interaction between old and new, global and local:

> Like teenagers the world over, the Anak Adi Rurum girls are big fans of pop and hip hop. While they enjoy learning and playing the songs of their ancestors, they're also keen to mix it up a little. At this concert, after several traditional melodies, the band pulls out guitars to accompany the *sapes* [local stringed instruments] and close their set with a hip-hop remix of an ancient melody.[11]

Cultural Differences Will Not Disappear

Evidence from research suggests that cultural values are far more resilient than we might imagine and that they have important implications for consumer behavior. In "Mapping Cultural Values for Global Marketing and Advertising," Marieke de Mooij demonstrates that Geert Hofstede's values of national culture impact product purchasing and media consumption behavior. She concludes: "Countries may be converging with respect to income levels but they are not converging with respect to values of national culture."[12]

A look at recent data from Global TGI reveals findings consistent with those of de Mooij. Similar values exist between rich and poor within a country, but there are big differences between people with relatively high standards of living across countries. People who have both higher incomes and experience of international travel are most likely to buy foreign brands. As global warming makes air travel less affordable, these "internationalists" may become an even smaller proportion of national populations than they are today, further amplifying cultural differences.

Table 16.2 Opposing Trends (Homogeneity/Diversity)

Trends in . . .	Trend toward Homogeneity	Trend toward Diversity
Language	English is increasingly the international language of business. The primary language of more than 400 million people and the second language of hundreds of millions more, English is essential in science, technology, economics, publishing, air traffic control, and finance. Due to the wide distribution of American popular culture, even more people are exposed to English than can speak it. The number of people who will learn English as a foreign language is expected to continue to grow until 2030.[a]	After a steady decline in the last century, the Welsh language is undergoing a revival. Long overshadowed by English, Welsh is the subject of renewed interest due to the rise of Welsh nationalism and the establishment of Welsh television and radio. At the end of the twentieth century, it became compulsory for all schoolchildren in Wales to learn Welsh up to age 16. Other European languages experiencing revivals are Catalan, Basque, and Breton.
European Union	Huge celebrations marked the accession of Romania and Bulgaria to the European Union on January 1, 2007. Their entry raised the number of member states to 27.	A 2006 Eurobarometer poll found that among people from the 15 states that were part of the EU before 2004, only 41 percent supported further expansion of the union.[b]
Retailing	Retailers like Wal-Mart, Tesco, Carrefour, and Metro AG continue to spread across the globe. In the grocery retail segment, for the top three players, 58 percent of sales come from outside the company's home market.[c]	The number of local farmers' markets in the United States almost doubled over the last 10 years, growing 19 percent between 2005 and 2006 alone.[d] In England, the first farmers' market was established in London in 1999. Now there are now 16 certified farmers' markets in London, with 550 nationwide.[e]
Media	In 1983, there were 50 dominant media corporations; today there are 5. The combined influence of Time Warner, Disney, Viacom, News Corporation, and Bertelsmann is enormous in terms of what is watched, read, and listened to around the world. Global news and entertainment	In 2007, Technorati tracked 70 million weblogs, with a new one being created every second.[f] The vast majority of blogs are focused on people's daily lives rather than world events. Technorati's list of the 100 most popular online sites included 22 blogs. While Japanese and English battle it out

Continued

Table 16.2 Continued

Trends in . . .	Trend toward Homogeneity	Trend toward Diversity
	channels like CNN, BBC World, Discovery, and MTV reach millions around the world daily.	as the most popular blogging languages, Farsi entered the top 10 list in 2007 with 1 percent of the posts measured.

[a] David Graddol, *The Future of English?* The British Council 2000. Book first published by The British Council in 1997 www.britcoun.org/english/enge2000.htm.

[b] http://news.bbc.co.uk/2/hi/europe/6220591.stm.

[c] www.atkearney.com/shared_res/pdf/GRDI_2005.pdf.

[d] www.ams.usda.gov/farmersmarkets/FarmersMarketGrowth.htm.

[e] www.thelondonpaper.com/cs/Satellite/london/food/article/1157140114749?packedargs=suffix%3DSubSectionArticle.

[f] http://technorati.com/weblog/2007/04/328.html.

Local Communities Can Be Virtual

The Internet allows individuals to form communities based on common interests that cut across geographies. These communities enable sharing of information, and sometimes much more. For example, 20,000 members of MyFootballClub contributed £35 each to own a share in the United Kingdom's Blue Square Premier football (soccer) team, Ebbsfleet United. When the landmark deal goes into effect in 2008, members will vote on player selection, transfers, and all major decisions. The deal has attracted investors from around the world, including over 1,500 from the United States. Many soccer enthusiasts and commentators suggest that the interest in the club is in part a reaction to the lack of connection that many fans feel with big soccer brands like Manchester United.

The connectivity promoted by Yahoo!, Google, MySpace, Facebook, and Bebo has prepared the way for brands to engage people online. For instance, *Contagious* magazine draws our attention to Dole's attempt at engagement by banana. Stickers on every bunch of organic bananas sold by Dole in the United States include summary information on the fruit's origin as well as a three-digit code. Consumers who enter this code at www.doleorganic.com can see who grew that banana and where it was picked. What better way of creating a sense of connection that crosses borders? As this example illustrates, brands don't have to create elaborate social networks or games to succeed online; they just need to come up with something engaging that fits with their promise. As the review in *Contagious* states, "When a banana goes digital, the future does too."[13]

The Middle Ground Will Become Increasingly Dangerous

If the future really does call for more local thought and local action, companies that have moved too far in the direction of global consistency may be ill-equipped to deal with it. In that case, they may have little alternative but to hold their ground as best they can by leveraging their advantages of scale.

But companies fight to survive in the same way that species do. They evolve and adapt to changing circumstances. Sir Martin Sorrell expects the global/local divergence to cause companies to reorganize into an "hourglass" shape, knocking out regional management in favor of strong global and local teams. Strong local teams will ensure that the expression of a global brand is as effective as possible in each market; the global team will highlight best practice and encourage a search-and-redeploy mentality.

Extrapolating from existing trends, we may expect to see two or three dominant global brands in each product and service category, counterbalanced by an ecosystem of local and specialist brands. Strong global brands, premium specialists, and value players are all likely to survive. The bland regional and midpriced brands are most likely to be at risk.

Go West, Young Brand

The world economy may be shifting from West to East, but to be a truly global brand, you still need to compete successfully in the West. Many brands from China, India, and elsewhere are eyeing the developed markets as the next frontier.

Lenovo, the company that bought IBM's Thinkpad brand, produces a line of well-designed pocket PC phones that hold their own against products from Samsung, Sony, and Nokia. Lenovo and appliance giant Haier are shaking off the cheap, low-quality image associated with Chinese brands. In the near term, a Chinese brand with a proposition based on quality and value could prove very attractive to price-sensitive westerners.

Cheaper prices may not be the only thing consumers find appealing about Chinese brands. As China's influence grows, we can expect Chinese style to have a major influence on fashion and product design. Shanghai Tang, China's first global luxury brand, is already making its presence felt in the world of fashion. Inspired by Chinese history and art, the brand has found success on the global stage with its revitalized Chinese fashions from the 1920s and 1930s. A 2006 *Fast Company* article credits the brand's creative director, Joanne Ooi, as saying "I decided it was really, really imperative to create cultural roots for every single product."[14] The brand now has stores in 11 countries, including the United States, the United Kingdom, and France.

The westward march of Asian brands will only add to the pressure on existing western brands. Unlike Shanghai Tang, many of the incomers will be positioned as value brands. This strategy worked well for Toyota, Sony, Hyundai, and Samsung. Global warming permitting, it seems likely to work well for Chinese and Indian companies too. Once established, they will need to start the long climb upward, adding features and benefits to their offerings in order to increase their price points, at the same time building their brands to offer something more than just an economical deal. Western brands will have two options: fight fire with fire and lower prices or continue to build their own value proposition through innovation and brand building.

The Fragmentation Frontier

We all know the fundamental issue: Consumers are suffering from attention deficit disorder brought on by too much choice. Now the moral imperatives brought on by concerns over global warming—to buy local, to buy green—are layered on top of an already bewildering variety of alternatives. People are recognizing that every purchase decision has consequences, but figuring out what the consequences really are is tough.

In theory, new media give consumers control over this complex world. When people can rouse themselves to use them, search engines, product ratings, and social networks can help shoppers make better purchase decisions. In reality, however, the online world of search and word of mouth is just as complex and confusing as the offline world. As a result, I believe that people will still be drawn to a simple, straightforward brand promise. If they find that a brand lives up to its promise, they are likely to stick with it. Why make another decision? If and when a brand exceeds their expectations, they are likely to recommend it to others. Advocacy will spread the word more effectively than search engine rankings or branded TV shows.

That said, a brand still needs to make its promise heard, and people need to find that promise personally relevant. They need to feel they can trust the company behind the brand to act in their best interests. Given the diversity of interests out there, many brands will need to align themselves with ever-narrower communities. If a brand cannot maintain broad, mass-market appeal, it will have to focus on the needs of specific segments of consumers, which may be defined more by shared attitudes than by demographics. A brand that can serve the needs of a specific target group better than any other can compensate for lack of mass appeal and trade volume by charging a premium price.

A really strong brand can rise above a specific product category. Apple offers the same philosophy and sense of design across computers, laptops, music players, and phones. Dove offers the same promise across soap, body lotion, antiperspirant, and hair care. Disney spans theme parks, cruise ships, movies, and games.

In the future, it will be far tougher for a brand to rise above an established connection with one community in making a broad appeal to others. The more a brand draws strength from a sense of community among users, the more likely it is to have a polarizing effect. Apple has set itself up against PCs in its "Mac versus PC" advertising. In doing so, it may alienate PC users with its superior and self-satisfied tone. Dove, in seeking to appeal to western values of personal self-worth, may undermine its appeal to women who still appreciate the adulation that outer beauty might bring. Disney, being firmly associated with family fun, will not make my short list of vacation destinations.

Walking the Talk

Nike, Guinness, and Dole are just a few examples of well-established brands that are happily surfing the new media wave. Increasingly, however, engagement is going to mean more than creating an engaging brand experience. For many brands, engagement will come to mean standing for something—a belief or a set of values—and inviting customers to stand with you. Brands need to declare their beliefs and act on them. Brands that are succeeding in doing this today include Whole Foods, Innocent, Newman's Own, Body Shop, and Patagonia.

Declaring and living out values should not be confused with merely supporting a good cause. Yoplait, M&M's, and Lee Jeans prominently supported the Susan G. Komen Breast Cancer Foundation in the United States during 2007. Assisting such a worthy cause is a laudable corporate action, but if a related value, such as the promotion of women's health, is not part of a brand's DNA, then the association with the cause may be viewed as nothing more than a marketing tactic. People know which brands are really committed to something and which ones are just trying to sell more stuff.

The future is uncertain, but one thing is sure: People pay a lot more attention to what companies do than to what they say. People respect companies that try to do the right things. If they believe companies are acting out of enlightened self-interest, as in the case of Wal-Mart, they are less likely to be cynical about their motives. Companies that seek to market their brands through "greenwashing" could find themselves pilloried online and off.

Surfing the Wave

Successfully riding the wave of the future will require anticipation, poise, and agility. It will require us to become far better at understanding our target audiences and anticipating their needs. Marketers will need to find ways to make their brands stand up and stand out, going beyond functional benefits to create a sense of purpose and identity.

We will need to be adaptable, changing to meet shifting conditions. The future of global brands does not lie in one-size-fits-all offers and cookie-cutter marketing. Successful global brands will embrace the diversity of individuals, communities, and cultures around the world. They will be comfortable appealing to a mind-set, not an age bracket. They will deliver great brand experiences, and they will orchestrate that experience across a wide variety of communication channels. To do so effectively and efficiently, these brands will have to allow local team members the freedom to act quickly and sensitively. Advantages of scale will be realized not from the application of rigid rules and rote systems but from a broad, shared understanding of the brand and the functional, emotional, and social benefits that it brings to its customers.

Addendum
From Leamington Spa to Beijing: How Millward Brown Became a Successful Global Brand

Dominic Twose
Global Head of Knowledge Management, Millward Brown

Millward Brown is one of the largest market research companies in the world. The story of how the company evolved to this position, with a globally consistent brand in just 35 years, is a classic example of vision and determination, combined with innovation and a pioneering culture.

Beginnings

Millward Brown was formed in the United Kingdom in 1973 by Gordon Brown and Maurice Millward, who had both worked as client-side researchers at General Foods. Gordon and Maurice set up shop in Leamington Spa, a town in the English Midlands. Their offices were above a row of real estate agents, and because they did not have their own computer, they used the town hall computer at nights.

Maurice summarized the Millward Brown philosophy early on: "Our objective has always been to provide our clients with information which allows them confidently to make the correct marketing and management decisions."

Gordon elaborated on how the company would approach this: "Where there are benefits to be derived from doing so, we always aim to develop new methods. But our fundamental belief is that techniques and technology should be regarded as adjuncts to thinking, not as substitutes for it."

As the company developed, Maurice focused on the operational side of the business; his particular forte was in finding practical solutions to intractable sampling and technical problems. Gordon concentrated on the company's intellectual developments.

Continuous Tracking

In 1976, Maurice and Gordon set up their first continuous tracking study for Cadbury Schweppes. The objective was to explore the issue of ad wear-out. Cadbury spent millions on advertising each year and needed a research tool that told it when executions ceased to be effective for its brands.

The continuous tracking methodology involved interviewing hundreds of different people every week across the country, taking great care to ensure that the samples were consistent, so that any changes measured were due to activity in the market. By plotting the resulting trends against marketing activity over time, it was easier to identify cause and effect than it was using traditional research approaches.

This was a time of great learning for the company. The continuous tracking study offered a unique way of looking at how advertising affected brand health over time. Because the findings confounded all the prevailing theories of advertising, Gordon came up with a new model, which allowed Millward Brown executives to make powerful recommendations in debriefs. Rather than simply describing what was seen in the data, Millward Brown began to be accepted as a partner in developing great advertising.

Along with his new philosophy, Gordon's quantitative approach to advertising assessment represented an enormous challenge to the conventional wisdom of the time. An emphasis on qualitative research in the advertising planning process had led everyone to believe that consumers were highly involved with advertising. Gordon said that they weren't. This led to a degree of intellectual confrontation between Millward Brown and London advertising agencies.

In 1984, Gordon published a paper, "Advertising Tracking Studies and Sales Effects," in which he presented analysis that combined econometric modeling with tracking data for three Cadbury brands. He showed that for each brand, the ads that achieved high ad awareness also produced stronger sales effects. In 1986, Gordon published another paper, "Modelling Advertising Awareness," in the journal *The Statistician*. In this paper, Gordon introduced the Awareness Index (AI), a measure of an ad's efficiency in generating awareness. The AI proved to be a valuable tool over the years and is now a widely used metric for aiding the assessment of advertising.

Going to America

As early as 1980, David Jenkins, the international research manager of Cadbury Schweppes, invited Gordon on a lecture tour of Cadbury's companies in the United States. He also introduced Gordon to Cadbury's U.S. research suppliers. At a time when most U.K. research companies were considering expansion into Europe, Maurice and Gordon recognized the huge potential the United States had to offer. To raise Millward Brown's profile in the States, Gordon secured speaking engagements at the Advertising Research Foundation in New York.

Responding to client interest, Gordon and company began conducting tracking studies in the United States. These studies were run out of the United Kingdom, and it quickly became evident that to ensure adequate quality control, Millward Brown would need its own field force in the States. And if it was to become a significant force there, the company would also need its own offices. The most practical solution to these problems was for the company to buy a U.S. research agency. In 1985, Millward Brown was floated on the U.K. Unlisted Securities Market to raise the needed funds. Sharon Potter, the company's finance director, was instrumental in easing the process of completing the transaction, since neither researchers nor financiers were familiar with what the other group did.

The purchase of the U.S. company Ad Factors was completed in 1986. Bob Meyers, executive vice president of Ad Factors, became chief executive of the new company, which was called Ad Factors/Millward Brown until the Ad Factors name was dropped in the company's second year. David Jenkins, who had joined Millward Brown from Cadbury Schweppes, moved to the United States. Armed with his in-depth understanding of the unique Millward Brown offer, he helped the U.S. business grow at a rapid pace.

Development of Link

Despite this growth, Millward Brown was facing a serious commercial problem in the United Kingdom. It was pretesting ads, using a fairly standard approach, but the results observed in tracking, particularly the Awareness Index, did not always match the pretesting outcomes. Given the emphasis the company was putting on the Awareness Index, this represented a significant commercial challenge. But it also represented a unique opportunity. Gordon Brown, together with Nigel Hollis, developed the Link pretest based on what they had learned from tracking. Link was launched in the United Kingdom in 1988.

Going Global

The success of the move into the United States, along with the globalization of its biggest clients, led to the decision to make Millward Brown a global company. The process started in 1987, with moves into Europe led by Tony Copeland, who had joined the company in 1984. In 1989, Gordon and Maurice sold the company to WPP, the marketing and communications conglomerate being assembled by Martin Sorrell. The sale was meant to provide Millward Brown with funds for continued global expansion; however, global economic conditions were such that WPP did not have the capital to invest. But by arranging a series of license deals and joint ventures, Millward Brown continued to extend its global reach to Italy, France, and Germany.

There was a pioneering spirit in the way the company established its international presence, driven by a desire to meet client needs. A number of individuals played a key role in this development. Cath Barnes moved to Asia and introduced the brand there. Andrea Bielli was enlisted to head up the Italian office and later took over Continental Europe. Rosi Ware was recruited to head up the U.K. company. Coming as she did from the advertising world, she understood the prevalent criticisms of Millward Brown and was able to change the way the company was perceived. This was critical to establishing the Link business in the United Kingdom and reducing tension between agencies and Millward Brown.

Gordon continued to play an active role within the company. In 1991, he published "How Advertising Affects the Sales of Packaged Goods Brands." In this document, known internally as "The Black Book," Gordon laid out his views on how advertising works. He then turned his focus to print advertising. Recognizing that print was different from TV in many respects, Gordon, together with Gordon Pincott, conducted a series of experiments and tailored studies. These projects led to a new understanding of the value of print advertising, proving that it was as effective as TV.

In 1992, Maurice retired, to pursue a number of interests including a passion for music. Gordon retired two years later to sail around the world on his yacht. The mantle of leadership then passed to David Jenkins. David had been in charge of business development in the United States and continued the focus on the global expansion of Millward Brown in order to service the company's most global clients. By 1994, considerable progress had been made in this area; Jean McDougall had expanded the relationship with United Distillers across Europe, Latin America, and Asia Pacific, until Millward Brown was servicing that client in 20 countries.

Another major opportunity presented itself when Unilever decided to standardize its pretesting and tracking methodologies worldwide. Millward Brown was chosen to become its preferred supplier, with Sue Gardiner taking on the role of global account director. Sue declared that the secret of her success was to be there whenever there was a Unilever research or marketing meeting. Saying "They can't escape me," she traveled the globe building strong local and regional client relationships.

In 1994, the same year David Jenkins took over as CEO, Nigel Hollis, who took on the role of group director of research and development on Gordon's departure, published a groundbreaking paper. Drawing on work by Paul Dyson using econometric sales modeling, Nigel demonstrated a link between the AI and sales across brands and categories. This work was subsequently developed to incorporate the effect of persuasion. This analysis, demonstrating the relationship between key metrics and sales, helped establish the value of the Millward Brown approach around the world.

Understanding Brand Equity

As CEO, David Jenkins turned the company's emphasis to understanding brand health. Millward Brown had a good understanding of how the main media worked, he argued, but it needed a better understanding of brand equity and how to measure it. David invested in a massive research and development project, run by Nigel Hollis, Paul Dyson, and Andy Farr, which resulted in the launch of BrandDynamics™ in 1996.

Behind BrandDynamics was the understanding that senior management needed robust, straightforward, easy-to-understand metrics to guide their understanding of a brand's health, while the marketing teams needed a detailed understanding of what comprised that brand health in order to know what action to take. BrandDynamics proved to be so successful that WPP later adopted and adapted it as BrandZ, a research tool with its own massive database for use across the WPP network.

Knowledge Management

Recognizing that, with so many employees spread around the world, it would be hard for them to keep up with the latest developments, David introduced one other major innovation: the Knowledge Management system. An intranet site was developed, which over the last 10 years has grown into a major resource for the company. A team of knowledge managers around the world act as a focal point for queries, ensuring that every member of staff has access to the best thinking within the Millward Brown world.

Continued Global Growth

At the end of 1997, David Jenkins left Millward Brown for a role with WPP. Bob Meyers become the global CEO. Rosi Ware took over the U.S. company and doubled its size over the next three years. Bob, Rosi, and chief financial officer Mike Gettle also expanded the company into Latin America, initially setting up a Millward Brown company in Mexico with Fabian Hernandez at the helm and partnering with other companies throughout the region. Over the next eight years, many of these partnerships and licensing agreements evolved into wholly owned Millward Brown companies. Sue Gardiner and Sharon Potter, then joint managing directors of the U.K. company, continued to expand the company's footprint to Africa and the Middle East.

In 2007, Eileen Campbell became the worldwide CEO following a very successful stint as CEO of North America and as chairman of global development, during which time Millward Brown acquired ACRS in China. In 2008, Millward Brown combined forces with IMRB (Indian Market Research Bureau) to create a joint venture in India. Millward Brown will have a majority share in Millward Brown India with offices in Mumbai, Delhi, and Bangalore.

Millward Brown Today

Today Millward Brown helps clients build and grow their brands, providing guidance in areas from strategy development through to marketing execution and assessment. The company is a truly global brand. Recognized by many involved in marketing around the world, Millward Brown works with about two-thirds of the world's 100 biggest brands. The company's successful growth can be attributed to a number of factors, including:

1. Starting with continuous tracking, following through to Link and BrandDynamics, Millward Brown developed a unique set of research tools that offer genuinely useful insight into marketing issues.
2. The company was early to recognize the importance of an international offering.
3. There was a strong commitment to providing the best resources to every office.
4. The company recruited great people: goal oriented, self-motivated, insightful, forthright, and entrepreneurial.

The company has developed expertise in many new and relevant areas, including the ever-expanding world of media as well as sponsorship and public relations. Dynamic Logic, a company specializing in online research, was acquired to enable Millward Brown to offer a range of tools to measure the effectiveness of every sort of online advertising. Millward Brown Optimor was established to quantify the value that brands can bring to business. As it becomes increasingly necessary for marketing teams to justify their budget in return-on-investment terms, brand valuation is a growing and valuable field. Millward Brown Optimor's annual "Top 100 Most Powerful Brands" study, the only brand ranking to combine consumer measures of brand equity with financial data, is the result of combining the financial expertise of the Optimor team with BrandZ data. Published in conjunction with the *Financial Times*, it demonstrates the real financial value that successful brand management can deliver.

As of January 2008, Millward Brown employed approximately 5000 people in 76 offices in 44 countries. And the company now has its own computers.

Appendix A

Millward Brown Optimor BrandZ™ Top 100 Most Valuable Brands Ranking 2008

Position	Brand	Brand Value $M	% Change in Brand Value (vs.2007)	Position Change
1	Google	86,057	30%	=
2	GE (General Electric)	71,379	15%	=
3	Microsoft	70,887	29%	=
4	Coca-Cola[1]	58,208	17%	=
5	China Mobile	57,225	39%	=
6	IBM	55,335	65%	3
7	Apple	55,206	123%	9
8	McDonald's	49,499	49%	3
9	Nokia	43,975	39%	3
10	Marlboro	37,324	−5%	−4
11	Vodafone	36,962	75%	11
12	Toyota	35,134	5%	−2
13	Wal-Mart	34,547	−6%	−6
14	Bank of America	33,092	15%	−1
15	Citi	30,318	−10%	−7
16	HP	29,278	17%	−1
17	BMW	28,015	9%	−3
18	ICBC	28,004	70%	15
19	Louis Vuitton	25,739	13%	1
20	American Express	24,816	7%	−1
21	Wells Fargo	24,739	2%	−3
22	Cisco	24,101	28%	2
23	Disney	23,705	5%	−2
24	UPS	23,610	−4%	−7
25	Tesco	23,208	39%	7
26	Oracle	22,904	29%	4

Continued

Appendix A Continued

Position	Brand	Brand Value $M	% Change in Brand Value (vs. 2007)	Position Change
27	Intel	22,027	18%	−2
28	Porsche	21,718	62%	12
29	SAP	21,669	20%	−2
30	Gillette	21,523	20%	−2
31	China Construction Bank	19,603	82%	30
32	Bank of China	19,418	42%	6
33	Verizon Wireless	19,202	18%	1
34	Royal Bank of Canada	18,995	39%	5
35	HSBC	18,479	6%	−4
36	Mercedes	18,044	1%	−7
37	Honda	16,649	8%	−1
38	L'Oréal	16,459	34%	8
39	Pepsi[2]	15,404	15%	9
40	Home Depot	15,378	−16%	−14
41	Dell	15,288	10%	−4
42	Deutsche Bank	15,104	14%	−1
43	ING[3]	15,080	31%	10
44	Carrefour	15,057	29%	5
45	NTT DoCoMo	15,048	11%	−22
46	Target	14,738	27%	6
47	Siemens	14,665	61%	24
48	Banco Santander	14,549	20%	−1
49	Accenture	14,137	34%	13
50	Orange	14,093	42%	17
51	BlackBerry	13,734	390%	102
52	Chase	12,782	14%	7
53	Nike	12,499	21%	10
54	Canon	12,398	9%	=
55	AT&T	12,030	30%	15
56	Starbucks	12,011	−25%	−21
57	Goldman Sachs	11,944	45%	19
58	Samsung	11,870	−7%	−14
59	Nissan	11,707	5%	−1
60	Marks & Spencer	11,600	22%	8
61	Amazon	11,511	93%	31
62	Yahoo!	11,465	−13%	−20
63	Morgan Stanley	11,327	1%	−7
64	UBS	11,220	−3%	−13
65	eBay	11,200	−13%	−22
66	H&M	11,182	28%	7
67	Wachovia	11,022	10%	−2
68	Ford	10,971	−13%	−23

Continued

Appendix A Continued

Position	Brand	Brand Value $M	% Change in Brand Value (vs.2007)	Position Change
69	Chevrolet	10,862	−3%	−12
70	Budweiser[4]	10,839	9%	−4
71	Colgate	10,576	37%	7
72	Harley-Davidson	10,401	1%	−8
73	Subway	10,335	39%	7
74	Merrill Lynch	9,802	−16%	−24
75	JP Morgan	9,762	15%	−1
76	Hermès	9,631	39%	9
77	BBVA	9,457	N/A	N/A
78	State Farm	9,425	8%	−6
79	Gucci	9,341	43%	10
80	Cartier	9,285	32%	4
81	FedEx	9,273	0%	−12
82	Tide	9,123	N/A	N/A
83	T-Mobile	8,940	11%	−6
84	Zara	8,682	34%	6
85	Chanel	8,656	15%	−6
86	IKEA	8,507	15%	−5
87	Ariel	8,437	N/A	N/A
88	Telefónica Movistar	8,117	73%	20
89	MTS	8,077	N/A	N/A
90	Esprit	7,907	46%	9
91	TIM	7,903	−6%	−16
92	Motorola	7,575	−30%	−32
93	Barclays	7,382	12%	−6
94	Avon	7,209	10%	−6
95	Auchan	7,148	28%	1
96	VW (Volkswagen)	7,143	2%	−13
97	AXA	7,141	50%	8
98	AIG	7,102	21%	−4
99	MasterCard	6,970	52%	13
100	Standard Chartered Bank	6,855	73%	25

Notes:

(1) Coke's value includes both Coke and Diet Coke

(2) Pepsi's value includes both Pepsi and Diet Pepsi

(3) ING's value includes both ING Bank and insurance

(4) Budweiser's value includes both Bud and Bud Light

Appendix B

The Global Brand Survey

In order to explore the role of local culture on brand success, Millward Brown commissioned a global survey to better understand the strength of global versus local brands. The questions we wanted to answer were:

- What role do factors like heritage, culture, and local production have on people's likelihood to buy a brand?
- Is there a difference between global and local brands in terms of what motivates people to buy them?

The Nature of the Survey

The survey was conducted in eight countries: (from west to east) the United States, Mexico, Brazil, the United Kingdom, Germany, Russia, India, and China.

In each country, we compared two global brands to two local brands in each of five categories: cars, beer, fast food, shampoo/conditioners, and soft drinks.

In total, we interviewed 3307 people about 91 different brands. About 400 people were interviewed in each country. A single respondent could answer for up to three categories for which he or she qualified. (The qualification was that people were likely to buy or use a brand in the category.) Because they are more likely to make brand decisions about hair products, only women were asked questions in the shampoo/conditioner category. Because men buy and consume more beer, only men were asked questions in the beer category.

The fact that the survey was conducted online limited the sample to people with at least moderate levels of income and education (in whom brand marketers are most interested), and quotas were applied to achieve a balance across age groups.

Sample Sources Used

Partnering in the research with us were Lightspeed Research, Survey Sampling International, and Greenfield Online. From the high-quality panels provided by these companies, we recruited participants who met the survey criteria.

Questionnaire

Because the survey was short (taking approximately 10 minutes to complete), we needed to focus our questions on people's perceptions of brands. We were not attempting to provide a complete understanding of individual brand equity.

Which Brands Were Included?

Table B.1 summarizes the brands asked about by country. The global brands we selected for study were McDonald's, KFC, Budweiser, Heineken, Toyota, Ford, Pantene Pro-V,

Table B.1 Brands Asked, by Category and Country, in the Global Brand Survey

	Global Brand 1	Global Brand 2	Local Brand 1	Local Brand 2
Fast Foods				
U.S.	McDonald's	KFC	Quiznos	White Castle
Mexico	McDonald's	KFC	Vips	Taquería Local
Brazil	McDonald's	Pizza Hut	Habib's	Bob's
U.K.	McDonald's	KFC	Wimpy	Little Chef
Germany	McDonald's	KFC	Nordsee	Wienerwald
Russia	McDonald's	Rostics-KFC	Kroshka-Kartoshka	Yolki-Palki
India	McDonald's	Pizza Hut	Barista	Café Coffee Day
China	McDonald's	KFC	Lihua	Yong He
Beers				
U.S.	Budweiser	Heineken	Sam Adams	Corona
Mexico	Budweiser	Heineken	Corona	Victoria
Brazil	Miller	Heineken	Skol	Bohemia
U.K.	Budweiser	Heineken	Boddingtons	John Smith's
Germany	Budweiser	Heineken	Becks	Warsteiner
Russia	Miller	Heineken	Baltika	Stary Melnik
India	Foster's	Heineken	Kingfisher	Royal Challenge
China	Budweiser	Heineken	Yanjing	Tsingtao
Cars				
U.S.	Ford	Toyota	Saturn	Buick
Mexico	Ford	Toyota	Volkswagen	Nissan
Brazil	Ford	Toyota	Fiat	Volkswagen
U.K.	Ford	Toyota	Vauxhall	Mini
Germany	Ford	Toyota	Volkswagen	Opel
Russia	Ford	Toyota	Lada	Volga
India	Ford	Toyota	Maruti Suzuki	Tata Motors
China	Buick	Toyota	Chevy	FAW

Continued

Table B.1 Continued

	Global Brand 1	Global Brand 2	Local Brand 1	Local Brand 2
Shampoo/Conditioner				
U.S.	Dove	Pantene Pro-V	Suave	Pert Plus
Mexico	Dove	Pantene Pro-V	Caprice	Sedal
Brazil	Dove	Pantene Pro-V	Seda	Natura
U.K.	Dove	Pantene Pro-V	Timotei	Tresemme
Germany	Dove	Pantene Pro-V	Guhl	Schauma
Russia	Dove	Pantene Pro-V	Chistaya Liniya	Russkoe Pole
India	Clinic Plus	Pantene Pro-V	Sunsilk	Dabur Vatika
China	Rejoice	Pantene Pro-V	Haseline	Slek
Carbonated Soft Drinks/Drinks				
U.S.	Coca-Cola	Pepsi	Dr. Pepper	Mountain Dew
Mexico	Coca-Cola	Pepsi	Jarritos	Peñafiel
Brazil	Coca-Cola	Pepsi	Dolly	Guaraná Kuat
U.K.	Coca-Cola	Pepsi	Tango	Irn Bru
Germany	Coca-Cola	Pepsi	Bionade	Red Bull
Russia	Coca-Cola	Pepsi	Fiesta	Fruk Time
India	Coca-Cola	Pepsi	Thums Up	Limca
China	Coca-Cola	Pepsi	Feichang Coke	Kangshifu

Dove, Coca-Cola, and Pepsi. However, because truly global brands are scarce, in some countries we had to make substitutions for one or more of these brands. For example, in Russia, we replaced Budweiser with Miller, and in Brazil, KFC with Pizza Hut. It is not that Budweiser is not present in Russia but simply that its presence there is too low for it to serve as a meaningful example of a global brand.

We selected local brands on a similar basis in each country. They had to be well known enough for the majority of people to have an opinion of them. Again, we had to make some adjustments for certain countries and categories. For example, because there are no major car brands that are truly "local" to Brazil, we had to select two foreign-owned brands, Volkswagen and Fiat, which are regarded as local because they have been manufactured in Brazil for many years. In one or two cases we deliberately selected a brand in order to make cross-country comparisons (e.g., Buick in the United States and China, Corona in the United States and Mexico).

Cultural Responses Affect Cross-Country Comparisons

Table B.2 shows the average percentage of people agreeing with each of seven agree/disagree statements asked in our global survey. The differences between countries are due in part to the fact that culture influences the way people respond to survey questions. This effect can make it challenging to interpret cross-country studies.

Table B.2 Average Percentage Agreeing across Seven Statements

Country	U.S.	Mexico	Brazil	U.K.	Germany	Russia	India	China
% agree	48	52	52	46	40	49	58	58

To keep things as simple as possible, all tables in the book refer to "raw" data, and I have drawn attention to relatively high or low scores as necessary.

People Who Made the Survey Happen

I would like to extend my thanks to all the people who had a hand in the implementation of the survey. In particular, I would like to thank the following people, without whose help I might have had data, but not findings that made sense:

Doreen Harmon, Vice President, Millward Brown

Amy Womack, Account Executive, Millward Brown

Jim Spaete, Data Technologies & Processing Senior Manager, Kantar Operations

Paul Bierzychudek, Senior Research Analyst, Millward Brown

Notes

Introduction

1. Geoffrey Probert, "Meeting Client Needs Now and In the Future," (Presentation, Millward Brown CEO Conference, Arion Hotel, Astir Palace Resort, Vouliagmeni, Greece, April 8, 2003).
2. Millward Brown is one of the world's top 10 marketing research organizations, with more than 70 offices in 44 countries. A part of the Kantar Group (the information, insight, and consultancy arm of WPP), Millward Brown is dedicated to helping clients build strong profitable brands and services.

Chapter 1

1. Paul Feldwick, *What Is Brand Equity Anyway?* (Henley-on-Thames, United Kingdom: World Advertising Research Center, 2002).
2. Graham Page and Jane Raymond, "Cognitive Neuroscience, Marketing and Research: Separating Fact from Fiction," (ESOMAR, Annual Congress, London, September 2006).
3. Jeremy Bullmore, *Apples, Insights & Mad Inventors* (Chichester, England : John Wiley & Sons, 2006), 64.
4. If you do recognize the name, you either live in Brazil or have spent time there, and you are likely to remember one of the 300-plus ads featuring Carlos Menos that helped propel Bombril to iconic status in Brazil. No mean feat for a simple scouring pad!
5. Faris Yakob, "Brands: Socially Constructed Reality," Talent Imitates, Genius Steals, January 10, 2007, http://farisyakob.typepad.com/about.html.
6. Peter Brabeck, interview by author, November 12, 2007.
7. Jeremy Bullmore, *Apples, Insights & Mad Inventors* (Chichester, England: John Wiley & Sons, 2006), 143.
8. Maurice Saatchi, "The Strange Death of Modern Advertising," *Financial Times* (June 22, 2006).
9. Richard Swaab, "Where Great Minds Meet: Global vs. Local" (Panel session, Seminar on Global Advertising sponsored by Millward Brown, London, November 20, 2007).
10. Gerd Gigerenzer, Peter Todd, and the ABC Research Group, *Simple Heuristics that Make Us Smart* (New York: Oxford University Press, 1999).
11. Erik du Plessis, *The Advertised Mind* (London, England: Kogan Page, 2005).
12. A.G. Lafley, *P&G 2002 Annual Report*, Cincinnati: Deloitte and Touche, 3.
13. Andy Farr and Gordon Brown, "Persuasion or Enhancement? An Experiment," *MRS Conference Papers*, 1994, 69–77.

14. John Deighton, "The Interaction of Advertising and Evidence," *The Journal of Consumer Research*, vol. 11, no. 3, (Dec., 1984) 763–70.

Chapter 2

1. Simon Rothon, interview by author, November 16, 2007.
2. Theodore Levitt, "The Globalization of Markets," *Harvard Business Review* (May–June 1983).
3. Pankaj Ghemawat, "Assess Your Global Readiness," Pankaj Ghemawat: What in the World, October 8, 2007, http://discussionleader.hbsp.com/ghemawat/.
4. Daniel Tearno, "Forging a Global Strategy for a Global Brand: Heineken U.S.A. Inc.," *The Advertiser* (June 2002).
5. Bill Ramsay, "Whither Global Branding? The Case of Food Manufacturing," *Journal of Brand Management* (2003): 11, 9–21.
6. Kim Severson, "The World's Best Candy Bars? English, of Course," *New York Times*, July 11, 2007.
7. Martin Lindstrom, *"Localised globalism,"* BrandFlash video blog, October 17, 2007, http://www.martinlindstrom.com/site_files/main_content/blog_player.php/id__66.
8. Mary Dillon, "The McDonald's 'Recipe' for Sustaining Growth," Association of National Advertisers Annual Conference, Phoenix, Arizona (October 12, 2007).
9. "Selling P&G," *Fortune Magazine* (September 5, 2007).
10. Jeben Berg, interview by author, January 11, 2008.

Chapter 3

1. Paul Dyson, Andy Farr, and Nigel Hollis, "Measuring and Using Brand Equity," *Journal of Advertising Research* vol. 36, no. 6, Nov/Dec (1996), 9–21.
2. Tom French, "Customer-focused Growth: The Keys to Success," (Presentation at The CMO Summit: Driving Customer-Focused Growth, Evanston, Illinois, September 20, 2007).
3. We determined the percent of brands that gained or lost share. To qualify as a gain or loss, the share change had to be at least 0.2 percent. Then we subtracted the percent of brands that lost share from the percent that gained share, to arrive at the net percentage gained/lost.

Chapter 4

1. To qualify for the analysis, brands needed to have been included in the BrandZ survey in at least seven countries between 2000 and 2007. The analysis is conducted within product or service category and within country.
2. Salil Tripathi, "A Disingenuous Campaign against U.S. Colas," *International Herald Tribune*, August 25, 2006, http://www.iht.com/articles/2006/08/24/opinion/edsalil.php.
3. Rasheeda Bhagat, "New Products, Consumer Focus Put Fizz Back in Coke," *Hindu Business Line*, October 3, 2007, http://www.thehindubusinessline.com/2007/10/03/stories/2007100351570500.htm.

4. Fiona Gilmore, *Warriors on the High Wire* (Great Britain, Profile Business, 2003), 8.
5. Linda Ban, Allan Henderson, Penny Koppinger, Benjamin Stanley, "Changing Lanes for Success: Flexible Automotive Business Models in Times of Accelerated Change," *IBM Global Business Services* (Somers, New York, July, 2006).
6. Gerard Tellis and Peter Golder, *Will and Vision: How Latecomers Grow to Dominate Markets* (Los Angeles, Figueroa Press, 2006), 42.
7. ibid. 43.
8. ibid. 41.
9. http://en.wikipedia.org/wiki/History_of_mobile_phones.
10. "Nokia's Upward Mobility in Uncertainty," *Innovate*; March–April 2006, http://www.korekalibre.com/index.php?option=com_magazine&task=show_ma gazine_article&magazine_id=5&Itemid=28&cat_id=46.
11. Gerard Tellis and Peter Golder, *Will and Vision: How Latecomers Grow to Dominate Markets* (Los Angeles, Figueroa Press, 2006), 41.
12. http://www.solepedia.com/Nike.
13. "Palace Revolution," *Design Week* (December 12, 2007), http://www. designweek.co.uk/Articles/136974/Palace+revolution.html.
14. Jonah Bloom, "The awards shows need to tear down silos, but it won't happen," *Advertising Age* 78.26 (June 25, 2007): 21.
15. Louise Story, "The New Advertising Outlet: Your Life," *New York Times*, October 14, 2007.
16. Frederick Dalzell, Davis Dyer, and Rowena Olegario, *Rising Tide: Lessons from 165 Years of Brand Building at Procter & Gamble* (Boston: Harvard Business School Press, 2004), 271–76.
17. Douglas Holt, *How Brands Become Icons* (Boston: Harvard Business School Press, 2004).
18. Andy Milligan, Shaun Smith, *Uncommon Practice: People Who Deliver a Great Brand Experience* (Pearson Education, Great Britain, 2002), ix.
19. "Nokia's Upward Mobility in Uncertainty," *Innovate*, March–April 2006, http://www.korekalibre.com/index.php?option=com_magazine&task=show_ma gazine_article&magazine_id=5&Itemid=28&cat_id=46.
20. "Our Impacts and Values," CR Report 2007, http://www.nokia.com/A4942323.

Chapter 5

1. Elise Ackerman, "Google earnings report upbeat," *Oakland Tribune*, April 20, 2007, http://findarticles.com/p/articles/mi_qn4176/is_20070420/ai_ n19038737.
2. Christine Canabou, "Masters of Design: Kun-Hee Lee," *Fast Company*, Issue 83, June 2004.

Chapter 6

1. "For whoever hath, to him shall be given, and he shall have more," *The Economist*, August 9, 2007, http://www.economist.com/displaystory.cfm?story_id=9616888.

2. Keith Bradsher, "A Revisionist Tale: Why a Poor China Seems Richer," *New York Times*, December 21, 2007, http://www.nytimes.com/2007/12/21/business/21yuan.html?ex= 1355979600&en=f08f623d737fa252&ei=5124&partner=permalink&exprod=permalink.

3. Geert Hofstede, "Geert Hofstede Cultural Dimensions," Itim International, http://www.geert-hofstede.com.

4. Geert Hofstede, "Geert Hofstede Cultural Dimensions," Itim International, http://www.geert-hofstede.com.

5. Geert Hofstede, *Masculinity and Femininity: The Taboo Dimension of National Cultures* (Sage Publications, 1998).

6. Diana Farrell, Ulrich Gersch, and Elizabeth Stephenson, "The Value of China's Emerging Middle Class," *The McKinsey Quarterly* (June 2006): 64.

7. BBC News, "India Population 'To be Biggest,'" August 18, 2004, http://news.bbc.co.uk/2/hi/3575994.stm.

8. Steve Hamm and Nandini Lakshman, "Widening Aisles for Indian Shoppers," *BusinessWeek*, April 19, 2007, http://www.businessweek.com/globalbiz/ content/apr2007/ gb20070419_814459.htm?link_position=link2.

9. V. Shashidhar, "Mera Des, Mera Gaon," *USP Age* (March 2006): 25.

10. Sangeeta Gupta, "Unravelling the Diversity of the Indian Market" (ESOMAR, Global Diversity Congress, London, September 2006).

11. Robert Galbraith, "Courting the new Russian and Indian luxury consumers," *International Herald Tribune*, September 30, 2005, http://www.iht.com/articles/ 2005/09/29/opinion/rforeign.php.

12. Steve Liesman, "The Spending Power of Russians has soared since the Fall of Communism," Sept. 24, 2004, http://www.msnbc.msn.com/id/6082215/.

13. TGI Russia, 2005.

Chapter 7

1. Debdatta Das, "HLL, Amul Gun for Top Slot in Ice Cream," *Hindu Business Line*, January 27, 2007, http://www.thehindubusinessline.com/2007/01/27/stories/ 2007012701460500.htm.

2. Saritha Rai, "Battling to Satisfy India's Taste for Ice Cream," *New York Times*, August 20, 2002.

3. Das, "HLL, Amul Gun for Top Slot in Ice Cream."

4. Dilek Dölek Başarir, interview by author, January 25, 2008.

Chapter 8

1. International Monetary Fund, "World Economic and Financial Surveys— Regional Economic Outlook: Sub-Saharan Africa—October 2007," Washington, D.C., 2007.

2. All macroeconomic data quoted excludes Zimbabwe, where triple-digit inflation, ongoing shortages, collapsing infrastructure, and an aging dictator are grim reminders of the old Africa.

3. Nicholas Norbrook, "ICT: Welcome to the Permanent Revolution," *Africa Report Quarterly*, No. 5 (2007), 23.

4. Karen Attwood, "SABMiller brews up a partnership with African farmers," *The Independent*, March 2, 2007, http://www.independent.co.uk/news/business/news/sabmiller-brews-up-a-partnership-with-african-farmers-438533.html.
5. Wanjiru Waithaka, "Small Is Beautiful and Profitable in Kenya," *Mambogani Business Daily*, May 8, 2007, http://www.mambogani.com/forums/index.php?showtopic=6433&hl=small.
6. Patrick Cescau, "Social Innovation: How values-led brands are helping to drive Business Strategy," (Speech, Business as an Agent of World Benefit: A global Forum, Cleveland, Ohio, October 24, 2006).
7. Stephen Williams, "Business Meeting the Challenge," *African Business*, Issue 328 (2007), 36–37.

Chapter 9

1. "Building Brands in China," *BusinessWeek*, November 22, 2005, http://www.businessweek.com/bwdaily/dnflash/nov2005/nf20051122_8451_db016.htm.
2. Tom Doctoroff, "The new multinational brand strategy in China," (Panel discussion 2006 CEO Summit, Peking University, May 19, 2006).
3. Richard Lee, "Winning the battle in China" (Panel discussion, 2006 CEO Summit, Peking University, May 19, 2006).
4. "MILO Announces the Investment of 43.5 Million Bhat," Thailand4.com/news, June 12, 2007, http://www.thailand4.com/news/2007–06–12/0103-milo-announces-the-investment-of-435/.
5. Michelle Krebs, "Chinese Lessons: What GM Has Learned in China," *Edmunds inside Line*, http://www.edmunds.com/insideline/do/Columns/articleId=117775/subsubtypeId=.
6. "GM vehicle designed in China to debut at Detroit auto show," Space Mart: Profiting from Space Today, http://www.spacemart.com/reports/GM_vehicle_designed_in_China_to_debut_at_Detroit_auto_show_999.html.
7. Fara Warner, "Made in China," *Fast Company*, Issue 114, April 2007, http://www.fastcompany.com/magazine/114/open_features-made-in-china.html.
8. Paul Eisenstein, "Buick Riviera Concept Will Morph into Next LaCrosse," TheCarConnection.com, January 11, 2008, http://blogs.thecarconnection.com/blogs/paul_blog/2007/buick-riviera-concept-will-morph-into-next-lacrosse/.

Chapter 10

1. Tony Palmer, interview by author, January 25, 2008.
2. Peter Brabeck, interview by author, November 12, 2007.
3. Jeremy Bullmore, "In Praise of Interior Decorators (or at Least Some of Them)," *WPP 2006 Annual Report*, 95–97.
4. Julia Moskin, "The Breakfast Wars," *New York Times*, January 10, 2007.
5. Janet Adamy, "McDonald's Takes on a Weakened Starbucks," *Wall Street Journal*, January 7, 2008.
6. Warwick Nash, interview by author, February 1, 2008.

7. Eric Salama, interview by author, November 28, 2007.
8. Del Levin, interview by author, November 14, 2007.
9. Richard Swaab, "Where Great Minds Meet: Global vs. Local" (panel session, seminar on Global Advertising sponsored by Millward Brown, London, November 20, 2007).

Chapter 11

1. Simon Rothon, interview by author, November 16, 2007.
2. Peter Brabeck, interview by author, November 12, 2007.
3. Randall Frost, "Putting a Local Spin on Your Global Brand," *Brand Packaging* 10, no. 3 (April 2006): 4.
4. Karen Hamilton, interview by author, December 6, 2007.
5. Ralph Blessing, interview by author, November 7, 2007.
6. Del Levin, interview by author, November 14, 2007.

Chapter 12

1. Valerie Curtis, Sandy Cairncross, "Effect of Washing Hands with Soap on Diarrhea Risk in the Community: A Systematic Review" *The Lancet Infectious Diseases*, May 2003, 275–81.
2. Valerie Curtis, "Where Great Minds Meet: Global vs. Local" (panel session, seminar on Global Advertising sponsored by Millward Brown, London, November 20, 2007).

Chapter 13

1. Brian Fetherstonhaugh, interview by author, October 11, 2007.
2. Tony Palmer, interview by author, January 25, 2008.
3. Richard Swaab, "Where Great Minds Meet: Global vs. Local" (panel session, seminar on Global Advertising sponsored by Millward Brown, London, November 20, 2007).
4. Much of the content reviewed here originated from a joint project between Millward Brown and Ogilvy & Mather in 2005, which included over 23,500 ads. Since then, additional data from qualitative research, tracking, and sales analyses have been incorporated as well as further insights from additional international advertisers.
5. Jeben Berg, interview by author, January 11, 2008.
6. Flávia Lacerda, *Laços* (Ties), *You Tube*, November 9, 2007, http://www.youtube.com/watch?v=gl74J-aAnfg.

Chapter 14

1. Toby Horry, James Miller, "Nicorette—Sold not Dispensed: The Power of Consumer Brands vs. Pharmaceutical Brands," *IPA*, London, (2006).
2. Richard Swaab, "Where Great Minds Meet: Global vs. Local" (panel session, seminar on Global Advertising sponsored by Millward Brown, London, November 20, 2007).
3. Lisa D'Innocenzo, "Inside P&G: How the Giant CPG Co. went from behind the Times to Leading Edge," *Strategy Magazine* (June 2006): 13.

4. Rob O'Regan, Constantine von Hoffman, *Magnosticism: Marketing and Media in the Age of Great Cynicism,* October 25, 2006, http://magnostic.wordpress.com/best-of-cmo/interview-jim-stengel-procter-gamble/.

5. Scott Davis and Michael Dunn, *Building the Brand-driven Business* (San Francisco: Jossey-Bass, 2002), 60.

6. Jaroslav Cír, "Where Great Minds Meet: Global vs. Local" (panel session, seminar on Global Advertising sponsored by Millward Brown, London, November 20, 2007).

7. Brian Fetherstonhaugh, interview by author, October 11, 2007.

8. David Wheldon, interview by author, January 17, 2008.

Chapter 15

1. Ben Haxworth, interview with author, November 2, 2007.

2. Ben Haxworth, interview with author, November 2, 2007.

3. James Eadie, "Where Great Minds Meet: Global vs. Local" (panel session, seminar on Global Advertising sponsored by Millward Brown, London, November 20, 2007).

Chapter 16

1. "How Companies Think about Climate Change: A McKinsey Global Survey," *McKinsey Quarterly,* February, 2008, http://www.mckinseyquarterly.com/article_page.aspx?ar=2099&pagenum=1.

2. Brittany Sauser, "Ethanol Demand Threatens Food Prices," *Technology Review,* February 13, 2007, http://www.technologyreview.com/Energy/18173/.

3. Emily Bryson York, "Kraft, Kellogg to Boost Ad Spending despite Earnings Drop," AdAge.com, Chicago, January 30, 2008, http://adage.com/article?article_id=124751.

4. Jack Neff and Emily Bryson York, "Recession, Eh? P&G, Colgate Boost Ad Bucks," *AdAge* (February 4, 2008).

5. "Poll: Americans See a Climate Problem," March 26, 2006, http://www.time.com/time/nation/article/0,8599,1176967,00.html.

6. "Wal-Mart Releases Sustainability Update," Facts & News section of walmart stores.com, November 15, 2007, http://walmartstores.com/FactsNews/NewsRoom/6926.aspx.

7. Jack Neff, "Why Wal-Mart Has more Green Clout than anyone," *Advertising Age,* (October 15, 2007).

8. Amanda Griscom Little, "Wal-Mart CEO explains his green creed," April 14, 2006, http://www.msnbc.msn.com/id/12316725/.

9. Martha Lagace, "Businesses Beware: The World is Not Flat (Q&A with Pankaj Ghemawat)," Harvard Business School Working Knowledge, October 15, 2007, http://hbswk.hbs.edu/item/5719.html.

10. Martin Sorrell, "The Advertising & Marketing Services Industry: China and the internet," *WPP 2006 Annual Report,* p. 85.

11. Michael Switow, "Reclaiming Borneo's Music," PRI's The World, February 1, 2008, http://www.theworld.org/?q=node/15739.

12. Marieke de Mooij, *"Mapping Cultural Values for Global Marketing and Advertising,"* (ESOMAR, Marketing Research, Edinburgh, September 1997).

13. *Most Contagious 2007*, (London, Contagious Communications), 19, http://www.contagiousmagazine.com/mostcontagious2007.pdf

14. Linda Tischler, "The Gucci Killers," *Fast Company*. January 2006, http://www.fastcompany. com/magazine/102/shanghai.html.

Index